THE RISE AND FALL OF COMMUNISM
IN EASTERN EUROPE

Also by Ben Fowkes and from the same publishers

**COMMUNISM IN GERMANY UNDER THE
WEIMAR REPUBLIC**

The Rise and Fall of Communism in Eastern Europe

Second Edition

Ben Fowkes

First Edition 1993
Second Edition 1995

Published in Great Britain by
MACMILLAN PRESS LTD
Houndmills, Basingstoke, Hampshire RG21 6XS
and London
Companies and representatives
throughout the world

ISBN 0–333–65108–1 hardcover
ISBN 0–333–65106–5 paperback

A catalogue record for this book is available
from the British Library.

10   9   8   7   6   5   4   3   2
04 03 02 01 00 99 98

Printed in Great Britain by
Antony Rowe Ltd
Chippenham, Wiltshire

Contents

List of Plates

Preface

History books are written about events, structures or a combination of the two. This book is about events. In that sense it is marked by the circumstances of its birth. I was induced to write it by the tremendous and rapidly unfolding spectacle of the collapse of communism in Eastern Europe: a series of events *par excellence*. Who could remain unmoved by the fall of a system which had seemed such a permanent feature of the world's political landscape? Who could fail to see the significance of the event, of the transitory occurrence, of the critical instant, in such a situation?

So it seemed in 1989. Not any longer. The event has lost its importance. The political crises in present-day Eastern Europe are, and will continue to be, superficial phenomena. Events will once again, as in the interwar years, 'pass across the stage of history like fireflies', to use Braudel's expression, barely denting the surface. The important movement will be that of the deeper structure, a structure by no means motionless, but rapidly evolving. Then will be the time for a structural analysis of communist Eastern Europe. Today even the preliminary studies are lacking for this important task. I hope in the meantime that I have provided a clear guide to the successive crises which have shaken Eastern Europe during the communist epoch without altering, until the end, the fundamental structures put in place after the Second World War.

One comment should be made here about the political terminology I have used. Political expressions like 'left' and 'right' tend to appear with their signs reversed in the communist context. For instance, it is difficult to find an appropriate word, without misleading connotations, for thoroughgoing opponents of the communist system. People who in the West might well have been labelled 'right-wingers' or 'conservatives' turn up in the East under the description 'progressives' or 'radicals'. Such at least is their self-image. I have tried to avoid attaching labels of this kind, but where I have they should be understood within the context of the Soviet bloc. I have tried in general to avoid using political shorthand, except where the alternatives would be unbearably circumlocutory.

There are many good books on aspects of communist Eastern Europe. I have drawn freely but I hope not too uncritically on the information they provide, and my debts are recorded where appropriate in the notes at the end of the book. What has been missing so far, and what the present work attempts to supply, is an overall study of the period from a historical point of view. The book that comes nearest to this is Joseph Rothschild's excellent *Return to Diversity*, but, firstly, his bias in terms of content is strongly towards the Second World War and its immediate aftermath, and, secondly, he is concerned with continuities rather than crises. I would therefore see my work as complementary to his.

Finally, I should like to acknowledge two debts of gratitude. One is to my current and former students, particularly Jim Browne, Bülent Gökay and Norman Laporte for inspiring me to undertake this task; the other is to the institution where I work, the University (formerly Polytechnic) of North London, for permitting me two months of study leave.

May 1992   BEN FOWKES

List of Abbreviations

AK	*Armia Krajowa*: Home Army (Poland)
ÁVH	*Államvédelmi Hatóság*: State Defence Authority (Hungary)
AVNOJ	*Antifašističko veće narodnog oslobodjenja Jugoslavije*: Anti-Fascist Council of National Liberation of Yugoslavia
ÁVO	*Államvédelmi Osztály*: State Defence Department (Hungary)
BCP	Bulgarian Communist Party
CBKP	*Centralne Biuro Komunistów Polskich w ZSSR*: Central Bureau of Polish Communists in the USSR
CC	Central Committee
CDU	*Christlich-Demokratische Union*: Christian Democratic Union
ČKD	*Českomoravská Kolben Daněk*: The Kolben Danek (Engineering) Works of Bohemia and Moravia
CMEA	Council of Mutual Economic Aid (Comecon)
CPCz	Communist Party of Czechoslovakia
CPSU	Communist Party of the Soviet Union
CPY	Communist Party of Yugoslavia
CRZZ	*Centralna Rada Związków Zawodowych*: Central Council of Trade Unions (Poland)
ČSSR	*Československá Socialistická Republika*: Czechoslovak Socialist Republic
DBD	*Demokratische Bauernpartei Deutschlands*: Democratic Peasants' Party of Germany
DiP	*Doświadczenie i Przyszłość*: Experience and the Future (Poland)
DISZ	*Dolgozó Ifjúság Szövetsége*: Federation of Working Youth (Hungary)

DWK	*Deutsche Wirtschafts-Kommission*: German Economic Commission
DZV	*Deutsche Zentralverwaltung*: German Central Administration
FJN	*Front Jedności Narodu*: Front of National Unity (Poland)
GDR	German Democratic Republic
GOM	*Gminny Ośrodek Maszynowy*: Communal Machine and Tractor Station (Poland)
HCP	Hungarian Communist Party
HDF	Hungarian Democratic Forum
HSWP	Hungarian Socialist Workers' Party
HWP	Hungarian Workers' Party
JZD	*Jednotné Zemědělské Družstvo*: Unified Agricultural Co-operative (Czechoslovakia)
KAN	*Klub Angažovaných Nestraníků*: Club of Committed Non-party People (Czechoslovakia)
KKP	*Krajowa Komisja Porozumiewawcza*: National Coordinating Commission (of Solidarity)
KOR	*Komitet Obrony Robotników*: Workers' Defence Committee (Poland)
KPD	*Kommunistische Partei Deutschlands*: Communist Party of Germany
KPN	*Konfederacja Polski Niepodległej*: Confederation for an Independent Poland
KPP	*Komunistyczna Partia Polski*: Communist Party of Poland
KRN	*Krajowa Rada Narodowa*: National Council of the Homeland (Poland)
K231	Club of Those Imprisoned under Article 231 (Czechoslovakia)
KSR	*Konferencja Samorządu Robotniczego*: Conference of Workers' Self-Government (Poland)

KSS   *Komitet Samoobrony Społecznej*: Social Self-Defence Committee (Poland)

LCY   League of Communists of Yugoslavia

LDPD   *Liberal-Demokratische Partei Deutschlands*: Liberal Democratic Party of Germany

MADOSZ   *Magyar Dolgozók Országos Szövetsége*: Hungarian National Workers' Federation (Romania)

MEFESZ   *Magyar Egyetemi és Főiskolai Egyesületek Szövetsége*: Federation of Hungarian University and College Associations

MKS   *Międzyzakładowy Komitet Strajkowy*: Interfactory Strike Committee (Poland)

MKZ   *Międzyzakładowy Komitet Założycielski*: Interfactory Founding Committee (Poland)

NDF   National Democratic Front (Romania)

NDH   *Nezavisna Država Hrvatska*: Independent State of Croatia

NDPD   *National-Demokratische Partei Deutschlands*: National Democratic Party of Germany

NMP   Net Material Product

NSF   National Salvation Front (Romania)

NSZ   *Narodowe Siły Zbrojne*: National Armed Forces (Poland)

NS   National Socialists (Czechoslovakia)

ORMO   *Ochotnicza Reserwa Milicji Obywatelskiej*: Volunteer Reserve of the Citizens' Militia (Poland)

OZNA   *Odeljenje Zaštite Naroda*: Bureau for the People's Protection (Yugoslavia)

PGR   *Państwowe Gospodarstwa Rolne*: State Farms (Poland)

PKWN   *Polski Komitet Wyzwolenia Narodowego*: Polish Committee of National Liberation

POM   *Państwowy Ośrodek Maszynowy*: State Machine and Tractor Station (Poland)

PPF   Patriotic People's Front (Hungary)

PPR	*Polska Partia Robotnicza*: Polish Workers' Party
PPS	*Polska Partia Socjalistyczna*: Polish Socialist Party
PSL	*Polskie Stronnictwo Ludowe*: Polish Peasant Party
PZPR	*Polska Zjednoczona Partia Robotnicza*: Polish United Workers' Party
RCP	Romanian Communist Party
ROH	*Revoluční Odborové Hnutí*: Revolutionary Trade Union Movement (Czechoslovakia)
ROPCiO	*Ruch Obrony Praw Człowieka i Obywatela*: Movement for the Defence of Human and Civil Rights (Poland)
RPPS	*Robotnicza Partia Polskich Socjalistów*: Polish Socialist Workers' Party
RWP	Romanian Workers' Party
SB	*Służba Bezpieczeństwa*: Security Service (Poland)
SBZ	*Sowjetische Besatzungszone Deutschlands*: Soviet Occupation Zone of Germany
SD	*Stronnictwo Demokratyczne*: Democratic Party (Poland)
SED	*Sozialistische Einheitspartei Deutschlands*: Socialist Unity Party of Germany
SL	*Stronnictwo Ludowe*: Peasant Party (Poland)
SMAD	*Sowjetische Militäradministration Deutschlands*: Soviet Military Administration of Germany
SNB	*Sbor Národní Bezpečnosti*: Corps for National Security (Czechoslovakia)
StB	*Státní bezpečnost*: State Police (Czechoslovakia)
SZOT	*Szakszervezetek Országos Tanácsa*: National Council of Trade Unions (Hungary)
TOZ	*Tovarishchestvo po Sovmestnoy Obrabotke Zemli*: Association for Joint Cultivation of the Soil (Soviet Union)
UB	*Urząd Bezpieczeństwa*: Security Office (Poland)

UDBA *Uprava Državne Bezbednosti*: Administration of State Security (Yugoslavia)

ÚRO *Ústřední Rada Odborů:* Central Council of Trade Unions (Czechoslovakia)

VVB *Vereinigung Volkseigener Betriebe*: Association of Publicly Owned Enterprises (GDR)

WOG *Wielka Organizacja Gospodarcza*: Large Economic Organisation (Poland)

WRN *Wolność, Równość, Niepodległość*: Freedom, Equality, Independence (Polish Socialist Underground 1939–45)

WRON *Wojskowa Rada Ocalenia Narodowego*: Military Council of National Salvation (Poland)

ZBoWiD *Związek Bojowników o Wolność i Demokrację*: Union of Fighters for Freedom and Democracy (Poland)

ZMP *Związek Młodzieży Polskiej*: Union of Polish Youth

ZMS *Związek Młodzieży Socjalistycznej*: Union of Socialist Youth (Poland)

ZPP *Związek Patriotów Polskich*: Union of Polish Patriots

ZSL *Zjednoczone Stronnictwo Ludowe*: United Peasant Party (Poland)

Introduction to the
Second Edition

Prediction is always a risky business, and I generally eschewed it in the first edition of this book. One prediction I did venture to make was that 'the event would lose its importance' in Eastern Europe, to be replaced by the movement of 'deeper structures'. I see no reason to revise this remark. The five years since the collapse of communist rule have seen a working out of trends already observable at the time, and a complete absence of decisive political occurrences. Elections have come and gone, contested by parties with shared objectives and policies; the winners, sometimes former communists leading socialist parties, have formed fresh coalitions, pursuing the identical aims of transforming state-run into market economies, encouraging foreign investment, striving to enter the European Community and NATO. Political pluralism and the institutions of liberal democracy have not been challenged. Everywhere there is multi-party democracy, at least in theory. Some countries have moved faster, some more slowly, along the path mapped out for them.

The economic picture has not been very bright. It was thought at first that 'shock therapy', or an immediate transition to a fully-fledged market economy, was the answer. Václav Klaus in Czechoslovakia and Leszek Balcerowicz in Poland were the most powerful advocates of this policy and they were both in a position to implement it. The instant improvement expected from the removal of the dead weight of bureaucratic control has not materialised. The main trend has in fact been rather the reverse; a severe decline in output, both industrial and agricultural. The growth in services and the financial sector has not usually counterbalanced this. The depth of the depression has varied from country to country, with Albania suffering a practical economic collapse in 1991, from which it has since partially recovered, and Poland experiencing a fairly steep fall in output in 1990 but not subsequently.[1]

So far Poland alone has successfully turned the corner economically. Free market economists like to claim this as a testimony to the success of the rapid price liberalisation, currency stabilisation and encouragement of private entrepreneurship instituted by the Balcerowicz Plan in January 1990. It may well be so, but Poland also enjoyed some special advantages: in March 1991 the international financial community wrote off half the Polish foreign debt. Poland also received almost half of the total amount of money allocated to Eastern Europe by Western financial institutions such as the World Bank and the IMF in the period 1990–1992.[2] In 1992, after three years of continuous decline in the Gross Domestic Product, Poland achieved an increase of 1.5 per cent, raised to 4.0 per cent the next year. Hungary and the Czech Republic at least managed to turn decline into stagnation.[3] Slovakia (a special case, because of the economically damaging decision to separate from its Czech partner) has so far failed to bring its decline in output under control.[4] Nevertheless, the whole of East Central Europe can be said to have good prospects of completing the economic transition from communism to capitalism and moving into a new era. Inflation, an inevitable result of the post-1989 price liberalisations, stabilised at moderate levels in the Czech Republic, Slovakia, Hungary and Poland in 1992.[5] Even these relatively fortunate countries still have a considerable way to go, however. On present performance they are not likely to make up for their post-1989 losses until the year 2000.[6] The West could do more, certainly. The tendency so far has been to keep Eastern Europe at arm's length through fear of competition, fear of responsibility and sheer lack of spare resources. Associate status with the European Community was granted in 1991 to Poland, Czechoslovakia and Hungary. But the next step, to full membership, has not yet been taken.

What of the underlying structural changes in East Central Europe? Privatisation has been pushed ahead fairly rapidly. In the former GDR (a special case) it is now complete. Privatisation has been slowed down in many countries by uncertainty about the best method. Should state enterprises be simply sold on the open market? Should they be returned to the previous owners (in the case of collective farms)? Should the ordinary citizens of the country be given vouchers to invest with investment trusts? Should they be asked to buy vouchers? Should those who work in the enterprises themselves take them over? Apart from the last, all these methods have been tried. As a result there is now a flourishing private sector everywhere in East Central Europe, producing over half each country's GDP. Other measures give roughly the same results.[7] This does not necessarily mean the rise of a new class of entrepreneurs. In Hungary and Poland there has been a considerable amount of what Staniszkis calls '*nomenklatura* privatisation' whereby the former communist managers of the state enterprises have simply taken them over themselves.[8]

Deep and prolonged recession in Eastern Europe has meant that the time of transition has been a period of social crisis. Unemployment rose from 2 750 000 in 1990 to 7.5 million in 1993, or 13.8 per cent. The level of unemployment benefit varies, but is nowhere more than 60 per cent of former income. Where people did keep their jobs they suffered a sharp drop in real wages. In Poland the fall was 29.2 per cent between 1990 and 1993, in Hungary 13.3 per cent, in the Czech Republic 15 per cent. Milanovic estimates that ten million 'new poor' have emerged, on incomes of less than $120 a month at 1990 prices. Inequality has increased considerably, with skilled workers and public employees sliding down the scale, and private entrepreneurs and professionals pushing ahead. Income inequality has increased dramatically everywhere except in Slovakia.[9] A new middle class has arisen, composed of people who started small in the flourishing 'second economies' of the 1980s, together with those members of the *nomenklatura* who were able to make the transition to the new epoch.

Some indication of the path that is being followed is given by Tymowski's suggestion (for Poland) that the past five years have seen the destruction of the three main social strata: peasants, proletariat and intelligentsia. Peasants have become commercial farmers or moved to the service sector; the proletariat has become unemployed with the dismantling of the old factories; the intelligentsia, he alleges, has lost its *raison d'être* because the 'national idea' no longer needs to be 'articulated'.[10] There is some hyperbole here, but clearly the decline in industrial production since 1989 has hit the traditional industries, and the post-1993 recovery has taken place in other areas such as services, finance, business and communications. The decline of the Polish peasantry has been relative rather than absolute, with the number of private farmers remaining static while that of non-agricultural private sector employees increased.[11] There has, however, been a severe fall in the contribution of agriculture to Poland's GDP, from 12.9 per cent in 1989 to 6.9 per cent in 1992. Both Hungary and the Czech Republic have seen similar declines.[12]

The above comments on the post-communist transition apply mainly to East Central Europe. Further south the course of events has been different. Some people like to explain this by pointing to a historic divide between the Balkan lands, with their tradition of Eastern orthodox Christianity, Ottoman rule and political dictatorship, and the Catholic and democratic countries further north. 'Eastern Orthodoxy is morally passive and emphasises forms rather than substance', a mind-set which is allegedly not conducive to initiative, risk-taking or even ethical politics, says Shafir.[13] Such general explanations in terms of political culture are impossible to prove or disprove. I shall however try to point to certain common features of the Balkan scene. One problem in this context is the prevailing atmosphere of uncertainty and confusion. For instance, to what extent has the land been decollectivised in Romania? Have only 7 per cent of Romanians received the land to which they are entitled? Do many state farms remain intact?[14] Or has there been a gigantic turnaround, with 90 per cent of the arable sector now in private hands?[15] The 77 per cent of Albania's arable land allegedly in private hands by 1992[16] hardly squares with the 50 per cent of state farms still in the hands of the state in 1993 according to another source.[17] At least they can agree that privatisation of the industrial sector has been 'slow'. But how slow? Gale Stokes, in his general survey *The Walls Came Tumbling Down*[18] avoids the issue of Balkan privatisations entirely. Provisionally one may conclude that while privatisation of the industrial sector in Albania, Romania and Bulgaria has been slow because there is little enthusiasm for it among the public and less among the ruling parties, decollectivisation of agriculture has also been delayed by the conflict of interests between the present occupiers of the land and former owners. It is easier to be definite about price liberalisation. Post-communist governments everywhere in the Balkans moved immediately to market prices. The result has been an inflation far more severe than in East Central Europe. In 1993 retail prices rose 63.4 per cent in Bulgaria, 85 per cent in Albania, 256 per cent in Romania, 250 per cent in Macedonia, 1,517 per cent in Croatia and 196,885,000 per cent in the Yugoslav Federal Republic (Serbia and Montenegro).

Another feature allegedly common to the Balkan countries is ethnic conflict. One should however distinguish between ethnic conflicts so serious as to threaten the structure of the state and minor quarrels. The former have occurred only in Yugoslavia and Czechoslovakia. In the latter country, the 'velvet revolution' of 1989 was followed by the 'velvet divorce' of 1993, by which separate states of 'the Czech Republic' and 'Slovakia' came into existence. On the ruins of the former, a number of states of varying viability have been established since 1991. Slovenia and Croatia to the north, and Serbia and Montenegro in the centre seem certain to survive as states. Bosnia-Hercegovina cannot survive. There is some doubt about Macedonia.

Elsewhere it would be more accurate to speak of minor quarrels among nationalities. In Slovakia (Slovaks against Hungarians) Romania (Romanians against Hungarians) Bulgaria (Bulgarians against Turks) and Albania (Albanians against Greeks) there has certainly been discord between the majority nation and minorities. Anti-Semitism has experienced a slight resurgence, sometimes, as in Poland, an 'Anti-Semitism without Jews' (Lendvai).[19] And the Romanies have been scapegoats everywhere. Unscrupulous politicians like István Csurka (Hungary) and Gheorghe Funar (Romania) have dabbled in these muddy waters. But it would be wrong to exaggerate the seriousness of this trend, above all because there is little interest in irredentism among Hungarians, Turks or Greeks.[20] The communist rulers of Romania and Bulgaria manipulated ethnic discord to stay in power, but the similarity stops there. The policy has been continued in Romania, though more mildly, and dropped in Bulgaria. What is perhaps more important is the linked feature of a generally undemocratic approach to politics, often including the use of physical force against the other side. In Romania the National Salvation Front led by Ion Iliescu acts as the heir of the former communist party, winning elections through intimidation (May 1990), organising the beating up of political opponents by miners from the Jiu valley (June 1990), rejecting the demands of Transylvanian Hungarians for autonomy, demanding Dobrudja from Bulgaria, incorporating elements of the *Securitate* into the new state intelligence service, and retaining former party bureaucrats in high civil service and local government positions.[21] In Albania ethnic Greek politicians are jailed for espionage (August 1994). In Yugoslavia (reduced in area to Serbia and Montenegro on 27 April 1992) the communist-nationalist government of Slobodan Milošević has continued and deepened its demagogic policy of directing attention away from internal problems by repressing Albanians within Serbia and giving moral and material support to Serbian nationalist armies in Croatia and Bosnia-Hercegovina.[22]

But there are several exceptions, and it would be wise to treat each case on its merits. Bulgaria and Macedonia, for instance, appear to contradict the rule of perpetual Balkan political backwardness and dictatorship. Macedonia, under its able ex-communist president Kiro Grigorov, faces the severe external problem of Greek non-recognition, but has maintained a calm and statesmanlike approach to its national minorities. In Bulgaria the failure of the democratic, non-communist forces to win the elections of June 1990 was subsequently cancelled out by the victory of the UDF (Union of Democratic Forces) in the October 1991 elections, and of its leader Zhelyu Zhelev in the presidential elections of January 1992. Two years later, on 18 December 1994, the Bulgarian Socialist Party (the renamed communist party) returned to power with an absolute majority of seats in parliament, and on a democratic programme emphasising the need for pragmatic reforms leading towards a market economy. In fact the delay in implementing structural reforms in Bulgaria was a result less of socialist opposition than of political uncertainty because of the lack of a clear majority for any party.[23]

These comments about the Bulgarian socialists are also of more general application. Communism may be dead, but ex-communists thrive. Support for them is driven not by nostalgia for the past but by the protest against the very painful phenomena accompanying the transition to a market economy. They do have an alternative programme but it is not radically different from their opponents'. This is clearly apparent in Hungary, for example. The

Hungarian Socialist Party, which won an absolute majority of the seats at the elections of May 1994 (54.2 per cent), was pledged to continue the privatisation process, although not by the 'mass privatisation' method adopted by the previous government.[24] The communist and post-communist parties differ only in paying somewhat more attention to the sufferings of the victims of the process of transition. In no case do they intend to reverse what is now irreversible. A broad political consensus in fact developed almost immediately after 1989 in the countries of Eastern Europe. Parties of the extreme left or the nationalist right have made little headway. The one exception is the former Yugoslavia, where civil war on ethnic lines either continues (Bosnia-Hercegovina) or may recur (Croatia) or may begin (Kosovo and Macedonia). I shall conclude by expressing the hope that Yugoslavia may finally cease to be the Eastern European exception, that the coming of peace will help the pollution of national intolerance to drain away, and that all the peoples of the region cease to be, in the words of Slavenka Drakulić, 'pinned to the wall of nationhood',[25] and start to recognise what binds them together as human beings.

January 1995   BEN FOWKES

NOTES

1. The average cumulative decline in GDP for the countries of Eastern Europe between 1989 and 1993 was 27.4 per cent. Albania's Net Material Product fell by 36 per cent, Poland's GNP by only 13.8 per cent overall. The rest fell between these limits, except certain parts of former Yugoslavia where the special circumstances of war and blockade made for truly catastrophic declines (the Federal Republic of Yugoslavia's Gross Material Product fell by 58.1 per cent and Macedonia's fell by 41.9 per cent).

2. The Polish foreign debt in 1991 was $33 billion. Poland received $25.3 billion of the total $57.1 billion allocated, 1990–92. See the World Bank's newsletter on Eastern Europe, *Transition*, vol. 5, nos. 2–3, Feb.–March 1994, p. 10.

3. GDP fell by 2 per cent in Hungary and by 0.5 per cent in the Czech Republic in 1993. The Czech Republic reported an increase of 2.2 per cent in industrial output in 1994, which might well imply an actual rise in GDP (*Financial Times*, 19 December 1994).

4. GDP declined by 7.0 per cent in Slovakia in 1992 and by 4.7 per cent in 1993.

5. Annual rates for 1992 (1993 in brackets): Czech Republic 11.1 (23.0), Slovakia 10.0 (23.2), Hungary 23.0 (22.5), Poland 43.0 (35.3).

6. *Economic Survey of Europe in 1993–1994* (New York 1994), p. 52. Many

observers, however, are inclined to downplay the seriousness of these declines, given the nature and quality of the products, and the statistics, previously produced.

7. Figures for 1994: Czech Republic 65 per cent, Poland 56 per cent, Hungary 55 per cent, Slovakia 55 per cent (*The Economist*, vol. 334, no. 7898, 21–27 January 1995, p. 76). There are slightly different figures for the size of the private sector in terms of employment, and for the proportion of state enterprises sold off.

8. J. Staniszkis, 'Political Capitalism in Poland', *East European Politics and Societies*, 5, 1991, pp. 127–41.

9. The coefficient of income inequality, on a scale from 0 (complete equality) to 100 (absolute inequality), has increased on average by 6 points between 1987 and 1993, from 24 to 30. See B. Milanovic, 'A Cost of Transition: 50 Million New Poor and Growing Inequality', *Transition*, vol. 5, no. 8, October 1994.

10. A. Tymowski, 'Poland's Unwanted Social Revolution', *East European Politics and Societies*, 7, 2, p. 200.

11. There were 4.0 million private farmers in 1989 and 4.1 million in 1993. The corresponding figures for non-agricultural private sector employment are 4.2 million and 5.3 million. See R. Blaszczyk, 'The Progress of Privatisation in Poland', *Moct–Most*, 2, 1994, p. 205.

12. *Economic Survey of Europe 1992–1993* (New York 1993), table 3.1.2, p. 78.

13. M. Shafir, *Romania – Politics, Economics and Society: Political Stagnation and Simulated Change*, (Boulder, 1985), pp. 150–8.

14. The World Bank's newsletter *Transition* makes this claim, in vol. 5, nos. 2–3, Feb.–March 1994, p. 18.

15. Economist Intelligence Unit, *Country Profile: Romania 1994–95*.

16. Economic Intelligence Unit, *Country Profile, Bulgaria and Albania 1994–5*.

17. *Economic Survey of Europe 1993–1994* (New York, 1994), p. 14.

18. G. Stokes, *The Walls Came Tumbling Down. The Collapse of Communism in Eastern Europe* (Oxford 1993), chapter 6.

19. P. Lendvai, *Anti-Semitism Without Jews* (New York, 1971).

20. On 5 September 1994 the Hungarian government recognised the 'permanence' of the border with Romania.

21. K. Verdery and G. Kligman, 'Romania', in I. Banac, (ed.), *Eastern Europe in Revolution* (Ithaca, 1992), p. 128.

22. In August 1994 Milošević agreed to blockade Bosnian Serb territory, but this does not exclude continuing covert support.

23.. *Financial Times*, 20 December 1994.

24. It is too early to say whether the decision by the Hungarian government in January 1995 to abandon the sale of the HungarHotel chain means a change in policy. The reason given was that the bids received were far below the real value of the asset (*Financial Times*, 18 January 1995).

25. Quoted in J. F. Brown, *Hopes and Shadows. Eastern Europe after Communism*, (London, 1994), p. 219; the best book so far on the post-communist transition.

1 Introduction

The title, and the scope, of this book require some explanation. In recent years there has been a tendency to reject the term 'Eastern Europe', replacing it with some more fashionable formulation such as 'Central Europe', 'The Other Europe', 'The Lands Between', or 'East-Central Europe'. There are, however, considerable disadvantages involved in adopting these other descriptions. 'Central Europe', as advocated by the Hungarian writer György Konrád, extends too far to the West, and excludes too much of the East. Bulgaria is kept out; West Germany is brought in. 'East-Central Europe', the invention of the Polish historian Oskar Halecki[1], which was taken up by Joseph Rothschild in his book *Return to Diversity*, has the advantage of clearly excluding the Soviet Union, but in Halecki's original conception it also excludes all countries without a 'continuous Christian tradition'. They happen to be the mainly Greek Orthodox lands which lived under Ottoman rule for four hundred years, namely southern Yugoslavia, Albania, Romania, Bulgaria and Greece. Rothschild, in contrast, adopts an essentially political definition, by which 'the lands of East-Central Europe' are the areas under communist rule. But he leaves out East Germany, for no clear reason.

It may well happen in the future that the term 'Eastern Europe' falls out of use. Perhaps it will be replaced by the two expressions 'Central Europe' and 'Balkan Europe'. The greater power of survival displayed by ruling communist parties (under another name) in Balkan Europe may indicate such a division. Perhaps the East and the West will merge together into a common 'Europe'. For the historian, however, the term 'Eastern Europe' is indispensable. It denotes that part of the European Continent which came under sole communist rule after the Second World War. This allows the exclusion of Greece, Finland and Austria, where there was initially some doubt about the final outcome; and compels the inclusion of East Germany, despite the artificial character of that state.[2]

The chronological limits of the book are determined by the life-span of communist rule. I end in 1990 with the overthrow and collapse of Communist Eastern Europe, and I begin in 1944 when it started to look as if Stalin would have the determining say in what happened there. The scope of the investigation is thus an episode of history, the episode of Soviet-style communism. Communism survives as an ideal; and it will continue to do so as long as there are people who dream of replacing the anarchy of

capitalism by a rational and just organisation of society. But the governmental episode is over. I refer here to 'Soviet-style communism'. Stalinism
in the strict sense died long before 1990; what expired in 1990 in Eastern
Europe was something different: a post-Stalinist hybrid moulded on the
contemporary Soviet Union. I also refer on occasion to 'reform communism'. This too expired in 1990; perhaps it had already lost its chance as a
viable alternative in 1968.

The first question that needs to be answered in a book such as this is
'why did Eastern Europe fall under communist rule in the first place'? A
proper answer would require detailed reference to individual countries, and
I shall provide this in the next two chapters, but there is a simple, crude, but
nevertheless true reply: because Stalin wished it, and he was in a position
to impose his will towards the end of the Second World War. Even in
Yugoslavia, despite the supreme tactical skill of Marshal Tito, and the
sacrifices, and the ruthlessness, of the Yugoslav Communist partisans,
victory was only made certain by the withdrawal of German forces from the
country, ultimately under the pressure of blows delivered elsewhere by the
Red Army. If Stalin did not intervene in Yugoslavia at that stage to place a
more compliant leadership in charge of the Communist Party of Yugoslavia
(CPY) it was because he did not want to do so, not because he lacked the
power. Nothing could happen in Eastern Europe against Stalin's wishes in
1945. This, the international framework, must be the starting-point for any
discussion. It is absurd to suggest that the West gave away Eastern Europe
at Yalta. The Yalta agreements were rather an attempt to save what could be
saved for Western democracy.

To attribute the ultimate responsibility to Stalin in this way is not to
ignore the indigenous leftward swing all over Europe in 1945. There was a
mass rejection of capitalism by large sections of the people in many European countries. The communists, by and large, were the beneficiaries of
this. The non-communist left was either numerically weak or hamstrung by
the need to cooperate closely with the communists and deceived by its own
naive faith in working-class unity. Of course the forces of the centre and the
right had not disappeared, but one of the functions of the Red Army and
of Soviet control was to make sure that these forces played no part in
determining the political future in 1945. What we need to look at first,
therefore, is the strategy of the local communist leaders, who had so many
cards in their hands at this time.

The communist leaders who came to power in Eastern Europe after 1945
shared a commitment to what they called 'Marxism-Leninism', i.e. the
ideology and practice developed by Stalin out of Bolshevism during the late
1920s and early 1930s. In more general terms, adherence to communism

meant identification with the Stalin model and therefore a wish to transplant it to Eastern Europe. Whether this involved a completely slavish adherence to the model is doubtful. Z. A. Pełczyński's comment about Poland applies elsewhere as well: 'It is inconceivable that, left to themselves, the Polish leadership . . . would have adopted all the policies and institutional structure which resulted from [Stalinism] . . . National traditions would have been flouted less ruthlessly and Soviet models copied more critically.'[3]

It is hard, however, to distinguish between willing acceptance of a given policy for ideological reasons and simple obedience to Soviet instructions. Those responsible for communist policy were unlikely to admit that they were simply carrying out Stalin's orders. All that can be said with certainty is that the postwar situation was the net result of decisions taken by communists either in Moscow or at home, according to certain general principles which were hardly changed at all in response to local conditions.

The implementation of Marxism-Leninism in internal policy will be examined in chapter four; here I am concerned with the implications of this theory for the seizure of power. The communist leaders certainly aimed at seizing power in one form or another: their long-term goal was, after all, the construction of socialism, and they could not do this without taking power. But during and immediately after the war the higher consideration of the defence of the Soviet Union operated to modify this. The 'National Front' strategy worked out and applied all over Eastern Europe during the war was aimed at the more limited objective of defeating the 'German and Italian fascist brigands'.[4] This would be achieved through a 'great national front of . . . people of all possible parties, religions and world views'.[5] Once Fascism had been defeated a more positive programme could be put into effect.

The positive programmes of the various National Fronts of Central and Eastern Europe were clarified and spelled out in more detail between 1943 and 1945. They included (a) measures of social reform, such as expropriation of the big estates and a certain amount of nationalisation of industry: all this was meant to ensure that the old upper classes did not return to power; (b) grass roots participation in political power through National Committees, Factory Committees and Citizens' Militias: in short the replacement of the pre-war administrative infrastructure; (c) establishment of a broad National Front alliance of political parties, with the communists playing a leading part in government; and (d) the solution of the national problem by the creation of homogeneous national states, involving expulsions and transfers of population; where this was impossible appropriate guarantees of rights and autonomy would be provided for minority national groups.

None of this amounted to a fully-fledged 'socialist' system. But it did involve a substantial reduction in the power of the old ruling classes, thereby creating a power vacuum, and it was open to the communists, if they wished, to become 'the hegemon of the nation' (Gomułka).[6]

The above strategy had not been worked out by the party theorists of Eastern Europe; it was an instruction from the very highest level, i.e. Stalin himself. Stalin's own intentions at this time for Eastern Europe are shrouded in mystery, as always. He made contradictory statements to different people. His remarks to the Yugoslav communist Milovan Djilas have often been quoted: 'This war is not as in the past; whoever occupies a territory also imposes on it his own social system. Everyone imposes his own system as far as his army has the power to do so. It cannot be otherwise.'[7]

This appears to be a very clear statement. But the context of the discussion should be considered. They were talking about different roads to socialism, and Stalin had just told Djilas that 'Revolution is no longer necessary everywhere [and] socialism is possible even under an English king'. It was in fact a tacit admission of the possibility of reaching socialism by varied routes, and a recognition that the Yugoslav revolution, though national in origin, had had far-reaching social consequences, which he, Stalin, did not wish to reverse. There lay behind it as well a recognition that 'socialism' was out of the question in the areas occupied by the Western allies. What it did not imply was an intention to impose 'socialism' on Eastern Europe. For Poland, for instance, we have Stalin's categorical reply of October 1944 to Mikołajczyk when he asked whether 'the Polish constitution would be communist': 'Of course not. Poland must have democratic rule. Private ownership and a free economic life should be maintained . . . There are no conditions in Poland for a communist system.'[8]

Accordingly, anyone who spoke of establishing 'Soviet power' in their country was sharply called to order, either by Dimitrov (in Slovakia in 1945, and he tried to do the same thing in Yugoslavia) or by Vyshinsky (he compelled the Romanian communist leaders Pauker and Luca to give up the idea of seizing power there in November 1944)[9] or by some responsible local leader (in Hungary, Révai[10]).

But the phrase 'Soviet power' was ambiguous. It might mean the *political* rule of the proletariat, i.e. of its vanguard party, the communist party; or it might mean the overthrow of capitalism as an economic and social system and its replacement by a Soviet system on the USSR model. Leftists within the communist parties were concerned with the former rather than the latter (which could come later); leftists within the Social Democratic or socialist parties wanted to achieve the latter, without the former. This was a basis for both cooperation and misunderstandings. A major feature of the wartime situation was the radicalisation of elements within the socialist parties. Sometimes this went so far that new parties appeared to the left of the existing ones. This happened in Poland, for instance, with the formation of the RPPS (Polish Socialist Workers' Party). Left-wing socialists of this kind, despite their radicalism, were not always inclined to cooperate with the communists.

Another trend among socialists during the war was the growth of a group of 'fellow-travellers' prepared to accept communist hegemony. This phenomenon should be clearly distinguished from the above. Radicals of this type, such as Stefan Matuszewski in Poland, Zdeněk Fierlinger in Czechoslovakia and György Marosán in Hungary could be seen as on the left not so much because they were radical on social and economic policy as because they favoured a cooperation with the communists so close as to amount to complete surrender to them. They were to be found in all the socialist parties of Eastern Europe after 1945, and the communist parties encouraged them to remain where they were for the moment rather than taking the logical step of actually changing their party allegiance. They were more useful under cover. Later on they played an important part in preparing the socialist–communist mergers of 1947–8, and they often occupied important positions in the united workers' parties that emerged as a result.

The many differences in the method and pace of the communist seizure of power in Eastern Europe after 1945 necessitate separate treatment of each country. I shall begin with Poland, where Stalin was in a hurry to settle things in 1945; then I shall examine the countries of the Northern tier, or East Central Europe: finally I move southwards, making a tour through the Balkan countries which ends in Albania.

2 The Seizure of Power
Part One: The Northern Tier

POLAND: A SADDLE FOR A COW?

Military factors played an overwhelming role in the establishment of communism in Poland. It was made possible by the victory of the Soviet Red Army; and alongside the latter there marched a 100 000 strong 'Polish Army', established in 1943 under Colonel Zygmunt Berling and consisting largely of former Polish prisoners of war conscripted within the Soviet Union. Nevertheless, the manner and the speed with which communist rule was established were determined by the interplay between Stalin's strategic objectives, the Comintern conception of the 'National Front', which lived on even after the quiet dissolution of that organisation in 1943, and the situation on the ground.

Stalin's initial plan, entirely in line with the 'National Front' policy, was to establish cooperation with the 'London Poles', i.e. the Polish exile government in London, but this was made impossible by the discovery of the graves of 4000 Polish officers in the Katyn forest in 1943. The Poles were inclined to believe (correctly, as has now been admitted) that the massacre was committed by Soviet security organs and not by the Gestapo. Stalin had the choice between admitting the truth and breaking completely with the Sikorski government in London. He naturally preferred the latter course. This break had a decisive impact on the attitude of the Polish communists to the 'London Poles'. Whereas the first manifesto of the newly re-established communist party, the PPR (Polish Workers' Party), had held out the possibility of cooperation with the Sikorski government (March 1943), the second manifesto, in November 1943, entitled 'What we are fighting for', explicitly rejected the London Polish government in favour of a provisional government based on the 'anti-Fascist national front', and listed some far-reaching socio-economic demands such as the nationalisation of large-scale industry, banks and means of transport, the control of production by factory committees, and a 'transition to the socialist order made by the working class within the framework of the democratic state'.[1]

There were other serious obstacles to a National Front policy of broad alliances, quite apart from the break with London. The communists were committed to acceptance of Stalin's objectives, and one of these was the redrawing of Poland's boundaries so as to incorporate the Eastern territories into the Soviet Union. Very few non-communist Poles could accept this. None of the exiled political leaders who sat on the Political Representative Committee in London would collaborate with communism or with the Soviet Union. The only way of implementing the National Front was to discover, or perhaps create, left-wing, pro-communist parties in Poland itself. The method of creating pro-communist parties by splitting existing non-communist ones was later to be applied all over Eastern Europe, but in 1943 the PPR had to make do with what was there. There did exist a socialist party to the left of the PPS (Polish Socialist Party). It was called the RPPS (Polish Socialist Workers' Party) and had split from the former in January 1943. But most of the RPPS leaders were opposed to cooperating with the PPR. At a conference in September 1943 only four out of 24 leaders of the RPPS, led by Edward Osóbka-Morawski, declared themselves in favour of accepting the PPR's programme. Similarly, the SL (Peasant Party) voted to reject the PPR's invitation, saying that 'the Polish peasantry will not let itself be deluded by the misleading programme of "radical reforms" in the style of state socialism modelled on that of Russia. They do not want to become manorial serfs in the barracks of the collective farm'.[2] Of course, collectivisation was not part of the programme of the PPR, but the SL leaders were aware of what had happened in the 1930s in the Soviet Union.

When the KRN (National Council of the Homeland) was founded on 31 December 1943, it was, as Władysław Gomułka, by now leader of the PPR, himself later admitted, 'with the relatively slim participation of other groups'.[3] The KRN was the creation of communists in Poland itself, and its version of the national front was too narrow, too far to the left, for Moscow. The Polish Communists in the Soviet Union, organised in the CBKP (Central Bureau of Polish Communists) (set up in January 1944), and the ZPP (Union of Polish Patriots in the Soviet Union), feared that the radical socio-economic programme of the KRN, and its uncompromising rejection of the London Poles, would give the West the impression that they intended to establish communism in Poland.

The programme of the Polish National Committee, drawn up by the Moscow group, was significantly to the 'right' of that of the KRN. It called for a 'patriotic national front' instead of a 'democratic [i.e. narrower, more radical] national front', it offered 'fair compensation to landowners', it stressed support for the parliamentary form of government, and instead of the KRN's 'nationalisation' it promised to return enterprises to their rightful owners after a temporary period of state administration.[4]

During the first few months of 1944 the Polish Communists in Moscow and the Soviet leaders (represented in fact by the Bulgarian Comintern veteran Georgi Dimitrov) continued to exert pressure for the formation of a broad-based national front, to include the WRN (i.e. the right wing of the PPS), the SL, and even the National Democrats. The CC of the PPR (in other words Gomułka) replied in March 1944 to Dimitrov that the national front was made difficult 'not by our party's sectarianism but by its line on the issue of Poland's eastern frontier' and by the 'dishonest game played by the RPPS, inspired by their Trotskyite ideas', by which he meant their excessive leftism. Moreover, the only way to deal with the problem of the SL was to establish a rival party, led by Władysław Kowalski. This took the name SL-*Wola ludu* and started to issue a newspaper printed and distributed by the Communists.[5]

In fact the Polish situation made any genuine national front impossible, and to that extent the local communists won this particular intra-party battle. Stalin was forced to recognise the KRN as the 'kernel of the new Polish government' in May 1944 and to hand over the administration of liberated areas of Poland to it.[6] But the Moscow Poles counter-attacked successfully, and the KRN was suddenly instructed by Molotov to set up a Polish Committee of National Liberation (PKWN) dominated largely by the ZPP. Although the chair was to be Osóbka-Morawski (left RPPS, former deputy chair of the KRN) both deputy chairs were members of the ZPP, as were ten out of the fifteen members of the Committee. The manifesto of the PKWN (22 July 1944) was based on the ideas of the Moscow Poles, not Gomułka's radical KRN manifesto. It called for nationalisation, but only of German factories. Other factories were to be placed 'under provisional state management' with compensation for the former owners. Small and medium enterprises would remain in private hands, or be restored to the original owners if they were Polish. Large landed estates owned by Germans and traitors would be confiscated, but otherwise there was a lower limit of either 50 or 100 hectares on the estates earmarked for land reform, depending on the region. The confiscated land would become a land fund, for later distribution among the peasantry. The property of the Catholic Church would not be touched.[7]

This moderation could hardly have the desired effect, given the political situation. Moreover, class antagonisms quickly emerged within liberated Poland itself. Factories abandoned by the Nazis in the course of their retreat were taken over by the Polish workers, acting through factory committees, without instructions from any political party or trade union. The entry into the 'Lublin Committee' (as the PKWN came to be described) of a few splinter groups from the socialist and peasant parties did not prevent the polarisation of political life into pro- and anti-communist camps. In October 1944, after a period in which the communists attempted to pursue a national front policy by differentiating between 'the reactionaries in the AK (Home Army)' and others,[8] there was a drastic turn towards repression, under the slogan of 'disarming the terrain'. Mere membership of the Home Army was now a ground for arrest.[9] Since the party's own security forces were not yet strong enough it was in practice left to the Soviet NKVD to hunt them down. The campaign of repression 'wrought devastation over the whole country', as General Berling later admitted.[10]

The 'October turn' also involved a more radical social and economic policy. Andrzej Witos, veteran leader of the SL-*Wola Ludu*, in charge of agriculture in the liberated parts of Poland, wanted to delay land reform until the end of the war. He was now dismissed from his post, and the estates were rapidly divided up. The land reform was completed by December, with the distribution of 212 084 hectares among 110 000 households. Nationalisation of industry began, with a large role being envisaged for the spontaneously developed factory councils. Whereas in September the PPR had attempted to replace the councils with a 'troika' system headed by the director of the factory, now party spokesmen told factory militants that 'the workers themselves should take the entire responsibility for the factories'.[11]

This position was formalised, after some delay, by a decree of 6 February 1945, which established factory councils in all enterprises employing over 20 people, giving them parity with the director of the enterprise. It was actually drawn up by the left socialist Bolesław Drobner. The factory councils often took a very radical line, opposing piecework, demanding equality of payment for everyone, and in general acting independently. They also had a tendency to organise strikes against the food shortages of the time. Gomułka later claimed that the factory councils 'were refusing to distribute their products to other factories in the production chain'. He went on to blame the workers for their 'lack of discipline', which had further reduced the level of industrial production. In April 1945 it stood at 19 per cent of its 1937 level. Of course, there were plenty of other reasons for that.[12]

The April 1945 resolution of the PPR-controlled Central Commission of the Trade Unions, insisting on piecework and payment according to qualifications and professional skills, was a sign of the impending abandonment of radical experiments. The 'October line' was definitively reversed at the May Plenum of 1945. There the party leaders shifted away from workers' control to the improvement of discipline and the raising of labour productivity. According to the resolution adopted at that time: 'the director of the enterprise alone is to decide all matters relating to economic and technical management.'[13] According to Reynolds, this amounted to 'the abolition of workers' control'.[14]

Politically this change was associated with a reversion to the broad national front strategy of attempting to draw in the Mikołajczyk wing of the Peasant Party. Mikołajczyk was permitted to return to Poland and join the Provisional Government of National Unity in June 1945. Five ministers out of 21 were London Poles, including Jan Stańczyk a leader of the right wing of the Socialist Party (PPS). International, and particularly Soviet, pressure played an important part in this decision. It had been agreed in February 1945 at Yalta by the Allies that the 'Lublin Committee' should be reconstructed 'on a broader democratic basis with the inclusion of democratic leaders from Poland itself and from Poles abroad.' Moreover, a partial amnesty was proclaimed in order to persuade 'honest' members of the Home Army who were still underground to give themselves up to the authorities.

The construction of a broad national front emphatically did not mean a communist surrender of power. Gomułka pointed this out to Mikołajczyk on his return: 'It is we who are in power. We sincerely wish to come to terms with you . . . But please do not think our existence depends on it. We shall never surrender the power we have seized.'[15]

So much for the Yalta pledge to hold 'free and unfettered elections' in Poland. If Mikołajczyk wanted a share of power he would have to fight for it. By February 1946 he had indeed drawn this conclusion. He refused to enter an electoral bloc with the PPR, preferring to rely on the growing strength of his own party, the PSL, which now had over 600 000 members. The PPR reacted to this by shifting back to its previous radicalism. Now it was decided that the national front would be replaced by a 'democratic bloc', an alliance of the two working-class parties against 'the reactionaries'. But the socialist leaders were against this. They continued to hope for a broad national front. The PPR had to wait six months before implementing its plan, because it did not feel strong enough to act on its own. The PPS actually had more members than the PPR in the towns (78 000 as against 65 000). It was only slightly smaller overall (194 000 against 235 300). It continued to act independently at this stage. Moreover, the PPR was not yet sure of the allegiance of the Polish army and the security forces.[16]

Within the PPS, the 'centrist' faction led by Osóbka, Hochfeld, and Cyrankiewicz were able to beat off a challenge from the fellow-travelling 'left', led by Matuszewski, the Minister of Information. The results of the June 1946 referendum (in which, even on the official, falsified returns, the

PSL secured a respectable vote of 32 per cent against the abolition of the Senate) encouraged the 'centrists' of the PPS in their endeavours to bring that party into an electoral bloc for the forthcoming elections. They offered Mikołajczyk a quarter of the parliamentary and cabinet seats. But he refused. At this point the PPS gave up trying and joined the PPR in its campaign to crush the PSL. By September 1946, therefore, the National Front had shrunk to the dimensions of a 'democratic bloc' of the PPR and the PPS, associated with two smaller parties: the *Wola Ludu* (WL, the communist-inspired peasant party) and the SD (Democratic Party). Now it was possible for the PPR to go forward with the organisation of the elections. A fifth of the PSL lists were invalidated; the PSL was excluded from the conduct of the elections; arrests and the suppression of the PSL press completed the picture.

The PPS Centrists still wanted to retain an independent and equal role for their party in the government to be formed after the elections. Hence the pact of November 1946 between Gomułka and Cyrankiewicz was a compromise. The PPR had wanted a merger of the youth movements of the two parties, as prelude to the eventual creation of a single working-class party.[17]

The PPS resisted this demand, but they had to agree to fight the PSL and to view it as 'a legal extension of the reactionary underground' and to 'struggle uncompromisingly against the influence of anti-Soviet ideology' within their own party. They also agreed on the need to ensure a decisive majority in the next *Sejm* (parliament). The allocation of parliamentary seats and the membership of the next government were also settled at this meeting. Osóbka would be replaced as prime minister by Cyrankiewicz.

Opposition within the PPS to this pact was neutralised by the control exercised by the Centrists over the party machine. Cyrankiewicz, the General Secretary, ensured the subordination of all the party's provincial committees. Rightists were purged everywhere, and Żuławski, the leader of the right, was forced to resign. Even so, the Centrists did not see the November Pact as a surrender to orthodox communism. They continued to advocate the 'third road to socialism, the Polish road'. Optimism in this regard was strengthened by Gomułka's own declaration in November that 'Our democracy is not equivalent to Soviet democracy, any more than our social order is comparable with that of the Soviet Union.'[18]

The PPS Centrists were able to convince themselves that the January 1947 elections were a peaceful means of overthrowing the opposition. Officially, the Democratic Bloc of the PPR, PPS, WL, and SD secured 80 per cent of the votes, the PSL only 10 per cent. The real results were probably different: where PSL tellers were allowed to witness the count they found figures of 68 per cent in their favour and 22 per cent for the Democratic Bloc. The elections were supervised by the Polish security forces rather than the Red Army, assisted by the ORMO (Militia Volunteer Reserve), a 100 000 strong force formed largely from PPR members 'to combat banditry'.

'Banditry', in the sense of the existence of armed resistance groups, was indeed a feature of the situation in Poland between 1945 and 1947. There were several thousand armed men hiding in the forests from 1945 to 1947, usually members of the NSZ (National Armed Forces), who had not taken advantage of the amnesty of August 1945. There were also 'bandits' properly so-called, such as Captain Ogień, who terrorised the Zakopane area until 1947. Then there were the *banderovci*, or adherents of the Ukrainian nationalist Bandera in the east of the country. The post-1945 underground resistance never achieved any notable successes. The forces arrayed against it (both Russian and Polish) were far too strong. By the summer of 1947 the authorities had achieved complete physical control of Poland. In fact the existence of an anti-communist underground was an advantage to the communists in their drive to secure absolute power. They could accuse the PSL of helping the 'bandits' and spreading civil war.

The international impact of the defeat of the PSL was smaller than one might have expected in view of the agreements of Yalta and Potsdam. The British reaction was abruptly to drop Mikołajczyk; even from the USA the protests that came were mild. Moreover, some members of Mikołajczyk's own party began to express doubts about his leadership and about the whole idea of resisting the communist takeover. Ten out of the twenty eight PSL deputies in the *Sejm* began to advocate a programme of 'worker-peasant alliance' which was clearly communist inspired. The year 1947 was marked by increasing communist pressure on the PSL, both from within and externally. A government offensive against 'speculators' and 'rich peasants', ostensibly non-political, enabled the security organs to drag supporters of Mikołajczyk into the labour camps alongside genuine speculators. The campaign against the PSL coincided with the general hardening of positions in the Cold War during 1947. Peasant parties in Hungary (resignation of Ferenc Nagy as Prime Minister in May) Bulgaria (arrest of Petkov in June) and Romania (arrest of Maniu in the same month) were all simultaneously under attack. This was not a coincidence. Eventually Mikołajczyk, in fear for his life, decided to flee the country (October 1947). His party now came under the control of the leftist supporters of cooperation with the PPR, led by Józef Niećko, and it eventually merged with the SL (November 1949) to form the ZSL (United Peasant Party), an obedient rural 'transmission belt' in subsequent years.[19]

There remained the problem of the PPS. Gomułka proposed to deal with this by merging it with the PPR; the Centrists in the PPS had hoped to preserve their separate status but were forced to take the initiative themselves by the threat of being outflanked by the PPS Left under Matuszewski. Cyrankiewicz put up an obstinate resistance but finally changed course and started to advocate a merger of the parties after a visit to Moscow in March 1948. In December 1948 the PPR and the PPS merged to form the PZPR (Polish United Workers' Party).

The political struggle for complete communist control was paralleled by a social struggle for the control of the workers' movement, which also reached its height in 1947. The factory councils were integrated with the trade unions in January 1947, and the latter were gradually converted into a 'transmission belt' over the next two years by the extrusion of the influence of the PPS oppositionists. Although initially the independence of the trade unions had been proclaimed by the communists themselves in 1945, it was reduced by the declaration of 1947 that 'the workers' parties should have the dominant ideological influence in the trade union movement'. That was only the first stage, given the extremely strong position of the PPS (also a workers' party) within the trade unions. In 1947 38 per cent of factory council members belonged to the PPS, as against 31 per cent PPR members; the PPS had the support of 562 district trade union leaders, as against the PPR's 381; and it had 346 members in the central trade union leaderships as against the PPR's 329. The problem of PPS influence in the trade unions naturally ceased to exist with the PPR–PPS merger of December 1948, which was in reality a PPR takeover.[20]

A further task for the Polish communists at this time was the imposition of strict industrial discipline on the workers, with the aim of extracting maximum production. The system of 'socialist emulation' on the Soviet model was introduced in July 1947. It started with the coalminer Wincenty Pstrowski, the 'Polish Stakhanov', who achieved a 270 per cent overfulfilment of the norm, and challenged his workmates to do better. The campaign coincided with a 20 per cent fall in the average wage, and the extra wages received by the 'leading workers' were a cause of resentment. The communist-controlled press avoided publicising workers' resistance, but there is evidence that a strike took place in September 1947 in the Łódź textile mills. It lasted several weeks, was directed against 'socialist emulation', and probably had to be put down by force of arms.[21]

With the suppression of the strike of September 1947, the flight of Mikołajczyk in October 1947, the removal of the PSL and the PPS from the political scene in 1948–9, and the ending of the last traces of armed resistance, Gomułka and the Polish communists were in a position to impose their own 'Polish road to socialism'. Later on we shall examine how this conception was replaced after 1949 by a single model shared with all the other People's Democracies and derived purely from Soviet experience.

CZECHOSLOVAKIA: A NATION TURNS TO THE LEFT

We shall now turn to Poland's southern neighbour, Czechoslovakia, which had in common with Poland its position as a 'victor' power in the Second World War, a relatively highly developed industry and strong working-class organisations. Where it differed was in the breadth of the possible political coalition after 1945 and the consequent delay in the completion of the communist seizure of power.

The CPCz (Communist Party of Czechoslovakia) emerged from the Second World War in a very strong position. This was not simply a question of the presence of the Red Army on Czechoslovak soil (after all, it only remained there until November 1945) but of a definite move to the left among the industrial workers, already a large class, with mining and manufacturing accounting for 38 per cent of those gainfully employed in 1934. There was a feeling that the old capitalist order had failed, and that new structures were required. An extremely powerful Works Council movement developed during 1945, pressing for nationalisation of the mines and industry, and in fact establishing workers' control over 10 000 enterprises (i.e. 45 per cent of the total) in the Czech lands during mid-1945. This was initially opposed by the CPCz, as it did not want to break up the National Front, but when it turned out that the other parties would accept nationalisation, the party leader began to give his support, while stressing, in July 1945, that private enterprise would still have 'wide areas in which to operate'. Hence the nationalisation decrees of October 1945 only covered 61 per cent of the industrial work-force, and 16 per cent of all enterprises. The Social Democrats, especially the left-wing Minister of Industry, Bohumil Laušman, wanted much more nationalisation, and were joined in this view by rank and file trade unionists, but the CPCz insisted both on a moderate degree of nationalisation, and on compensation for former owners (except for Germans, Hungarians, and collaborators). The party did not want to go beyond the 'national democratic' programme yet or split the National Front by offending the 'middle-class parties'.

The Works' Council movement of 1945 strongly favoured workers' control, advocated by the left-wing Socialist Evžen Erban, but also by the communist František Jungmann. As Jungmann said on 16 May 1945: 'the works' councils shall be the power on which the whole economic structure of the state rests.'[22] There was much sympathy for this idea among the trade unions at first, until the election of the leading communist trade unionist Antonín Zápotocký, to replace Erban at the head of the union executive, ÚRO, in June 1945.[23]

Official CPCz policy was directed towards limiting the role of the Works' Councils and subordinating them to the trade unions. This was naturally welcome to the CPCz's coalition partners in the National Front, and the presidential decree of 24 October 1945 made it clear that the function of the Works' Councils in management was purely 'advisory', that the manager of a nationalised enterprise had to run it on 'sound business lines', and that only 'part' of the managing committee would consist of employee representatives.[24] Bruno Köhler, a leading CPCz functionary, later congratulated himself on his success in restraining the Works' Councils' 'attempts to build a state within a state', and his involvement in the presidential decree on the Works' Councils.[25] As a result, they became mere 'transmission belts' for carrying out the instructions of the trade unions.[26]

While resisting further nationalisation and workers' control, the CPCz made sure of its grip on the unified trade union movement, the ROH, which represented a very large proportion of Czech workers (2 250 000 members by December 1947). The executive of the ROH, the ÚRO, was overwhelmingly dominated by communists (94 out of 120 members).[27] This was not a manipulated result but a true reflection of the strength of the CPCz in the industrial working class. 58 per cent of the 1 100 000 members of the CPCz (counting the Czech lands alone) were industrial workers in 1946.[28]

Domination of the trade union movement was a useful adjunct to the political power of the party in the years 1946 to 1948. The ROH resolved at its first national conference in January 1946 that it would 'support every government which aims at socialism, but not a government which would want to check and sabotage the path to socialism'. The ÚRO resolution of 17 October 1947 similarly threatened to withdraw support from the political parties of the NF if 'their activity was in conflict with the mission of our national revolution to support a popular democratic development to socialism'.[29]

The CPCz had a large number of other cards in its hands as well. Its hegemony was in practice entrenched in the governmental system of the National Front. The post-1945 National Front coalition in Czechoslovakia did not allow the existence of an opposition; the number of political parties was limited to six (the two communist parties, Czech and Slovak, the Social Democrats, the National Socialists, the People's Party, and the Slovak Democrats) and all others were banned. The communist party obtained seven cabinet seats out of twenty-five in the postwar government, but

Professor Nejedlý (non-party) was in fact linked to the communist party, as were Zdeněk Fierlinger (Social Democrat, and prime minister 1945–6), and Jožka David (National Socialist). This made a total of ten reliable votes: still a minority. But the non-communist parties did not attempt until 1947 to use the majority they enjoyed in theory, because they were committed to the idea of national cooperation, based on the Košice Programme. The communist view of these matters was put by Václav Kopecký, speaking to the Central Committee in February 1946: 'We envisaged the CPCz as the guiding force, and closest to it would be the Social Democrats, headed by their left-wing leadership.'[30]

There was the less need for conflict in that the Košice Programme, a moderate document drawn up by the communist leader Klement Gottwald during the war, was the agreed basis of policy for all the government parties. As he said in April 1945, 'We shall base the National Front not on our communist programme with its goal of Soviets and socialism but on the government programme.'[31]

The Košice programme was a 'popular democratic' programme on lines familiar over the whole of Eastern Europe. There would be free elections to a Constituent Assembly; foreign policy would be based on a close alliance with the Soviet Union; the Czechoslovak army would be 'genuinely democratic and anti-Fascist' (point 3); elected National Committees would administer local affairs (point 5); Czechs and Slovaks would have equal rights (point 6); traitors would be punished (point 9) and lose their property (point 10); Germans and Hungarians, unless proven anti-Fascists, would lose their citizenship (point 8) and their property (point 10); enemy landed property would be confiscated and divided among the small farmers (point 11). Nationalisation was not mentioned, except in regard to factories confiscated under point 10.[32] Only 8 per cent of Czechoslovaks opposed this programme, according to a survey made in 1946.[33]

Thus the Czechoslovak communists decided not to seize power in 1945, although they were fully capable of doing so, especially given the presence of the Red Army. This was precisely in line with Stalin's policy at the time. Attempts by leftists in the Slovak communist party to move towards the introduction of a fully-fledged Soviet system were sharply rejected by Georgi Dimitrov, the Bulgarian Comintern veteran who had Stalin's ear, with the words: 'You people in Slovakia who are in far too much of a hurry as regards Soviet power must calm down. The question of Sovietisation is not to be posed. Only when the time is ripe.'[34]

Nevertheless, the National Front system set up in 1945 had elements of instability. Although they had momentarily renounced the prospect of seizing power, the CPCz leaders did not intend to let go of the commanding position they already had. Gottwald himself let this be known publicly before the 1946 elections: 'If we do not achieve a favourable result, the working class, the working people, our party, have sufficient means and weapons to hand to correct the results of mechanical voting. We have enough power in our hands to produce a favourable result for the working class.'[35]

The implicit threat did not need to be activated. The election victory of May 1946, in which the communists received 38 per cent of the votes and the Social Democrats 12 per cent, could be presented as a victory for the working class, a joint communist and social democratic victory. The CPCz and the Social Democrats together had 151 out of the 300 seats in the National Assembly. At 40 per cent the communists' success was much greater in the 'Czech lands' of Bohemia and Moravia than in Slovakia, where the CPS (Communist Party of Slovakia) had only received 30 per cent of the vote as against the Slovak Democrats' 62 per cent. Hard-liners in the Slovak party reacted to this by demanding harsh measures against the Democrats but were restrained by their Czech colleagues.[36]

Instead, the non-controversial 'Construction Programme' was issued. This was essentially a continuation of the Košice Programme, but it also contained a Two Year Plan for economic reconstruction, with the moderate target of a level of industrial production in 1948 10 per cent higher than had been achieved in 1937.[37] The 'Construction Programme', like its predecessor, had been worked out by the communists and then approved unanimously by their coalition partners (on 7 July 1946). Gottwald affirmed in parliament that 'the campaign of nationalisation . . . is concluded'. The plan called for 'the consolidation of nationalised industry and its coexistence with the private sector of the economy'. Politically the system of 'people's democracy' was presented by Gottwald as 'our own specific road to socialism'.[38] He had it on Stalin's own authority that the Soviet road to socialism was not the only possible one.[39]

There now began a process of gradual takeover, in which, by barely perceptible transitional stages the government behind the scenes (the party leadership) became the real government. Gottwald replaced Fierlinger as prime minister in 1946; by the end of 1947 127 out of the 160 District National Committees in the Czech lands were chaired by communists; of the 17 district commanders of the SNB (the police force) 12 were communists and four unaffiliated; of the 13 members of the central command of the SNB 10 were communists and three social democrats. The commander in chief of the army, General Ludvík Svoboda, was so pro-communist that in 1945 he asked Gottwald whether to join or not.[40] The officer corps was only 15–20 per cent communist before February 1948, but this mattered less, given Svoboda's position.[41]

All that was lacking was an overall electoral majority, which Gottwald proclaimed in January 1947 to be the chief political aim, with the slogan of 'the conquest of an absolute majority' or '51%'. Then everything would be 'settled at one go' he added.[42] The non-communist parties regarded this as incompatible with the cooperation enshrined in the National Front. The principle of the National Front, according to them, was that the decisive components of the national life should rule together; one should not dominate the others. However, the agreement of February 1947 not to nationalise any further sections of industry calmed the political atmosphere. The US ambassador in Prague, L. A. Steinhardt, reported in June 1947 that democracy was well rooted in Czechoslovakia, and the economic situation was satisfactory. Moreover, trade with the USSR was declining while it was increasing with the West, and Gottwald 'had the extremists in the communist party well under control'.[43]

If Steinhardt was proved wrong, it was largely for reasons of international policy. The year 1947 saw the definitive breach between Stalin and the West and start of the Cold War: a turning point in the history of postwar Europe. The policy turn of 1947 was both political and economic. Politically the suppression of non-communist opposition was accelerated all over Eastern Europe. The coalition system of People's Democracy was dismantled, or at least emptied of any real content. In the economic sphere, the idea that, as Imre Nagy said in 1947, 'people's democracy is compatible with residual capitalism', was henceforth rejected. The degree of nationalisation of industry (slight until 1947) was increased sharply in the former enemy countries of Bulgaria (16% in 1947; 95% in 1948); Hungary (45% in 1947, 81% in 1949); and Romania (11% in 1947, 95% in 1948), while the small sector which still remained in private hands was mopped up in Poland (20% in 1947, 8% in 1950); Czechoslovakia (22% in 1947, 4% in 1948); and Yugoslavia (18% in 1947, 0% in 1948). In foreign policy the countries of Eastern Europe ceased to have room for manoeuvre between East and West.

International factors were of decisive significance in Stalin's decision to consolidate his grip on the lands east of the Elbe. The promulgation of the Truman Doctrine in March (itself a reaction to the Greek insurgency) and the removal of communists from office in Italy and France (in April and May respectively) indicated a hardening of the West's position; the rejection of the Marshall Plan in July (imposed upon the unwilling Poles and Czechs after Stalin had vetoed it) and the establishment of the Information

Bureau of the Nine Communist Parties (known as the 'Cominform') in September at Szklarska Poręba in southern Poland indicated a hardening of Stalin's position, which was immediately transmitted to all the European communist parties. There was also an economic factor: the progressive decline of Eastern Europe's trade with the Soviet Union in 1947 made a political intervention into economic affairs urgently necessary. The Soviet share of Czechoslovakia's foreign trade, for example, had fallen progressively: it was 25% in 1945, 12.5% in 1946 and 6% early in 1947. Stalin had to resist the gradual reintegration of the Eastern European economies into the Western capitalist network. It did not matter that economic relations were pulling in the opposite direction.

The impact of the reorientation of Soviet policy was felt particularly strongly in Czechoslovakia. This was indicated first of all by its rejection of the Marshall Plan, on direct Soviet instructions. But the transition to the new line was gradual. Important as it was for Czechoslovakia's foreign policy and economic development, the decision to reject the Marshall Plan did not in itself mean a change in communist strategy. Initially the Czechoslovak government had been in favour of the Plan. Gottwald had made soundings in Moscow through party channels without receiving a definite reply. He would hardly have supported the Marshall Plan in the knowledge that Stalin was against it. The same applies to the rest of the Czechoslovak government; the original decision to accept Marshall Aid (4 July) was not an anti-Soviet move but a simple misunderstanding of Stalin's intentions.[44] The Czechoslovak delegation to Moscow, led by Gottwald, was criticised by Stalin for failing to consult him beforehand, and asked to retract the decision to participate. After some argument, the Czechoslovaks fell into line, feeling that once Moscow had spoken there was no alternative. On 10 July the cabinet in Prague decided unanimously 'to renounce participation' in the Marshall Plan conference 'in the light of this clear expression of Soviet views'.[45]

This was a recognition of the Soviet Union's veto power over Czechoslovak foreign policy; but it had no immediate domestic consequences. The basic strategy of the CPCz remained that of preparation for the next elections. Only in the improbable case of an offensive by the non-communist parties, said Gottwald on 21 August, would the party reply by a general strike or where appropriate by the formation of a new government including the mass organisations. Otherwise, it would encourage left factions in the other parties and raise the slogan 'reactionaries out of the National Front'. It would 'renew the Socialist Bloc' by including left Social Democrats and National Socialists in it.[46] The CPCz also made a demagogic proposal to pay for grain price subsidies by raising a 'millionaires' tax' (rejected in cabinet on 2 September). A more radical land reform was proposed too (it was rejected on 12 September). This was all part of the general strategy of driving a wedge between 'leftist' and 'rightist' elements of the National Front, but did not involve a complete change of approach.

The decisive turning-point for Czechoslovakia and for Eastern Europe generally was not the Marshall Plan rejection but the meeting of representatives of nine major communist parties in September 1947, which set up the Cominform. Attention has centred on the severe criticisms made there of the French and Italian Communist Parties for their failure either to engage in a revolutionary struggle against their governments or effectively resist their exclusion from office in the spring of 1947. But the Czechoslovak and Hungarian communists were attacked too.[47]

A Soviet delegate referred to the fact that, unlike the rest of Eastern Europe, 'the power contest in Czechoslovakia still remains undecided at the end of 1947'.[48] The leader of the Polish party, Władysław Gomułka, rebuked the CPCz leaders for allegedly having left it too late to seize power. The Yugoslav Kardelj attacked the 'illusions of the CPCz about the peaceful, parliamentary and electoral road'.[49] When Rudolf Slánský, the chief Czechoslovak delegate, returned to Prague he reported to his colleagues that several delegations had felt that 'more than any other Slav state, Czechoslovakia is stuck in the shackles of formal parliamentary democracy.' The conclusion he drew was that 'on the domestic front just as in the international field we should go onto the offensive'.[50]

What forms would this offensive take? The party's leftists (e.g. Čepička) wanted a direct seizure of power. This was not Gottwald's way. He preferred to step up the pressure on the non-communist parties, by methods already applied before September. The CPCz decided to exploit the 'discovery' (in fact the invention by State Security) of a conspiracy in Slovakia by Democrats who had been members of the collaborationist Hlinka People's Party during the war (15 September). The party now demanded the establishment of a de facto communist majority on the Slovak Board of Commissioners by including representatives of the mass organisations (the ROH and the Peasant Commissions – both under communist control). The demand was rejected, thanks to the firm opposition of the non-communist parties, with the result that the communists remained in a minority on the Slovak Board (five out of 15 posts). The 'left' of the CPS wanted to react forcibly to this defeat by 'regenerating' the National Front through the creation of new National Front committees containing representatives of the mass organisations (Karol Šmidke's proposal of 4 December).[51]

The CPS leaders rejected this idea. Meanwhile, in the Czech lands

Gottwald's strategy continued to be to prepare for the elections, though this time by establishing a single list, which would 'bring together everything that is really progressive and democratic in the country'.[52] The single list would include candidates from the other parties who were prepared to swing their policies behind those of the communist party. A department of the CPCz, headed by O. Hromádko, was set up for work within the other parties. Each party had 'left-wingers' within it, people who were prepared to stand jointly with the CPCz on a single list: Fierlinger and Erban within the Social Democrats; Šlechta and Neuman within the NSs; Plojhar within the People's Party; even the Slovak Democrats had their leftists. The CPCz's own information led it to believe that it would receive 55 per cent of the votes in the next elections; but a single list was a safer way of winning.

Nevertheless, there was nothing here to suggest a plan to seize power. Power would be gained, certainly, but in a gradual way. It was in fact the National Socialists who took the initiative, feeling that they had to stop the rot, on 13 February 1948. The issue was the 'largely fortuitous matter of measures taken by the director of the Bohemian region of State Security'.[53]

The NSs managed to gain a cabinet majority on 13 February to instruct the communist Minister of the Interior, Václav Nosek, to dismiss eight district police chiefs. When he failed to do so they mounted a collective resignation by twelve ministers (20 February). But the Social Democrats (on whom they had placed great hopes, in view of the replacement of the pro-communist party chairman Fierlinger in November by the 'centrist' Laušman) failed to join in. Instead they condemned the resignations, hoping to play the part of mediators. Hence a majority of ministers (fourteen) remained in office. The resignations of 20 February were a windfall for the communists, who now began to drive for power in earnest. As Gottwald said later: 'I prayed that this stupidity over the resignations would go on and that they would not change their minds.'[54]

The CPCz could now make the reasonable-sounding demand that the resignations be accepted, and the places of the absent ministers be filled by President Beneš. He had in fact promised the NSs that he would not do so, and on one level the events of the next six days were aimed at compelling Beneš to take back this promise. The method chosen was the idea, already broached and rejected in December, of 'renewing' the National Front by setting up 'Action Committees'. These would act as executive organs and be entirely staffed by communists or their sympathisers.[55] This was Gottwald's strategy; the radicals in the party leadership like Ďuriš, Kopecký and Zápotocký 'like horses champing at the bit' would have preferred an open confrontation.[56]

Neither the armed forces nor the security services were needed. Even a general strike was unnecessary (although a highly effective demonstrative strike lasting one hour was called). The threat of force was certainly present in February, in three aspects: 5000 Slovak communist partisans had kept some weapons from 1944; units of factory guards were set up in the big factories at the end of 1947; above all, the People's Militia was available. This force, commanded by Josef Pavel, originated out of 'emergency platoons' of trusted communist workers, and was set up officially on 21 February. It was 15 000–18 000 strong, and received 'tens of thousands of brand new rifles and automatics sent by armaments workers from Brno'.[57] The Red Army could also be called on if necessary; Valerian Zorin, the Soviet deputy foreign minister, was present in Prague throughout the crisis, and allegedly offered Soviet military assistance to Gottwald on 19 February.[58]

This kind of help was not needed. Gottwald's chosen method was rather a combination of direct pressure on President Beneš, whom he visited at least six times during the February crisis,[59] and the mobilisation of the mass organisations of workers (the Congress of Works' Councils) poor peasants (a Congress of Peasants' Commissions, scheduled for 28 February, and intended to overcome right wing opposition to Ďuriš's proposed land reform expropriating all landholdings of over 50 hectares) and the people in general (the Action Committees of the National Front). A Congress of Works' Councils had already been decided on by the CPCz leaders (11 February) and called by the ÚRO Presidium (12 February) before the resignation of the ministers; now it could be used as a further element of pressure. The resolution passed by the 8000 people present at the Congress of 22 February with only 10 contrary votes did not in fact mention the government crisis, but concentrated on the demands for further nationalisation, land reform, and the threat of a general strike if these demands met with opposition.[60]

The Action Committees, set up in response to Gottwald's call of 21 February, were overwhelmingly Communist (70 per cent) or left Social Democrat (17 per cent).[61] Their main function was to purge opponents of the CPCz from public life, starting at the top. The Minister of Transport, the Slovak Democrat Ivan Pietor, was ordered to leave his office by an Action Committee on 23 February. The same thing happened to Hubert Ripka (NS, Foreign Trade), and Jaroslav Stránský (NS, Education).[62]

Meanwhile the pressure from below was increased, with the one-hour general strike of 24 February by two and a half million workers, and the mass demonstrations of 25 February (250 000 in Prague, hundred of thousands in other cities). Beneš finally gave way at 4.30 p.m. on 25 February. He accepted the resignation of the twelve ministers, and agreed to the replacements Gottwald had nominated. In the new cabinet the communists had thirteen seats out of twenty five, and the rest of the ministers, whatever their party allegiance, were prepared to serve the new regime. The CPCz had much greater representation lower down the hierarchy, thanks to the purges begun by local Action Committees and then organised systematically by the Central Action Committee chaired by Zápotocký.[63]

Members of the non-communist parties were dismissed from positions in local government. 59 000 were removed from the National Committees; 20 000 Works Councillors and trade union officials were sacked; 15 000 officials of the Sokol gymnastic associations were removed; 28 000 people were dismissed from the civil service including a quarter of the army officers, 534 professors and lecturers and 145 judges; and 4000 workers were sacked for having refused to take part in the general strike of 24 February.[64]

But there the purges stopped. The left of the party (Kopecký and Čepička in particular) wanted an immediate transition to fully-fledged Stalinism. This was opposed by Gottwald, who wanted the other parties (duly purged) to retain a place within the 'renewed' or 'regenerated' National Front. As he told a CC Plenum in April 1948, 'It would be a good thing if there were one or two opposition parties.' But, he added in June, 'we have to be careful that they do not become an arena of the reaction'.[65] He also wanted the Works Councils, trade unions, and 'Peasants' Commissions' to retain a certain degree of independence. Economically the government did not go beyond the programme of February: although further sectors of industry were nationalised during 1948, leaving virtually no private enterprise with more than twenty employees in existence, the retail trade was initially left alone, as were peasants and artisans. Moreover, political repression was limited at this stage: leading opposition politicians were left untouched (although 10 deputies were imprisoned for their alleged part in a 'reactionary plot').

The shift to severer, specifically 'Stalinist' policies occurred later in the year, in the context of Stalin's break with Tito, and the campaign against 'separate roads to socialism' that followed it. Before we examine this transition, however, the seizure of power over the rest of Eastern Europe must be treated, beginning with East Germany, where Stalin, far from being in a hurry as he had been in Poland, was extremely doubtful for a long time about the whole project.

GERMANY: HALF IN AND HALF OUT

Many studies of communist Eastern Europe exclude the eastern half of Germany from their subject. There are certainly a number of good reasons for doing this. In terms of policy, Stalin long continued to recognise the special status of his occupation zone of Germany as half of a country destined ultimately for reunification; in its economic and social structure, it remained in the stage of transition far longer than any of the People's Democracies. The very title assigned to East Germany in 1949, 'the German Democratic Republic', seemed to accentuate what separated it from its neighbours to the south and east. Yet there are stronger grounds for inclusion. The ultimate fate of East Germany was the same as that of the rest of Eastern Europe. The differences, marked at first in certain spheres, gradually diminished as Soviet policy evolved towards admitting the permanence of Germany's division. By 1961 at the latest the clock in Pankow was keeping time with the clocks in Prague, Warsaw and Budapest at least as well as they kept time with each other. This was even more apparent in 1989.

The communist 'seizure of power' in East Germany after 1945 is more accurately described as an orderly transfer of responsibilities. Two events in June 1945 laid the foundations for this. On 9 June the Soviet Military Administration in Germany (SMAD) was set up to administer the Soviet Zone of Occupation (SBZ). Marshal Zhukov was in charge of the SMAD until April 1946, then Vasily Sokolovsky, but the real maker of policy was Colonel S. I. Tyulpanov, head of the CPSU party organisation within the SMAD.

The other major event was the refounding on 11 June of the Communist Party of Germany (KPD). KPD leaders were in place from the very start of the Soviet occupation of East Germany. Three 'initiative groups' were flown there in April, headed by Walter Ulbricht, Gustav Sobottka, and Anton Ackermann. They soon put a stop to attempts by indigenous Anti-Fascist Committees to revolutionise German society. Their aims were strictly limited. Hence the programme of the KPD explicitly ruled out the Soviet system, as it 'does not correspond to the present conditions of German development'. The aim the party set itself was 'the establishment of an anti-fascist, democratic regime, a parliamentary democratic republic' from which 'feudal survivals had been completely removed.' Thereafter the familiar roles were played out. Non-communist parties such as the CDU (Christian Democrats) and the LDPD (Liberal Democrats) emerged alongside the KPD, and were encouraged by it. Their programmes differed little from the latter's, in view of its studied moderation. The SPD was also restored. Its programme was marked by a strong commitment to socialism and working-class unity. At this stage the KPD opposed such ideas. Instead it advocated a 'National Front', which found expression in the establishment of a bloc of the four anti-Fascist parties (11 July 1945). After initially resisting the SPD's idea of a fusion of the two working-class parties the KPD altered course in October 1945. The merger, and the establishment of the SED (Socialist Unity Party) followed in April 1946. As elsewhere, the 'united party of the working class' was the old communist party writ large. There was a considerable degree of opposition, and much pressure had to be exercised to bring the obstinate Social Democrats into line.[66]

The Conference of the Sixty, a meeting of thirty officials from each party held in December 1945, was the scene of bitter comments from Social Democrats about the sudden change in communist policy. Otto Grotewohl, later prime minister of the GDR but at that time an SPD leader, complained that the KPD remained as 'centralist and undemocratic in its party structure as before,'[67] and he pointed out that unification on a local level would make 'unification of the German workers' movement impossible'. Despite this, he and all those present with one exception voted for the KPD resolution in favour of further organisational steps towards unity. The reason was that the SPD in the east had the choice between self-dissolution (recommended by the western SPD) and entering the united party in the hope of retaining some influence.

Resistance by the other parties was dealt with by the founding of competing organisations which would appeal to the same constituency. The DBD (Democratic Peasants' Party) was founded in June 1948 to cut into the support of the CDU; the NDPD (National Democratic Party) to undermine the LDPD. There were also 'mass organisations' which played the role of 'transmission belts' for the SED. The German Democratic Women's League is one example. This technique was also standard throughout Eastern Europe.

One cannot assign a specific date to the SED's achievement of a monopoly of power. The process was one of gradual strangulation of the opposition, with the active (and indispensable) assistance of the SMAD; once the decision was made to establish the German Democratic Republic power could simply be transferred in full from the Soviet authorities to the SED. But a separate German state was not part of the original plan. It was only after 'long hesitation' (Staritz) that Stalin decided to reply to Western moves towards unifying West Germany by converting the SBZ into the GDR. As late as December 1947 a 'People's Congress for Unity and a Just Peace', entirely dominated at it was by the SED, called for 'the formation of an all-German government'.

Inability to abandon the perspective of German unity had an impact on economic and social policy. A comparison with the rest of Eastern Europe shows that there was a built-in delay of about three years in this area. There are various views on the date of the decision to establish socialism. Some people suggest November 1946. This seems too early. To speak of 'economic planning', as Ulbricht did then, is not to call for the construction of socialism. Everyone was talking about economic planning, in the context of post-war reconstruction. In any case, whatever Ulbricht's personal views, he had to wait for Stalin. When Otto Grotewohl, on behalf of the SED, proclaimed in June 1948 that 'our orientation is exclusively and unreservedly to the East', he was called to order by Stalin, who told the party leaders in December 1948 that 'discussions of how Germany is to be organised are stupid. First you must win'. The Third German People's Congress in May 1949 proposed to reply to the practical foundation of the Federal Republic by calling for 'German unity and a just peace treaty.' Even the founding of the GDR in October 1949 was not in itself an option for the 'building of socialism'. It was rather a counter-move to the unification of the Western zones, and the decision of the West Germans to go for full integration with the Western Alliance. The SED leaders still in 1949 found it impossible to think of 'socialism in half a country as an acceptable perspective'.[68]

At the SED's First Party Conference (January 1949) Grotewohl proclaimed that 'there can be no question of transition to a "people's democratic" development in the immediate future'. The party's aim continued to be 'the all-round establishment of the anti-Fascist democratic order'.[69]

Naturally one should distinguish the needs of propaganda from the real situation. Although the establishment of the GDR was delayed until 1949, unified economic institutions had long been in place. Order No. 17 (25 July 1945) set up German Central Administrations (DZVs) which were in effect ministries for the whole of the SBZ. In June 1947 a German Economic Commission (DWK) was set up, to draw up an economic plan and organise the delivery of reparations to the Soviet Union. Despite its purely economic function it was the kernel of the later government, and its permanent secretariat was dominated by members of the SED like Heinrich Rau, Bruno Leuschner and Fritz Selbmann. The nationalisation of 65 per cent of industrial capacity by June 1948 placed tremendous power in the Commission's hands.

But this power could not be used to establish socialism, even after the GDR had been set up. Stalin was against it, because he did not want to preclude a possible re-unification of Germany on a neutral basis. Only after the failure of the West to respond to Stalin's note of March 1952 offering a peace treaty with a 'unified, independent, democratic and peace-loving Germany' was Ulbricht permitted to go ahead with the 'construction of socialism'. It was the task of the Second Party Conference (July 1952) to proclaim this objective, which involved the mopping up of the remains of private industry (still responsible for 19 per cent of production in 1952) and trade (37 per cent) and the gradual collectivisation of agriculture.[70]

Now for the first time the GDR was described as a 'people's democratic order'. In other words, it began to follow the course taken by the other People's Democracies after a delay of three years. Nevertheless, once the decision had been taken the GDR adopted the Stalinist pattern as quickly as possible, and it never really departed from it. But before considering this pattern in more detail we shall examine the differing routes to power taken by the communist parties of the southern, more agrarian and generally less developed parts of Eastern Europe.

3 The Seizure of Power
Part Two: Hungary and the Agrarian South

We have now to consider the countries to the south of Czechoslovakia, which were still characterised in 1945 by a continuing predominance of the agrarian sector, a minority urban population, an undeveloped working class, and a concomitant pre-war weakness of both socialism and communism.[1] These statements apply in general terms to the Balkan lands. They are less true for Hungary, which did have a large urban population and an industrial working class, although politically the severe repressive measures of the interwar years had taken their toll of the socialist and communist movements. Hungary was on the boundary between north and south, both in its geography and its economic and social structure.

Nevertheless, Hungary, Bulgaria and Romania can be grouped together from certain points of view. They were defeated opponents in 1944–5, rather than liberated allies; they were under Soviet occupation; they were covered (unlike Poland and Czechoslovakia) by the Stalin–Churchill 'percentage agreement' of October 1944; their fate was determined in detail by Allied Control Commissions (ACCs) set up after the war; the decisions of the Soviet military chairmen of the ACCs were accepted, *faute de mieux*, by their British and American colleagues. This effectively counterbalanced the weakness of the indigenous communist parties. Without Soviet support they could hardly even have considered assuming power.

The 'percentage agreement' of October 1944, as modified subsequently by Eden and Molotov, assigned a 90 per cent influence in Greece to the West, giving in return Soviet predominance in Hungary (80 per cent), Romania (90 per cent), Bulgaria (80 per cent) and Yugoslavia (60 per cent).[2] Although this agreement was never confirmed by the United States, it indicates the degree of control that Britain was prepared to assign to the Soviet Union in the Balkans. What did Stalin intend to do with the powers thereby granted to him? Coalition governments with communist participation were on the agenda in all cases, in line with the 'National Front' policy valid for the whole of Eastern Europe. Whether Stalin placed the communists in control from the outset depended on the local situation, and in particular on the seriousness of the threat presented by surviving anti-communist forces.

In Hungary in 1945 any threat from the right was practically non-existent. The former ruler, Admiral Horthy, who had long collaborated with Germany, had tried to work the trick of changing sides at the last moment, but failed. Hence Hungary was reconquered by the Red Army from the Nazis and their puppet ruler, the Arrow Cross leader Ferenc Szálasi, and the coalition government that took over in April 1945 was faced with a political *tabula rasa*. The situation developed differently in Romania and Bulgaria. On 23 August 1944 King Michael of Romania successfully changed sides, hence Romania remained a monarchical state. In Bulgaria the regency council which took over after the death of King Boris III was thrown out by the coup of September 1944, but important elements of the pre-war élites retained power. The new premier of Bulgaria was Kimon Georgiev of the Zveno movement of army officers.

Hence if pro-Soviet governments were to retain power in Romania and Bulgaria, considerable surveillance and pressure was needed, whereas Hungary did not need to be kept on such a tight rein. So the Soviet military authorities in Hungary at first did no more than requisition supplies and dismantle and remove factories. They stayed neutral towards internal Hungarian politics. There seems no evidence of direct Soviet intervention in Hungary before October 1945 (when Marshal Voroshilov, the Soviet chairman of the ACC, insisted that the current coalition government be preserved regardless of the outcome of the general election).[3]

Until then the Hungarian Communists were left to make their own way to power. They did not make a very good job of it. Their initial position was strong, for they were the only organised force in the country. It was the communists themselves who encouraged the other parties to resume their activities in 1944–5, so as to have someone to enter a coalition with. As Ernő Gerő said in December 1944: 'It is not right that only one party should be active in the area controlled by the Soviet army. Let other parties take up activities as well.'

The Provisional Government set up at Debrecen on 23 December 1944 was a coalition with a moderate programme and only two communist ministers. The top leaders of the party, the 'Muscovites' Rákosi, Gerő, Farkas and Révai, were excluded from the government on Stalin's instructions, 'because they would be seen as hirelings of Moscow'.[4]

The new government contained three generals from the former Horthy régime: Béla Miklós (Prime Minister), János Vörös (Defence), and Gábor Faraghó (Food Supply). The communists Imre Nagy and József Gábor took over Agriculture and Commerce respectively, and the rest of the team was made up of Smallholders and Social Democrats. The government programme (which was also the programme of the Hungarian National

Independence Front) was a typically moderate National Front affair: liberal democratic demands predominated, and interventions into the economy were limited to an extensive land reform, the nationalisation of energy industries and 'state supervision' of banks and industrial cartels. The trial of war criminals, the dissolution of Fascist organisations, and a purge of Fascists from the administration also figured in the programme. There were some leftists within the party who wanted to go further, but Gerő told them: 'It is not a correct viewpoint to urge the construction of socialism upon the rubble of defeat.'[5]

The communists did, however, secure indirect control of the vital Ministry of the Interior owing to the appointment of Ferenc Erdei, a member of the left-leaning pro-communist faction of the National Peasant Party. The other means of exercising control was from below, through four bodies, which though set up at communist instigation (Révai was already advocating the setting up of 'revolutionary, democratic authorities at a local level' in December 1944[6]) displayed considerable spontaneity: 'national committees' to run local affairs; 'works' councils' to run factories seized by local radicals, either communist or social democratic, and legitimised but at the same time emasculated by the decree of 18 February restricting them to the supervision rather than the control of management; 'village land claims commissions', set up by the decree of 17 March 1945 to carry out the land reform, and consisting of landless labourers and poor peasants; and finally the 'people's courts', *ad hoc* tribunals used both to judge and condemn traitors, war criminals and Arrow Crossists, and to purge some officials of the former régime, using the so-called 'B lists'.

Yet these institutions only had a brief heyday. It is hard to see why. Rákosi himself said on 22 February 1945 that 'the central problem is the removal of officials of the old type . . . and the introduction of new people',[7] thereby giving official support to a thorough purge. It seems that the communist party just did not have things its own way in Hungary in 1945. The Smallholders strongly opposed the dismissal of officials of the former civil service and judiciary and at a local level they were often strong enough to prevent this. The communist line of coalition with 'democratic forces' implied listening to their objections. No effective purge of the civil service took place. By June 1945 only 20 per cent of the civil servants were new appointees. The old factory managers, army officers and local authorities soon returned. These omissions had to be remedied in the course of 1946. The communists were however able to gain immediate control of the Trade Union Council when it was set up in February 1945. They had a two to one majority over the social democrats on the secretariat, and the Secretary-General, István Kossa, was a communist. He used his powers to restrain the radicalism of the Works' Councils: 'Comrades who play a decisive role in the Works' Councils do not fully comprehend the party's political line on the recognition of private property.' (May 1945) They should hand back the plants they had seized, he added.[8]

Finally, two sets of elections in autumn 1945 turned out disastrously for the communist party. The first, the Budapest municipal election of 7 October 1945, gave an absolute majority (in a purely urban constituency) to the Smallholders (50.5 per cent) and 42.8 per cent to the Workers' Unity Front of communists and social democrats together. This failure resulted in the Soviet intervention already mentioned, but Voroshilov's further demand that the distribution of seats in the National Assembly be determined by advance agreement between the parties was not accepted; the USA warned that in that case recognition of the Hungarian government would be withheld. A genuinely free election thus took place in Hungary on 4 November 1945, and it produced another absolute majority for the Smallholders (57 per cent). The communists received 17 per cent, the social democrats 17.4 per cent. Voroshilov told the Smallholders' leader Ferenc Nagy that 'the Soviet Union wishes to base its friendship with Hungary on its relations with the Smallholders' Party'[9] but he insisted that the communists retain an important role in the coalition cabinet. They received three portfolios, the Smallholders seven; the balance was made up by three Social Democrats and one National Peasant. The Prime Minister was a Smallholder (Zoltán Tildy); but Voroshilov made sure that the Ministry of the Interior was given to Imre Nagy.

The communists' failure in the elections indicated the need for a change in the policy of both the Soviet representatives and the local party. A combination of pressure and manipulation was now used. Firstly, the masses were mobilised. The communist party had grown by October 1945 to 500 000 members, having started from a figure of 3000 in November 1944. Moreover, the Social Democrats (400 000 strong by the end of 1945) had a sizeable pro-communist left wing. The Left Bloc, formed on 5 March 1946 by the communists, Social Democrats and National Peasants, immediately called a monster demonstration of 400 000 workers in Budapest against Dezső Sulyok and other 'reactionaries' in the Smallholders' Party. Secondly, the moderate line taken in 1944 was now abandoned. Rákosi told the party's Central Committee in May 1946 that whereas in 1944 hotheads had had to be restrained, now 'the time has come to remind our party and the working class that we are also socialists.' The time when socialism would be realised was drawing near, he added. One way of achieving this would be to establish a single working class party by merging the communists with the social democrats. Thirdly, party control of the Ministry of the

Interior was used to bring communists into the police force. In March 1946 the hard-liner László Rajk replaced Imre Nagy, who was insufficiently ruthless, despite or perhaps because he was a 'Muscovite' communist. Rajk promptly got rid of 5000 policemen and 60 000 civil servants, using the 'B-list decree' of May 1946, which set up screening committees to evaluate the loyalty of state officials to the 'democratic reshaping of the country'. His methods were effective. By October 1946 69 per cent of the police were supporters of the left, and 52 per cent supported the communist party.[10]

Fourthly, Soviet pressure was brought to bear via the ACC. The party did not yet have control of the armed forces, so in October 1945 Voroshilov ordered the reduction of the Hungarian army from 70 000 to 20 000. This allowed a corresponding expansion of the Frontier Guard and its conversion under György Pálffy (a Smallholder sympathetic to the HCP) into a communist armed force. By June 1946 60 per cent of the officer corps were party members or sympathisers.[11]

Direct pressure was also exerted to persuade the Smallholders to get rid of 'reactionaries' in their midst. Ferenc Nagy, the Smallholders' leader, relates that he received a series of official notes on this subject in February 1946. He was finally forced to expel Sulyok and twenty other right-wing deputies from his party (March 1946). The motivation for his surrender, it seems, was less fear of the mass demonstrations mounted by the Left Bloc than hope for Soviet international support over a reduction of reparations and the retention of Transylvania, which was in danger of being handed to Romania. He was to be disappointed. Two months later the Council of Foreign Ministers assigned the whole of Transylvania to Romania, with the full agreement of the Soviet Union, a decision confirmed in August 1946 at the Paris Peace Conference.

This does not exhaust the list of methods of achieving power. The standard technique of leaving convinced communists in other parties, or actually inserting them, described graphically by Gomułka in the Polish context as the placing of 'plants'[12] was thoroughly developed in Hungary by Rákosi and Révai. As Révai told the founding meeting of the Cominform in September 1947: 'The National Peasant Party acts under guidance. The secretary is a communist, and one of the two ministers representing it in the government is a communist.'[13] The situation was similar with the Social Democratic left, led by György Marosán. In his memoirs, Marosán describes meetings with communist leaders to take instructions.[14] The right of the SDP, under Peyer, tried to protest, but to no avail. At the 35th Party Congress, in February 1947, Arpád Szakasits was confirmed as General

Secretary, and Marosán and Ries were elected as his deputies. All three were from the pro-communist left of the party.

Where the non-communist parties could not be controlled from within, their disintegration could be pursued from the outside. To do this, Rákosi utilised what he later boastfully described as the 'salami tactic'.[15] This was the method of destroying rival parties by slicing pieces off them, starting at the right and moving gradually left, so that finally they were reduced to their 'extreme left' and therefore pro-communist factions. The removal of Sulyok was followed by campaigns against Béla Kovács (Smallholder) and Imre Kovács (National Peasant). Béla Kovács was prevailed upon by Ferenc Nagy to resign in February 1947 and subsequently arrested for 'conspiracy against the republic', first by the secret police, then by the Soviet authorities (he was deported to the USSR); Imre Kovács was also forced to resign in February 1947, and replaced by the pro-communist Ferenc Erdei. A further group, led by Zoltán Pfeiffer, was expelled by Nagy from the Smallholders in April. By May Ferenc Nagy himself had reached the slicing end of the salami. While on holiday in Switzerland, he was accused of complicity in conspiracy against the republic, and forced to resign to secure the release of his five year old son, who had been held hostage. He was replaced as prime minister by Lajos Dinnyés, a 'left-wing' Smallholder, and the bogus coalition government continued.

This successful implementation of salami tactics set the stage for the holding of elections, now 'organised' so as to secure the right result. The August 1947 elections were marked by the disenfranchisement of known anti-communists (10 per cent of the electorate) and the printing of special blue tickets so that communists could vote several times. According to Bán there were 300 000 illegal votes.[16]

The election result was a testimony to the effectiveness of communist tactics. The groups that had been split off from the Smallholders stood in opposition to the ruling Left Bloc, and obtained a total of 35 per cent. The official Smallholders obtained 15.4 per cent. Hence they would still have retained an absolute majority of 50.4 per cent, if the party had held together. The HCP itself did slightly better than before, with 22 per cent, and the government coalition secured a total of 60.9 per cent. It was enough to qualify as a success. And it was quickly followed by the suppression of the Hungarian Independence Party (September 1947).

In this context the criticisms levelled at the HCP by the Yugoslavs at Szklarska Poręba seem rather wide of the mark. Kardelj attacked the HCP for its 'coalition fetishism' and 'failure to understand the meaning of People's Democracy'. It is clear, however, that the HCP already held the whip hand in the coalition. The upshot of the founding conference of the Cominform for Hungary was not so much a major shift of policy as an acceleration of existing policies. The tasks of the communist party in Hungary were now described as the 'exclusion of the bourgeoisie from power' and the formation of a 'popular front modelled on Yugoslav single-party experience.' After September 1947 the party set to work to eliminate the opposition. The Democratic People's Party was purged in October and the centrist elements in the SDP were expelled in February 1948. Rákosi announced in March that the Independence Front would be replaced by a 'People's Front', the main task of which was the dissolution of the other parties in the coalition by limiting their organisations to the capital city.[17]

A more radical economic policy was also implemented from October 1947 onwards. Gerő described this to the Politburo as exploiting 'the favourable conjuncture', i.e. 'the rapid development of the internal political situation'.[18] As in Czechoslovakia, however, there was an interval of approximately a year between the definitive seizure of power and the adoption of fully Stalinist policies.

THE BALKANS: ALLIED CONTROL COMMISSIONS AND COMMUNIST AGITATION

Bulgaria and Romania underwent the same process as Hungary only more quickly. The first stage in both countries was the setting up of a coalition government in the immediate aftermath of a coup. In Romania a coalition called the National Democratic Bloc had been formed underground in June 1944 between the National Peasant, Liberal, Social Democratic and Communist parties; but it hardly affected the course of events, which was determined by the advance of the Red Army towards the frontiers of Romania and the decision of King Michael to save what could be saved from the wreck by changing sides. On 23 August 1944 the king dismissed his pro-German premier, Antonescu, and agreed to the armistice conditions set by the Allies. He set up a largely military government but admitted the civilian politicians of the National Democratic Bloc to a partial share in power.

Only one communist, Lucreţiu Pătrăşcanu, was brought into the cabinet. He became Minister of Justice. The prime minister was General Constantine Sănătescu. The communist party, with a mere 2000 members, was in a weak position at first, but immediately began to organise various groups which were discontented with the apparent continuation of royal rule and the prewar governmental and social system. The Ploughmen's Front, led by a Transylvanian lawyer, Dr Petru Groza, represented the interests of the poorer peasants, in opposition to the wealthier peasants organised in the National Peasant Party; the Union of Patriots was an organisation of professional people; the Hungarian Workers' Federation (MADOSZ) represented the Hungarian minority in Transylvania; a workers' militia, the *Apărare Patriotică*, had existed since August. In October 1944 the communists set up the National Democratic Front as an umbrella to cover all these groups, with a programme of land reform, the reacquisition of Northern Transylvania and the removal from power of the 'historic' parties of the National Liberals and the National Peasants, tarred with the Fascist brush.

The Soviet Chairman of the Allied Control Commission, General Vinogradov, supported these demands. He described Maniu, the leader of the National Peasant party, as a Fascist, and banned a demonstration by that party. General Sănătescu was forced to give way to this pressure and remodel his cabinet on 4 November 1944, adding two communist representatives: Gheorghiu-Dej as Minister of Transport, and Vlădescu Răcoasa as Minister for Minorities. Dr. Groza, who was very close to the communists, became deputy prime minister. But the Ministry of the Interior was placed in the hands of Nicolae Penescu, of the National Peasant Party. This meant that the police force was controlled by an anti-communist.

So the NDF continued its agitation, seconded by Stalin's envoy Vyshinsky, who demanded a 'strong and efficient government.' But at this stage Stalin did not want to press matters too far. On 6 December 1944 King Michael replaced Sănătescu with another general, Nicolae Rădescu, who offered a compromise to the communists and the NDF which they accepted. Penescu would be dismissed; but Rădescu would take over the Ministry of the Interior himself with a communist under-secretary. He would disarm the *Apărare Patriotică*, and the bourgeois parties would retain a majority in the cabinet (nine out of 16 posts). Agrarian reform would be postponed until the end of the war. King Michael reported to Western representatives in Bucharest that 'the Soviet Union had no desire to see Romania become a communistic state' and that 'Vyshinsky had talked to some of the more viperous communists and advised them against stirring up trouble'.[19] This misled the West into thinking that Vyshinsky's statements should be taken at face value.[20]

Stalin's reaction to the very moderate compromise arrived at by King Michael was to summon two of the top Romanian communists, Ana Pauker and Vasile Luca, to Moscow to report. We do not know what passed at that meeting. Either they persuaded Stalin that he should let them off the leash, or he gave them instructions to seize power. The latter supposition is the more plausible. In any case, their return on 7 January was followed by a renewed upsurge of NDF agitation.

There was no shortage of combustible material. In the countryside the Ploughmen's Front encouraged the peasants to seize the large estates; in the towns there were street riots and demonstrations under the slogan of a purge of reactionaries, the removal of General Rădescu, and the democratisation of the army. The US envoy in Bucharest, Berry, reported in February that there was now 'overt Soviet help for the NDF'; the Romanian Foreign Minister (Constantin Visoianu) had told him the communists were acting under instructions brought from Moscow to create a crisis in the next few days.[21]

The British representative, Air Vice Marshal Donald Stevenson, reported shortly afterwards: 'underground action sponsored by General Vinogradov is taking place.' Rădescu was told by Vinogradov that to use force would lead to civil war, which could not be tolerated. The violent demonstrations continued, culminating in a clash in Bucharest on 24 February which left two people dead. Rădescu replied with a radio broadcast describing Pauker and Luca as 'horrible hyenas' and 'foreigners without God or Fatherland'. This chauvinistic manoeuvre was based on the fact that Ana Pauker was Jewish and Vasile Luca was a Hungarian from Transylvania. Rădescu was now unacceptable, and Vyshinsky was sent back to Bucharest to make this clear (26 February). At an interview on 27 February Vyshinsky told King Michael he had 'just two hours and five minutes to make it known to the public that General Rădescu has resigned', and left the room 'banging the door hard enough to crack the plaster round the door frame'.[22] Soviet troop movements gave his violent words and actions added weight.

Stalin's choice for a replacement was Dr Petru Groza. Iuliu Maniu, the leader of the National Peasant Party, advised King Michael to resist; but the British view was presented by Sir Orme Sargent in the following words: 'Disturbing as the situation is I cannot see what more could be done . . . The Soviet representative is backed by Soviet military force.'[23] The USA took the same view. Roosevelt later wrote to Churchill (11 March) 'Rumania is not a good place for a test case'.[24]

Groza was appointed on 6 March, and he formed a cabinet in which the communists still had only three ministries, but they were very important ones: the Interior (Georgescu), Justice (Pătrăşcanu) and Economics (Gheorghiu Dej). Moreover the other ministers were individuals selected by the RCP for their reliability. The genuine coalition had thus given place to a bogus one. It was not without a popular base: the local power of Workers'

Committees, Vigilance Committees and Peasant Committees. However, these groups had the purely negative function of destroying the local organisations of the National Peasant and National Liberal parties and purging the civil service of non-NDF elements.

The Groza government's policies can be summed up under four main headings: land reform, conciliation of the Hungarian minority in Transylvania, closer relations with the Soviet Union, and the punishment of Fascists. The land reform of 22 March 1945 was moderate in character. Holdings over 50 hectares were confiscated (with compensation, except for land belonging to German settlers, fascists and war criminals); ecclesiastical and royal estates were not touched. The result was that whereas 3.8 million hectares had been distributed in the post-1918 reform, only 1.1 million hectares were distributed after 1945. Nine hundred thousand families each received a small parcel of land.

Transylvania, with its large Hungarian minority, was handed over to Romanian administration on 9 March. This was a way of strengthening the Groza government by appealing to Romanian nationalism, and in fact the NDF leaders had promised that the new government would have a better chance of achieving this because of its greater acceptability to the Soviet Union. But steps were also taken to reconcile the local Hungarians with their new status. An autonomous Hungarian administration was set up in three Hungarian majority counties in the south-east, run by the MADOSZ; a state-supported Hungarian university was set up at Cluj (Kolozsvár); the number of schools where education was conducted in Magyar was increased. There were divisions in the communist party over this international approach, which was favoured by the 'Muscovites'; the 'local' party leader Lucreţiu Pătrăşcanu was inclined to a more nationalist line.[25]

Closer relations with the Soviet Union required the delivery of industrial equipment (some of which belonged to British and American oil companies), three hundred million dollars of reparations, and the strengthening of trade links. The Economic Agreement of 8 May 'assigned the entire exportable surplus of Romania to the USSR'[26] and set up Mixed Soviet-Romanian Companies, or *Sovroms*, covering oil (initially a third of Romania's productive capacity, rising to 100 per cent by 1950), transport, pig iron (46 per cent), steel (52 per cent), timber, aviation, and banking (40 per cent). The Soviet Union had a controlling interest in all these companies; they amounted to a third of the stock value of industry and finance in Romania by 1946.[27]

Finally, the punishment of Fascists received a legal basis in the Decree of 21 April prescribing the death sentence for political prisoners and those convicted of membership in a Fascist organisation i.e. Codreanu's Iron

Guard movement.[28] This played an important part in the consolidation of communist rule, as the hunt for Fascists was conducted by the communist Emil Bodnăraş.

The contrast between Bulgaria (where the opposition wanted to postpone the elections in 1945–6 and the communists wanted to hold them) and Romania (where the positions were reversed) can be explained by the success of King Michael in changing sides in August 1944, which allowed the old Romanian ruling classes to retain considerable power. The king felt strong enough in August 1945 to demand the resignation of Groza, and on the latter's refusal to stir up a political crisis by refusing to sign any decrees. In effect, the king had gone on strike.

There was some popular support for King Michael's action, shown by demonstrations in November 1945 in Bucharest on the occasion of his birthday. But the international context was not favourable. As we have seen, the paramount role of the Soviet Union was in practice recognised by the West, despite some complaints, and the decisions of the Moscow Conference of the Three Foreign Ministers in December 1945 merely constituted a face-saving gesture. The Moscow Conference recommended for both Romania and Bulgaria that the government be broadened by the inclusion of two opposition leaders; this broader government would hold elections and be rewarded by Western recognition. Whereas in Bulgaria the opposition refused to accept office without power, in Romania two minor leaders of the 'historic parties', Haţieganu (National Peasant) and Romniceanu (Liberal), were persuaded to accept Ministries without Portfolio (January 1946). This was followed by Western recognition of the Groza government (February 1946).

The elections still needed some preparation, however. The 'salami tactic' of splitting the non-communist parties was vigorously applied. Tătărescu's 'leftist'[29] Liberals opposed Brătianu, the leader of the traditional Liberal party; Maniu's National Peasant Party was split twice (first by Alexandrescu then by Dr N. Lupu, a genuinely leftist peasant leader). The Radăceanu group took control of the Social Democratic Party, driving out the right-winger Titel Petrescu, who set up his own party, the Independent Social Democrats, in March 1946.

Once a group of subservient allies had been assembled, they could be gathered together in a government bloc. The National Democratic Front had been too broad, embracing as it did a number of bourgeois parties; in May 1946 a Bloc of Democratic Parties (BDP) was formed, which comprised the RCP, the Ploughmen's Front, MADOSZ, the Radăceanu Social Democrats, the Tătărescu Liberals, and the Alexandrescu Peasants. The elections of November 1946, held in conditions of intimidation and fraud, completed the process by giving the BDP 372 seats out of 414. The communists received 276 seats. Only 33 opposition National Peasants and 3 opposition Liberals were elected. The defeat of the opposition made the continued presence of Romniceanu and Haţieganu in the government unnecessary. Groza remained in charge, and the signing of the Peace Treaty with Romania on 10 February 1947 was a clear indication of Western disinterest.

The subsequent mopping-up operations were unusually thorough, because of the relative weakness of Romanian communism and the initial strength of King Michael's position. Single-party rule was established not just in practice as elsewhere but formally. The opposition parties were naturally liquidated (by the dissolution of the National Peasant Party in July 1947 and the life sentence imposed on Maniu; the Liberal Party was dissolved in August); but the pro-communist splinter groups also disappeared, the Tătărescu Liberals and the Alexandrescu Peasants in November, and the Radăceanu Social Democrats in February 1948 by merger with the RCP, which was accordingly renamed the Romanian Workers' Party (RWP). King Michael was forced to abdicate in December 1947, and the Romanian People's Republic was proclaimed. A Constitution was promulgated in 1948, modelled on the 1936 Soviet constitution, although the parliament was renamed the Grand National Assembly to fit in with Romanian traditions.

As in Romania, the seizure of power in Bulgaria was marked by a combination of military coup, Soviet intervention and pressure from below organised by the communist party. The situation differed in Bulgaria, however, because of the readiness of a sizeable section of the Bulgarian army to cooperate. This was the group named *Zveno* (link). It was founded in 1927, under the direction of Colonel Kimon Georgiev, and it saw itself as 'an elitist group set on modernising Bulgaria by means of political guidance from above'.[30] This programme had more than a passing similarity to Stalin's version of communism, and it predisposed *Zveno* to accept an alliance when it was offered by the BCP in 1942. *Zveno* had already mounted one coup, in 1934; a counter-coup by King Boris III in 1935 removed them and established a royal dictatorship, which though neutral leaned towards Germany during the Second World War.

Hitler's attack on the Soviet Union naturally altered the situation considerably. The Bulgarian Communist Party, which had shrunk in size from 30 000–35 000 in 1934 to 10 600 in mid-1941[31] was able to come out of its sectarian corner and take action in two directions, the one with more success than the other. The first, the partisan struggle, faced a number of obstacles: Bulgarians were relatively prosperous during the war because of King Boris III's policy of neutrality and the Third Reich's need for agricultural produce, and even as late as September 1944 there were only between 8000 and 10 000 partisans in the mountains.[32] They had no discernable military impact. Bulgaria was not under German occupation; the patriotic motives which came into play in occupied Europe were not so evident here, although the resistance did assassinate a number of pro-German officials.

The other arm of communist policy was far more effective: the construction of a Fatherland Front of all patriotic groups, with a programme of the defeat of Fascism and the establishment of democracy. The Fatherland Front, set up in June 1942, comprised communists, left social democrats, Georgiev's *Zveno*, and the left, or *Pladne*[33] wing of the Agrarian Party. However the centre and right of the political spectrum (the Democrats, the Gichev Agrarians and the Pastukhov Social Democrats) preferred to stay outside the Front.

There was the usual division of party control between the local leadership of the BCP (Traicho Kostov, Tsola Dragoicheva and Anton Yugov) and the exiles in Moscow (the Comintern veterans Georgi Dimitrov and Vasil Kolarov, and the younger Vŭlko Chervenkov) but it did not result in differences over tactics.

When it became apparent in 1944 that Germany had lost the war, the royal government (now a regency) sensibly decided to change sides: but the Fatherland Front refused to negotiate with it, and Stalin sent his troops across the border (8 September), having remedied the legal difficulty of Bulgaria's neutrality by declaring war three days earlier. The royal government under the right wing Agrarian Kosta Muraviev tried to preserve itself by simply surrendering, and Stalin, whose objectives were military rather than political at this stage, instructed his local commander, General Tolbukhin, to agree to an armistice. The Royal Bulgarian Army was allowed to keep its weapons.[34]

At this point the Fatherland Front stepped in. The BCP Politbureau decided on 6 September to order a general uprising for the night of 8–9 September. Outside the capital there were elements of an uprising, but in Sofia it was more of a coup. On 9 September one military unit after another (including the officers) went over to the Front. The Ministry of War was seized by junior army officers from *Zveno* who unlocked the back door from inside; the Minister of War himself, General Ivan Marinov, assured them of his cooperation. He was later appointed Chief of Staff.[35]

A coalition government was set up, with the key positions shared between *Zveno* and the BCP. *Zveno* provided the premier (Georgiev) and the ministries of National Defence (Damyan Velchev), Foreign Affairs and Education. The communists had the Interior (Anton Yugov), Justice, and

Public Health. Nikola Petkov, one of the leaders of the *Pladne* Agrarians, was made Minister without Portfolio.

All parties were agreed that the administration should be purged of supporters of King Boris's royal dictatorship; and this gave the communist party the opening to set up Fatherland Front Committees, under Tsola Dragoicheva, who was answerable to the party alone. Control of the Ministry of the Interior and its state security force was an additional advantage. The police force was abolished in October 1944 and replaced by a People's Militia staffed by the BCP or its supporters. The judicial function was carried out by People's Courts. These institutions had a threefold function. They were used to take revenge on members of the former regime (the government itself admitted executing 2138 people);[36] to conduct a purge of the old state apparatus (by December 1944 800 army officers had been dismissed and replaced by former partisans and political prisoners; 63 district capitals out of 84, and 879 villages out of 1165 reported examples had communist mayors); and to confiscate factories (137 in 1944–5). Moreover it was decreed that supervision over all Bulgarian industry was to be transferred to the Factory and Workshop Committees which had emerged in September. Outside Sofia local committees of the Fatherland Front mushroomed in the later months of 1944. By December there were 7292 committees, and the BCP had twice as many representatives on them as the Agrarians.

This rather disorganised period did not last long. The party moved against both the right and the left. The Factory Committees were integrated into the communist-run trade unions; the Anarchists, who had played some part in the partisan movement and the Committees, had their newspapers and pamphlets confiscated and burnt, and in March 1945 they were rounded up and sent to labour camps.[37] This was consistent with the general policy of the communist party, and of Stalin, which was to restrain any attempts to go beyond the national democratic stage. The role of the Soviet Deputy Chairman of the Allied Control Commission (ACC), General Biryuzov, in this respect was recognised by the US representative in Sofia, who said 'The Russians appear to be exercising a restraining influence on the communists'.[38]

Biryuzov was the only person in a position to exert any influence in Sofia. In November 1944 he forbade the new government to communicate with his Western colleagues on the ACC, and when the Americans protested he simply suspended all ACC meetings between December 1944 and February 1945.[39] Biryuzov's policy, he later recalled, was 'to knock the stick out of the hands of our "partners", which they tried to insert into the wheel of history at every turn'.[40]

The percentage agreement of October 1944 between Stalin and Churchill had assigned an 80 per cent share of influence in Bulgaria to the Soviet Union, and when the British moved on Athens (December 1944) Stalin moved on Sofia. His help was certainly needed. The hold of the BCP was revealed to be alarmingly unstable by a report that the Agrarians were as influential as the communists in the majority of the villages surrounding Sofia.[41] In January 1945 General Biryuzov demanded the removal of Dr G. M. Dimitrov from his position as leader of the *Pladne* Agrarians. He was too independent and too pro-Western; if the Agrarians did not remove him Biryuzov would simply dissolve their party. The new leader, Nikola Petkov, initially acceptable because of his membership in the Fatherland Front, quickly proved to be no more reliable than Dimitrov. Elections due to be held in the spring were now postponed to allow more thorough political preparation (parts of *Zveno* were making trouble too). The next approved candidate to be produced was Alexander Obbov. At a congress of the *Pladne* Agrarians in May 1945 Obbov had Petkov expelled from the party and took control himself. The communist Minister of the Interior, Yugov, ruled that the assets and the organisation of the party belonged to the Obbov wing. Petkov's reply was to resign from the Fatherland Front, taking Kosta Lulchev (Social Democrat) with him (August 1945). He hoped to rely on the willingness of the West to defend democracy in Bulgaria.

This was a forlorn hope, but in the short run the West did make a certain show of firmness. An attempt was made in the summer of 1945 by Britain and the USA to give the non-communist opposition a fighting chance in the Bulgarian elections. 'Single list' elections had been scheduled for August 1945. But the US Secretary of State, J. F. Byrnes, sent a note to the Bulgarian government complaining of 'the endeavour by a minority government in power in the country' to 'prevent participation in the elections of a large democratic section of the electorate',[42] and asking for a postponement. The elections were postponed, at the last possible moment (24 August). This was an unusual retreat by Stalin, made for no clear reason, and a short period of political relaxation set in, with opposition parties being permitted to hold meetings.

The newspapers were briefly allowed to criticise the régime; even the Anarchist paper was permitted to reappear for a few issues. Three opposition parties were legalised (Petkov's Independent Agrarians, Kosta Lulchev's Social Democrats, and Nikola Mushanov's Democrats). The honeymoon did not last long. The return of the Comintern veteran Georgi Dimitrov in November to Bulgaria to head the BCP was a symbolic indication that no further concessions would be made. 'It is clear,' he said, 'that behind the opposition parties there stand Bulgarian reactionaries who are striving to restore the past.' The elections were finally held on 18 November 1945. Petkov decided to call on his supporters to abstain as he knew the authorities would not allow the voters a free choice. The result of these single list elections was an 88 per cent vote for the Fatherland Front. The abstention campaign was relatively unsuccessful, with 10.6 per cent of the voters presenting blank ballot papers.

Yet once again diplomacy produced an apparent retreat by Stalin. At the December 1945 Foreign Ministers' Conference in Moscow, the USA outlined conditions for the recognition of the Bulgarian and Romanian governments. Stalin refused to agree to fresh elections, but he was prepared to 'give the Bulgarians friendly advice to include some members of the loyal opposition' in the new cabinet. The concession was only apparent. Unconditional entry into the new cabinet would mean that Petkov was condemned to powerlessness; hence he demanded that the BCP give up the Ministries of the Interior and Justice. The Soviet reply was to send Vyshinsky to Sofia to examine the situation (9 January 1946). Vyshinsky advised that Petkov's conditions could not be met. Georgiev (still theoretically in control of the government) continued to try for compromise, and offered the opposition the Ministry of Justice and the Vice-Ministry of the Interior. On 28 March the Soviet Ambassador, Kirsanov, instructed the Georgiev cabinet to withdraw this offer.[43]

The new cabinet formed on 1 April 1946 left out the opposition and strengthened the hold of the BCP. The Ministry of Finance went to the communist Ivan Stafanov, and Kostov himself became Vice-Premier and Minister of Electrification and Natural Resources.

Further purges and arrests followed. The *Zveno* Minister of National Defence, Velchev, lost control of his ministry in July 1946 when its functions were transferred to the cabinet as a whole; 30 per cent of the officer corps was purged; the opposition press was suppressed; the leader of the opposition Social Democrats, Pastukhov, was arrested and tried for his comments on the army purge; 200 lawyers who protested about this were put in labour camps; two leading members of Petkov's party (though not Petkov himself) were arrested. The US representative in Sofia, Maynard Barnes, reported that 'Democratic freedoms have been so completely stamped out in Bulgaria that our continued presence on the ACC without some form of protest would be shameful.' He advocated instead that the Western powers recognise their impotence and leave the Commission.[44]

The West still possessed a certain leverage in the fact that no peace treaty had yet been signed with Bulgaria; hence the opposition was allowed to contest the elections of 27 October 1946 for the Constituent Assembly. It was not a fair contest: 15 members of the Socialist Party's Central Committee were in jail, alongside 35 out of 80 members of the Supreme Council of the Petkov Agrarians. Twenty four of Petkov's election agents were assassinated in the course of the campaign.[45]

The Fatherland Front gained 70 per cent of the votes. The opposition was represented in the Assembly by 99 members (89 of them members of Petkov's party); the communists in the Fatherland Front had 275 seats, the Obbov Agrarians 69, *Zveno* eight, and the Fatherland Front socialists nine. Barnes now advised US recognition of Bulgaria owing to the 'relatively satisfactory results of the elections, despite fraud'.[46] On 20 January the Bulgarian Peace Treaty was signed; on 11 February Britain recognised the Bulgarian government; and on 5 June the US Senate ratified the peace treaty. Petkov was arrested the same day, tried in August by a People's Court, and hanged in September 1947. The United States decided that 'non-recognition of the Bulgarian government would play into Soviet hands'. Recognition accordingly followed in October.

The definitive establishment of communist rule in Bulgaria coincided with the first Cominform meeting in September 1947 and the concomitant move towards state control of economic life. This was a new and sudden departure. The state sector inherited from the war was unusually small. The proportion of industrial production deriving from state-run firms actually fell during the war, from nine per cent to 5.6 per cent. The nationalisations of 1945–7 had only brought the proportion of firms under state control to 6.4 per cent by 1947, although they were generally large firms, accounting altogether for a quarter of total industrial production. After the Cominform meeting the party moved to the immediate nationalisation of all private firms (23 December 1947). By 1949 98 per cent of industry was state-owned. Collectivisation of land was slower: in 1947 only 3.8 per cent of the arable land was held in collectives[47] and in 1948 Dimitrov warned against the 'illusion' that the land could be collectivised straight away. By the end of 1949 the proportion of arable land in collectives was still only 11.3 per cent. A more rapid tempo was put in hand, as elsewhere, in response to the Cominform's anti-Tito resolutions of June 1948.

PARTISAN VICTORIES: YUGOSLAVIA AND ALBANIA

We now turn to the two countries where a communist party could claim to have achieved power by its own efforts: Yugoslavia and Albania. The victory of the Albanian communists was achieved under Yugoslav tutelage and as a by-product of the Yugoslav victory. The victory of the communist partisans in Yugoslavia was unquestionably their own work.

The Communist Party of Yugoslavia (CPY) was assisted by a number of unique advantages in its progress towards power. The Nazi invasion of Yugoslavia in April 1941 led to the rapid capitulation of the Yugoslav high command and the partition of the country into nine fragments, the largest of which was a much-expanded Croatia (the NDH, or Independent State of Croatia). In the resistance which emerged from the defeat of 1941 the communist party was from the first on an equal footing with the non-communists, owing to a combination of the shift in Soviet policy in an anti-German direction (which in this case predated Hitler's attack on the Soviet Union) and the foresight of the leader of CPY, Josip Broz Tito, who reacted to the news in 1939 of the Nazi–Soviet Pact by preparing for the all-out conflict he knew would eventually occur. The CPY was also in a position to take advantage of the national fragmentation of the country. It alone was capable of linking the different nationalities together. It was the only organisation to cover the whole of Yugoslavia, the sole repository of the 'Yugoslav' as opposed to the 'Serb', 'Croat' or 'Slovene' idea. It had both an internationalist policy, based on the principle of national self-determination, which implied a federal rather than a centralistic structure for a reborn Yugoslavia (in appearance at least), and a multinational leadership. Tito himself was a Croat, Kardelj a Slovene, Djilas a Montenegrin, Ranković a Serb. The other main resistance movement, the *četnik* force commanded by Draža Mihailović, was exclusively Serbian in composition.

The events of the resistance war strengthened these initial advantages. The terrible massacres committed by the *ustaše* on the territory of the NDH, particularly in Bosnia-Herzegovina, created a tremendous pressure for action among the Serbian minority; moreover, the Croat population itself was alienated by the requisitioning of the 1942 harvest for German military requirements. The royal Serbian *četnici* preferred a 'waiting policy' in the face of overwhelming German power. The massacre of the population of Kragujevac in October 1941 as a reprisal for partisan attacks showed the results of armed resistance clearly enough. The *četnik* policy of inaction led to conflict with the communist partisans (November 1941) and to the fateful decision by Mihailović to view the communists as the main enemy and collaborate with the German army and the forces of General Nedić the Serbian puppet leader. Tito was not above doing something similar in reverse, but his negotiations with local German commanders in March 1943 were brought to an end by Hitler's veto.[48]

The vital difference between the two sides was that Tito's sly manoeuvre only came to light many years later, and had failed before the arrival of the first British military mission (May 1943), whereas the behaviour of Mihailović became common knowledge, so that Winston Churchill was able to explain to the House of Commons in May 1944: 'The reason why we have ceased to supply Mihailović is a simple one. He has not been fighting the enemy, and . . . some of his subordinates have made accommodations with the enemy.'[49] The fact that Mihailović was keeping his powder dry in expectation of the proper moment to start fighting, whereas Tito and the partisans were engaged in a continuous struggle, was perhaps of even greater weight than any accusations of treason to the allied cause.

The National Front policy, compulsory for all communist parties, was also very useful in hiding Tito's real objectives, for those who wished to be deceived. The official policy was put well by Kardelj: 'The goal of the national liberation struggle cannot be other than to achieve national freedom and democratic rights.'[50] The limited character of the goal was stressed in November 1942 at the first session of the AVNOJ (Anti-Fascist Council for the Liberation of Yugoslavia), held at Bihać on liberated territory. The First AVNOJ Manifesto called for the liberation of Yugoslavia and the setting up of a broad democratic government recognising the rights of ethnic and religious groups. Private property was to be 'inviolable'; individual commercial initiative was to be encouraged; there would be 'no radical changes whatsoever in the social life and activities of the people'.[51]

Notwithstanding these soothing words, it was quite clear who would be in control. The only possible form of National Front (or 'People's Front' – the more usual term in this case, reflecting the country's multinational character) in Yugoslavia was the entry of former members of other parties into the communist-run People's Liberation Fronts as individuals. A document from Slovenia dating from March 1943 makes this clear. In this, leaders of the Slovene Sokols and the Christian Socialists announced their participation in the Slovene Liberation Front, accepting the 'vanguard role of the Communist Party of Slovenia' and renouncing 'any intention of forming their own separate party organisation'. The domination of the CPY was anchored firmly at local level on the People's Liberation Committees. These were not organs of the party 'in theory'; but 'in practice the best people were chosen for them. Such men were in the main communists . . . or people closely connected with the party'.[52]

Stalin had agents in the Yugoslav party and was well aware of the situation. He was not happy about Yugoslav radicalism, as it contradicted his own alliance policy. The second session of the AVNOJ, at Jajce in November 1943, increased his annoyance, and he described as a 'stab in the back' the decision to set up a provisional government and to warn King Peter of Yugoslavia not to come back unless invited by the people. 'The boss is furious' said Manuilsky.[53]

Yet he had to accept Tito's *fait accompli*, especially as the Western powers did not seem particularly upset. In August 1944 Tito crossed to Italy and made an agreement with Churchill that members of the exiled royal government of Dr Šubašić would join his provisional government, which would then become the recognised government of Yugoslavia. This meant in effect that the West had abandoned the non-communist forces. It is unlikely that Churchill was taken in by Tito's assertion that 'he had no desire to introduce the communist system into Yugoslavia'. A month later Tito flew to Moscow and made an agreement with Stalin that the Red Army would assist in the liberation of Yugoslavia, but withdraw immediately after it had done so. Stalin kept to this agreement, but he also insisted that Tito keep the agreement with Šubašić. Accordingly, in March 1945, Šubašić, Milan Grol (Democratic Party) and Juraj Šutej (Croat Peasant Party) were admitted to the provisional government as window-dressing. Šubašić had no illusions: 'The communist party will dominate the coalition' he said in July 1945, and 'the only alternative is civil war, which cannot be won without armed foreign assistance'.[54]

The official communist line, however, continued to be the retention of an opposition, albeit a tame one. As Tito said in June 1945 'we are not against parties, all the more as some are already cooperating usefully in the Popular Front; those outside the Front should also be formally allowed to operate . . . We say to whoever does not want to be in the Front, whoever wants his own party; let him go and form it.'[55] But Moša Pijade warned the opposition, especially the Democratic Party of Milan Grol, against voting systematically against the government: 'If these new fellow-travellers of ours . . . begin to set themselves apart . . . one day we may come into open conflict.'[56]

The true situation was that both the non-communist members of the Popular Front (such as Jovanović of the Agrarian Party, and Prodanović of the Republican Party) and the former exiles admitted to the coalition like Grol and Šubašić were powerless to alter the line of policy implemented by the CPY. As Milan Grol complained when he resigned (19 August 1945) 'An exclusive party programme is being implemented' which is 'sacrosanct, and excludes any divergence of views'.

In fact, despite Tito's independence of Stalin, the tactics of the CPY bore a remarkable similarity to those of all other communist parties in the immediate aftermath of the Second World War. First, form a coalition; then, strangle the opponents of the coalition; then, hollow out the non-communist parties within the coalition; finally, establish single party rule. It was not possible for Yugoslav historians to admit this publicly until the mid-1980s.[57]

There were no 'liberalising periods' in Yugoslavia which can be compared with the Czechoslovak historiographical renascence of 1964–9. Most English writers on the subject have adopted the view that the overwhelming majority of the Yugoslav people supported the communist partisans, and that their harshness towards political opponents reflected popular feeling and a hatred of quislings and collaborators. This may be true, but political manipulation played a part as well, as Koštunica and Čavoški have shown.

A two-stage process took place, whereby the opposition were suppressed, first outside the Popular Front, then within it. The opposition were prevented from agitating in 1945 by the traditional methods of banning their newspapers, beating up their supporters, and smearing them by association. Despite his later record, Milovan Djilas was not above taking part in the last-named activity. He warned supporters of the Democratic Party in November 1945 that they would be punished if they followed Milan Grol (who had appealed for a boycott of the elections), because 'the monsters of treason and crime (such as Mihailović, Pavelić and others) are hidden behind the "opposition"'. It was only logical, therefore, that fourteen Slovene intellectuals should be charged with espionage in July 1947 and given either death sentences (in three cases) or long jail terms.

The November 1945 elections were a race with one horse. It was possible to vote against the Popular Front but no candidate was allowed to stand for election against it. The opposition parties' boycott was unsuccessful. 88.6 per cent of those qualified to vote did so; 90.5 per cent of those who voted voted for the Popular Front. Some courage was required to drop a ballot in the separate box provided for those who wished to vote against (17 per cent did so in Slovenia). Victory at the elections was accompanied by terror against both former *ustaše* and former *četnici*, carried out by the secret police (OZNA, or Bureau for the People's Protection), under Ranković, who also replaced the priest Vlado Zečević as Minister of the Interior in February 1946.

Once the opposition outside the Popular Front had been dealt with, the coalition parties inside it could be brought into line. A large number of parties had joined the Front during the war. They were often left-wing splinters from existing parties, as in other parts of Eastern Europe at this time. But in some cases they had a genuine independence of outlook. This could not be tolerated. Tito claimed in January 1946 that 'there will be an opposition inside the Front, and a fairly strong one at that.' When Dragoljub Jovanović and Miloš Popović took him at his word, they were treated in the same way as previous oppositions. 'Where are your masters? Inside the country or outside it?' they were asked. And connections with Draža Mihailović were implied. The left-wing Agrarian Jovanović was particularly troublesome because he challenged the sole rule of the CPY and predicted the collapse of Yugoslavia 'because of political oppression, just as the old Yugoslavia perished because of nationalist oppression'. He also opposed collective farming. Djilas records an exchange between Tito and Ranković about Jovanović. 'He must be arrested,' said Tito. 'It will be hard to get anything on him,' replied Ranković. 'Then make him guilty of something.'[58] In October 1946 he was expelled from his own party. In May 1947 criminal proceedings were started; in October the trial took place. The charge was connections with the political emigration 'against the background of his opposition to the policies of the CPY'.[59]

The proper attitude for a bourgeois politician was shown by Josip Vidmar in his grovelling address of August 1945: 'What the CPY has achieved with its tireless education of us non-communists and with its tireless enlightenment of the masses in Slovenia . . . is that the people have moved towards complete unity and will never again want any other kind of party in the future.' This meant that only the CPY could exist in Yugoslavia as a real party. The second congress of the Popular Front, in September 1947, resolved that it represented 'the political unity of the workers, peasants etc. . . . under the leadership of the communist party.' Tito justified this with the argument that 'all the people have to be mobilised, and the political parties will start disagreeing. This would paralyze our strength'. He never departed from this position for the rest of his life.[60] The third congress of the Popular Front (April 1949) marked the final stage in this process by proclaiming that 'a member of the Popular Front cannot be a member of a political organisation whose programme is contrary to the communist programme'.

The destruction of opposition in Yugoslavia was an adjunct to the process of seizing power rather than a constituent element in it. Yugoslavia stood apart from the other People's Democracies in this respect. Power was essentially seized during the later stages of the war. Yugoslavia was unique, too, in the absence of any 'moderate', 'transitional' stage in internal policy such as characterised the rest of Eastern Europe between 1945 and 1947. Tito and his inner circle (Kardelj, Djilas, Ranković) went ahead immediately with the construction of Soviet-style socialism, despite the opposition of Stalin's men in the leadership, Andrija Hebrang and Sreten Žujović. Hebrang was forced to draw up a Five Year Plan of forced industrialisation despite having insisted in August 1945 on the need for methodical and slow development in the absence of large credits. He was then moved from the Planning Commission to light industry, and taken off the Central Committee.[61]

The Five Year Plan (1947–52) anticipated the plans of the other People's Democracies in its centralism, its stress on heavy industry and its tautness.

27 per cent of the national income was to be invested every year; the value of industrial production was to increase 200 per cent from the 1939 figure; metallurgicals were to increase 700 per cent; chemicals 900 per cent. The number of skilled workers was to double. All this was to be achieved by 'the mobilisation of millions of people for the labour offensive.' The only difference (a concession to the need to repair agriculture from the ravages of war) was the postponement of collectivisation. Instead, expropriated land was distributed to landless peasants and war veterans, and an upper limit of 35 hectares on landholding was established to prevent the formation of a rural bourgeoisie. But some of the land (18.3 per cent, or 287 700 hectares) was handed over to state farms under the law of August 1945. And a number of voluntary agricultural cooperatives were formed (covering an area of 121 000 hectares in 1946, rising to 324 000 in 1948, or 2.4 per cent of the total farm area).[62]

Yugoslavia was thus a model People's Democracy, though differing from the rest in two essential ways: her determination to move straight on to the second stage of development, despite Stalin's objections, and her independence. The US ambassador was well aware of communist Yugoslavia's independent position, and reported as follows in September 1947: 'Tito is free from Soviet interference in domestic policy', and 'Yugoslavia stands out as the Soviets' most faithful and conscientious collaborator rather than a satellite'.[63]

Stalin found this independence intolerable. He was particularly concerned about Yugoslavia's pretensions in foreign policy. Tito supported the communist insurgents in the Greek Civil War, when Stalin thought the insurrection would have to be brought to an end; he pursued the idea of a Balkan Federation, which would link Yugoslavia, Bulgaria, Albania and Hungary and thereby lessen Soviet influence; he refused to form any joint Yugoslav-Soviet companies after February 1947. Stalin replied by trying to divide the Yugoslav leadership, relying on 'Cominformists' who placed their loyalty to the Soviet Union first. He also tried to infiltrate his men into the secret police. Both tactics failed, and there began a furious exchange of correspondence (March 1948) culminating in an open and public breach (June 1948), with tremendous consequences for the development both of Yugoslavia and the rest of Eastern Europe, which we shall examine in Chapter 4.

A few brief comments are in order here on Albania, where a communist party was founded in November 1941. During the war it pursued an identical policy to that of Yugoslavia. While Tito was quarrelling with the *četnici*, the Albanian communists were quarrelling with *Balli Kombëtar* (the National Front), and for similar reasons, except that the relationship with Yugoslavia was also an issue, since *Balli Kombëtar* wanted to establish a Greater Albania, including Kosovo. Just as the Yugoslavs set up a National Liberation Movement and a provisional government, so did the Albanians. After victory, however, differences began to develop between Koçi Xoxe, the Organising Secretary of the Communist Party of Albania and also Minister of the Interior, and Enver Hoxha, the Secretary-General of the party and Prime Minister. Until 1948 Xoxe's faction was in control, since the Albanians did not feel strong enough to challenge Yugoslav hegemony. But the conflict between Tito and Stalin was Hoxha's opportunity to break free, purge Xoxe, and line up with the Soviet Union so as to pursue a policy of Albanian independence.[64]

4 High Stalinism

The completion of the seizure of power meant that the Stalinist model could now be imposed to its fullest extent on Eastern Europe, with the exception of Yugoslavia, where a different direction was chosen after 1948. Stalinism meant, first and foremost, uniformity. As we have seen, the seizure of power had taken place at varying speeds and under varying conditions. A start was made, roughly in 1948, with the 'construction of socialism' of the Stalinist variety. The local communist leaders themselves probably did not intend this at first. That is why Stalin's break with Tito was of such importance.

There were perhaps eight major features of the Stalinist model in its Eastern European version: first and foremost, exerting a determining and indeed distorting influence upon the rest, there is the endeavour to imitate the Soviet Union as closely as possible. The other features were as follows: complete intellectual and cultural uniformity on the basis of the ideology of Marxism-Leninism; single party control (in effect, oligarchic rule, since a narrow Politburo took all the decisions); the absence of the rule of law and the predominant role of the security organs; complete state control of economic activity ('the command economy'); planned economic development with a bias towards heavy industry and away from consumption; the removal of the former middle classes from political, social and economic influence and in theory the creation of a classless society, though in practice the consolidation of a new class. The above features are all specific to Stalinism. But Stalinism also implied a modernisation process, such that most of the aspects of modernisation picked out by Detlev Peukert in the German context as giving a 'recognisable picture of modernity', namely 'rationalized industrial production, bureaucratized administrative and service activity . . . an increasingly small agricultural sector . . . wage and salary discipline, an urbanized environment, extensive educational opportunities . . . a demand for skills and training . . . social planning . . . the expansion of the sciences . . . and the domination of media products in culture'[1] apply with little modification to the efforts of the Stalinist countries of Eastern Europe after 1948.

The drive to imitate the Soviet Union gathered strength with the breach with Yugoslavia, announced in June 1948 at the second meeting of the Cominform, held in Bucharest. The resolution of 28 June 1948 on 'the situation in the Communist Party of Yugoslavia' embodied binding instructions as to the direction the People's Democracies had to follow in constructing the new society.[2] The word 'nationalism' is employed in this resolution as meaning 'opposition to the Soviet Union', and becomes synonymous in Cominform parlance with 'Titoism' and 'anti-Sovietism'. Hence the first lesson to be drawn from this resolution was that the slightest deviation from the line pursued by the Soviet Union amounted to nationalism and was to be condemned. As the Italian communist leader Togliatti pointed out in July: 'There can only be one guide for everyone: in the realm of theory, Marxism-Leninism; in the domain of real forces, the country of socialism headed by a party steeled by three revolutions and two victorious wars.'[3] This meant the end of the 'specific roads to socialism' proclaimed with such a flourish in 1946. There was initially some resistance from the Polish party leader, Gomułka, who had committed himself deeply to the latter approach; but not from anyone else.

The second feature of the Cominform resolution was the thesis of the sharpening of the class struggle even after the seizure of power by the proletariat, as the building of socialism came to fruition. As Slánský put it on 27 June 1948: 'the road to socialism is accompanied not by a mitigation but by a sharpening of the class struggle'.[4] Capitalist elements, which had been treated relatively mildly hitherto, would now be suppressed, both politically (by merging social democratic and communist parties and removing surviving elements of independence from other parties) and economically (by ending the role of small-scale private enterprise in trade and agriculture). In Czechoslovakia the 'left' wing of the party leadership (Kopecký, Ďuriš, and Čepička), who had been held in check by Gottwald earlier in 1948, now began to proclaim the onset of the 'class war' and to attack the 'democratic illusions' and 'mistaken humanism' of some of the party's leaders.[5] In some countries there was a delay in the implementation of the Cominform Resolution. It would be wrong to speak of resistance, except in Poland, where Gomułka dragged his feet until he was removed from office.

The Polish leader had several reasons for opposing the Cominform resolution. He had already nailed his colours to the nationalist mast in 1944. His chief contribution to the establishment of communist rule had been as Minister for the Occupied Territories, where he was in charge of a land reform of a purely nationalist type, consisting in the expulsion of German farmers, large and small, and the settlement of formerly landless Poles in the territory vacated by the Germans. He had proclaimed in November 1946 that 'Poland will attain socialism without a dictatorship of the proletariat'. A less rigid man would have bent with the wind in 1948, but Gomułka was obstinate, and he dreamt of retaining a degree of Polish independence even under communist rule.

The Polish leader's objections to the new Cominform line were twofold. He did not accept that nationalism should be treated as the main danger, and he did not want to impose agricultural collectivisation. He criticised the Polish delegates at Bucharest for voting in favour of the part of the Cominform resolution which declared that 'the elimination of the last and biggest exploiting class – the kulak class' was possible 'only on the basis of the mass collectivisation of agriculture'.[6] To start collectivising, he said, would be 'greatly premature and tactically erroneous'. There was a clear policy difference involved here. The argument over nationalism was less clear. Gomułka seemed intent on dragging up old issues from the past. He attacked the prewar KPP for its alleged 'Luxemburgism' in the national question and praised the PPS for its traditional support of Polish national independence. He advocated an immediate merger of the PPS and the PPR without carrying out any more purges of the PPS. These were strictly unnecessary hostages to fortune for a man committed to communism in close alliance with the Soviet Union. As he himself said in his September self-criticism, 'It never entered my head that Poland could progress along the way to socialism without being supported by the Soviet Union.'[7]

On the face of it this was a quarrel over ideology rather than policy; underneath could be discerned the coded statement that Poland's peculiar national traditions and characteristics ought to be taken into account. Gomułka stubbornly insisted in September: 'There must be some elements of the Polish road to socialism.'[8] He simply had to go. His friend Spychalski failed to support him, and the CC Plenum of the PPR held in August–September 1948 condemned him for 'rejecting the part of the information bureau resolution dealing with collectivisation', for 'avoiding a class struggle against capitalist elements in the countryside' and for 'a tendency to keep quiet about the fact that . . . the Polish road to socialism is qualitatively nothing other than a copy which arose thanks to the prior victory of socialism in the USSR'.[9]

He was replaced as Secretary-General by Bierut during the September Plenum, and although he retained nominal membership of the CC his influence was at an end. There was no more opposition to the Cominform line, and Poland fell into step. When the new, merged, Polish United Workers' Party (PZPR) held its first Congress in December 1948 it adopted a party programme which stated: 'People's Democracy is the road to socialism' (i.e. not the Polish road to socialism). 'The system of people's democracy can and should effectively realize the basic functions of the dictatorship of the proletariat . . . Every tendency aimed at loosening collaboration with the Soviet Union endangers the very foundation of people's democracy in Poland.'[10]

The only other country where the break with Tito actually led to a change of leadership was Bulgaria. Here, however, the issue was different. The veteran leader of Bulgarian communism, Georgi Dimitrov, obediently reversed his 1946 definition of people's democracy in December 1948. Now he described the Soviet régime and people's democracy as 'two forms of one and the same power, the power of the working class' and 'two forms of the dictatorship of the proletariat'. This meant that 'Soviet experience is the best model for the construction of socialism for us and the other countries of people's democracy'.[11]

Dimitrov's colleague, Traicho Kostov, General Secretary of the party, a 'non-Muscovite', took a more independent attitude. He accepted the validity of Soviet experience, but objected to Soviet economic exploitation of his country. The Soviet Union was unloading cheaply purchased Bulgarian tobacco onto the world market at prices that undercut the Bulgarians themselves. Kostov complained about this, and he was therefore accused in March 1949 of being nationalist and anti-Soviet, and dismissed from the Politburo.[12]

Elsewhere, local communist leaders were slow to take the Cominform's advice on collectivisation, although not openly defiant. In Hungary Rákosi argued in July 1948 that the Cominform resolution 'does not mean collectivisation is on the agenda for the current year'.[13] The news of Gomułka's condemnation in September 1948 was an important factor in clarifying the views of the Hungarians. They did not want to suffer the same fate. On 26 December 1948, people's democracy was finally proclaimed by Gerö to be 'a form of the dictatorship of the proletariat'. After that there were no more hesitations.

The party leader in Czechoslovakia, Klement Gottwald, who was by now president as well (he replaced Beneš in June) stood by his rejection of collectivisation at first. Instead, he said, there would be a 'twenty year period of the voluntary formation of cooperatives' by the peasants themselves.[14] Gottwald was summoned by Stalin to the Crimea in the late summer of 1948 to straighten out his ideas. On his return the policy of the CPCz changed abruptly. In September 1948 the party's general secretary Rudolf Slánský told a meeting of regional party secretaries: 'We have been reproached with talking big and doing nothing. Before February we talked of a peaceful road to socialism, a Czechoslovak road. It is therefore natural that we made mistakes, underestimated the forces of reaction and exercised insufficient vigilance. Our sharp struggle with the reaction should have started earlier. We must implement sharp administrative measures against the reaction.'[15]

Slánský went on to suggest a Law for the Protection of the Republic (it was passed in October), firmer action against small traders and farmers, the setting up of labour camps and the forcible removal of 'reactionaries' from the towns. The Action Committees would be used to gather information on 'enemies'. That was the repressive side of the policy; the workers on the other hand could be offered improved food supplies and higher rations, in accordance with the principle of 'class provision'.[16]

Similar measures were implemented everywhere in the wake of the Cominform's anti-Tito resolution. By 1949 at the latest a large degree of uniformity prevailed over the whole area of the Eastern European People's Democracies (the German Democratic Republic travelled the same road a few years later; Yugoslavia and Albania had developed most of the typical features of Stalinism a few years earlier, though Yugoslavia subsequently dismantled some of them). As a result, the period between 1949 and 1953 lends itself well to historical generalisation. Whole books could be written on the application of Stalinism to Eastern Europe. Unfortunately, the necessary specialised investigations into fields such as the evolution of social structure, the intellectual and cultural atmosphere, the relations of society and the state and the texture of life in general are almost entirely absent. We shall therefore be content simply to examine a number of key aspects of the political and economic spheres, which have been much more thoroughly researched.

STALINISM IN ECONOMIC POLICY

The drive to secure state control of economic activity and thereby to approximate to the situation in the Soviet Union by establishing a 'command economy' was pursued at roughly the same speed everywhere, as far as industry was concerned (except in the GDR, where the pace was slower at first). The earlier distinction between 'ex-enemy countries' and 'liberated countries' (with the former displaying a very moderate degree of nationalisation) was effaced in the course of 1948. By 1949 there was almost complete uniformity. (Proportion of industry nationalised by 1949/50: Albania 97%; Bulgaria 95%; Czechoslovakia 96%; Hungary 81%; Poland 92%; Romania 95%; Yugoslavia 100%; GDR 76% of industrial production). By 1952 even small divergences in this respect had been wiped out (the respective proportions were 98%, 100%, 98%, 97%, 99%, 97%, 100%, and 81% for the GDR, increased to 89% by 1956). Small firms with under 20 employees were at first left untouched, as was the retail trade. But the years 1949 to 1953 saw retail trade squeezed out too (e.g. in Czechoslovakia the share of private trade in total turnover fell from 68.7% in 1948 to 20% in 1949, 8% in 1950 and 0.5% in 1953).

Stalin's theory of the 'sharpening of the class struggle during the period of the building of socialism' meant that private capitalists were assumed to be constantly committing 'sabotage' through the black market and the encouragement of speculation. Hence the decision on complete state control, while apparently economic, served a political purpose as well. It both made possible the development of the economy on a fully planned basis, and helped to destroy the last remnants of capitalist resistance. Let us look first at the peasantry. The weakest link in the chain was the persistence of capitalism in agriculture. Hence the call for collectivisation, which had several further motives. It was suggested that collective farms were more efficient. But this did not imply immediate and forcible collectivisation. For that to happen, direct pressure from the Soviet Union was needed.

In Czechoslovakia, for example, the year 1948 saw the completion of the policy of sharing out the land among the poorer peasants and encouraging cooperatives among them (in March 1948 all estates of over 50 hectares were confiscated with this aim in mind). This was not meant to be a prelude to collectivisation: 'Noone wants *kolkhozy* here. We can attain an increase in the productivity of peasant labour in our own way . . . Our old cooperative system can play a significant part.' (CC resolution of April 1948). But, as we have seen, the Cominform's resolution of June 1948 brought about a change in policy. By early 1949 the party had begun to carry out a big propaganda campaign in favour of collective farms, though it called them Unified Agricultural Cooperatives (JZDs) instead. The law of 23 February 1949 merged all the former cooperatives (which had a long tradition in Czechoslovak agriculture) into these new bodies. They were simply collective farms under another name.[17]

In fact the use of the term 'collective farm' was carefully avoided throughout Eastern Europe, owing to its associations with the forced collectivisation of the 1930s in the Soviet Union. It was thought that the peasants would be more inclined to join the collectives if they were renamed 'Agricultural Producers' Cooperatives' or some variant of this expression.[18]

The attack on the so-called 'kulaks' or richer peasants was another motive for collectivisation. There was certainly scope for this, owing to the moderate nature of the land reforms of 1945–8, which were directed against estate-owners and foreigners rather than wealthy indigenous farmers. The upper limit of permissible landholding was generally set at 50 hectares (except in Bulgaria and Albania where it was set at 20). In Hungary the decree of 15 March 1945 had ensured the temporary survival of the wealthier peasants by setting an upper limit of 115 hectares on peasant holdings, raised by 50 per cent for people who could prove they had taken part in the resistance movement.[19]

Hence when the Hungarian leader Rákosi announced the start of collectivisation in November 1948 he told the party CC that 'the land of the kulaks can be taken and used as bait to induce the peasants to join collective farms'. The only opponent of this policy, Imre Nagy, was forced in September 1949 to undertake a self-criticism and confess to his 'opportunism in agrarian matters'. But Rákosi had no illusions about the disadvantages of the collectives for the peasants: 'The peasant must be forced to sacrifice more for the building of socialism' he told the Politburo in November 1950.[20] In Poland Hilary Minc announced a rather moderate programme of collectivisation at first (a target of one per cent of all farms during 1949) though in introducing the Six Year Plan at the founding congress of the PZPR in December 1948 he spoke more ambitiously of 'increasing the output of state farms and developing collective farming'. Agricultural production, thanks to the collective farms and mechanisation, was set to increase by five to six per cent a year under the Six Year Plan. This was hardly likely, given that only 10 per cent of total investment was allocated to agriculture (and 35–40 per cent of that went to the state farms).[21]

The establishment of collective farms proceeded relatively slowly at first, with Czechoslovakia and Bulgaria at the top of the scale in 1950 (14% and 11% of cultivable land respectively) and Poland, Albania, Hungary and Romania at the bottom (2%, 3%, 3%, 3%). Even by 1953 only Bulgaria topped the 50% mark (53%); the others followed at some distance (Czechoslovakia 40%; Hungary 26%; Yugoslavia 19%; Albania 8%; Poland 7%; Romania 8%; German Democratic Republic nil). Full collectivisation occurred, where it did occur (i.e. everywhere except in Poland or Yugoslavia) not at the height of the Stalin era but in the late 1950s. This also applies to the GDR, which caught up rapidly after a late start (collectives covered 3.3% of the farmed area in December 1952, 84.2% in December 1960).[22]

It is not so much collectivisation as the attempt to achieve it for doctrinal rather than economic reasons, and the use made of it as a weapon against the wealthier peasantry, that is characteristic of the first period of People's Democracy. It seems the communist parties actually *expected* a drop in agricultural output to result from the campaign against kulaks, but according to the doctrine of 'the worse, the better' this would have favourable results in the long run. Given the priority assigned to industry in investment and the concomitant shortage of agricultural machinery no one expected any immediate gains.

The collective farms themselves were of various types. Following standard Soviet practice in the 1930s, they were subdivided into three and sometimes four categories, in ascending order from the 'lowest' type, which was closest to individual farming, to the 'highest', which was fully collective. In Type I, the Association for Land Cultivation, modelled on the Soviet TOZ of the late 1920s, only the land was collectivised and livestock and equipment remained in private hands. The product was divided according to the individual's contribution of land, labour and capital. In Type II, the Producers' Association, land, livestock and implements were all collectivised, and production was carried on collectively, but the product was still divided according to the individual's contribution of land, labour and capital. In Type III, the Producers' Union, the division of the product, or the income of the individual, was determined solely by the amount of labour contributed. Sometimes yet a fourth category was added between Types I and II. In theory, the existence of the various types of collective farm allowed the peasants to make a gradual ascent from individual to collective farming, as they became used to the idea. In practice, they were no more eager to join the lower than the higher types. Although party activists were rebuked for breaches of the 'voluntary principle' it seems that the stick played a greater role than the carrot. The usual method was to brand any obstinate farmer a kulak and proceed accordingly. The purges of the early 1950s were a further inducement to join. A CPCz CC resolution of February 1951 blamed the 'Slánský gang' in Slovakia for the way collectivisation was 'lagging behind' there. Brabec showed later that a sudden wave of collectivisation occurred in 1952 in the area of Prešov, in Eastern Slovakia, after 24 000 people were charged with crimes against the state. By 1953 68 per cent of the local peasants had entered the collectives.[23]

In Poland, similarly, there was the Gryfice case of 1951, where the local party committee used force to conduct searches for grain among the peasants. In Hungary the peasants were driven into the collectives by the threat, sometimes executed, of imprisonment. In Romania 80 000 peasants were arrested between 1949 and 1953 for resisting collectivisation. In Bulgaria Chervenkov relied on economic compulsion of an extreme kind. All privately owned machinery and farm equipment was compulsorily purchased by the state, and the definition of a kulak was extended from a person owning 10 hectares (1949) to one owning five hectares (1950). Higher delivery quotas were imposed on 'kulaks'; they also had to pay more to hire machinery and equipment. From April 1950 onwards holdings over 10 hectares owed the state 75 per cent of their grain crop. In December 1953 the screw was tightened still further on private holdings, while the collectives had their delivery quotas reduced. This policy was highly successful in forcing the peasants into the collectives. By 1953 60 per cent of the agricultural area was under collective farms.[24]

In Czechoslovakia the lowest type of collective farm (JZD Type I) was favoured at first (96.1% in 1949) but by 1952 it was down to 15.7% of the total. Types III and IV rapidly became predominant (25.9% in 1950, 56.9% in 1952, 96.8% in 155). When the collectivisation drive was re-launched over the whole of Eastern Europe apart from Poland and Yugoslavia after 1956 the highest type of collective farm was favoured.[25]

Alongside the collectives there were two other rural institutions copied directly from Soviet experience: the state farms and the machine and tractor stations. The basis for the state farms was provided by the big estates expropriated after 1945: some had been subdivided among the poorer peasants and landless labourers, but a substantial area was always retained by the state. These were allegedly to be model farms, but in Poland the purging of former estate managers in 1949–50 meant a shortage of skilled people to run them. The machine and tractor stations (MTSs) had both political and economic functions. Their political departments controlled the local party organisations, enforced labour discipline and calculated the remuneration of labour on the basis of labour norms. Their economic task was to organise the compulsory grain deliveries from the collectives and to provide them with farm machinery and equipment.

They were also supposed to encourage further collectivisation. In fact Jakub Berman, who was in charge of Polish culture at this time, made even greater claims for them in an address to writers in February 1950, thereby killing two birds with one stone: 'The role of the MTSs goes far beyond their productive functions. They are to become political and cultural centres, radiating proletarian elements onto the peasant masses in order to cement the worker-peasant alliance. Hence in your work you should pay attention to the MTS.'[26] Perhaps the abolition of the MTSs everywhere except in Albania and Romania after 1956 is the best comment on this.

One reason for striving to achieve complete state control of the economy was to enable economic development to proceed in a planned fashion. (Another was simply to strengthen party control: 'to frustrate the class enemy and win the class struggle.') The need for planned economic development was common ground at least on the left after 1945. There was a tendency to blame capitalism for the horrors of the Second World War, and the preceding economic depression, which had hit Eastern Europe particularly hard. Moreover, state involvement in the promotion of both industrial and agricultural development was nothing new. It already existed in the 1930s, particularly in Poland.[27] What was new was the element of overall planning, and the use made of Soviet experience. One needs however to distinguish 'planned economic development' from 'breakneck expansion of heavy industry'.

The latter strategy, which is the distinctive Soviet contribution, was not arrived at all at once. As we have seen, the immediate postwar period saw moderate reconstruction plans lasting two or three years. The trend towards Five Year Plans (Six Years in the case of Poland) begins with the Cominform resolution of 1948 and the definitive defeat of social democratic planners. In October 1947 in Czechoslovakia the CPCz and the Social Democrats had put forward rival plans, the latter's being more moderate (87 billion crowns of investment as opposed to 133 billion) and more balanced (40 billion crowns on agriculture as against 28 billion) than the former's. The victory of February meant the adoption of the communist variant, a purge of the Central Planning Commission, and the setting up in February 1949 of the State Planning Office.

In Poland a similar conflict between the Social Democratic experts entrenched in the Central Planning Board and the communist-run Ministry of Trade and Industry (under Minc) resulted naturally enough in the victory of the latter at a special conference in February 1948. The issues were clear enough: the Planning Board did not accept the primacy of production over consumption in planning, it exaggerated the share of private commerce in producing national income, and it ignored Soviet planning experience. It was purged immediately, and dissolved in February 1949.

In Hungary too there was a conflict between the Office of Materials and Prices (controlled by the Smallholders), the Planning Office (left Social Democrats) and the Supreme Economic Council (controlled by its Chief Secretary, the communist Zoltán Vas). It ended in the usual way, with the Supreme Economic Council gaining control of the planning process (it was replaced in June 1949 by a People's Economic Council). The common characteristic of all these planning bodies was that they were directly imitated from the Soviet model; they were chaired by leading members of the Politburo and their job was to implement the objectives set by the party.[28]

The victory of communist planning was only the first stage in the process of transformation. The plans of 1948–9 were not yet mere copies of the Soviet plans of the 1930s. That was to come after 1949, under direct pressure from Stalin. The twin instruments of this pressure were the Cominform (or Information Bureau) and the Council for Mutual Economic Assistance, (CMEA, known in the West as Comecon), a body set up in January 1949 to coordinate the efforts of all the countries of the 'socialist bloc'. It was long considered that Comecon was largely inactive between 1949 and 1953, given Stalin's preference for bilateral rather than multilateral negotiations, but evidence from Czechoslovak archives presented by Karel Kaplan shows that it did intervene even at this stage.[29]

In August 1949, at the second full meeting of the CMEA Council, held in Sofia, the Soviet side complained about 'inadequate cooperation' between Czechoslovakia and its partners, and excessive Czechoslovak trade with the West. Evžen Löbl, the Minister of Foreign Trade, had to carry out a 'self-criticism' and promise decisive changes in this area. The pressure was renewed a year later (October 1950). 'Sharp criticisms' were levelled at Czechoslovakia by members of the CMEA Bureau for her 'continuing trade with capitalist states' and 'failure to make her surplus goods available to other People's Democracies'.[30] The Czechoslovaks made amends by re-routing their trade eastwards, so that the CMEA countries' share of Czechoslovak foreign trade turnover rose from 32.6 per cent in 1948 to 54.6 per cent in 1950 and 72 per cent in 1953.

The Cominform too was used to exert pressure on Eastern European economic policy. At the Matra meeting of November 1949 the participants agreed to 'intensify efforts at economic independence from the capitalist world, and . . . speed up the industrialization process, so as to extend their own economic potential and strengthen the defensive capacity of the whole socialist camp' in view of imperialism's 'direct preparations for war'.[31]

Greater stress was accordingly laid on machine production, as well as a faster pace of collectivisation. Even this was not enough for Stalin. In the summer of 1950 he intervened directly, informing Čepička that Czechoslovakia had untapped sources of mineral wealth and could bear a much faster rate of industrial growth; to underestimate this and rely instead (as hitherto) on imports of raw materials from the West was reprehensible 'bourgeois cosmopolitanism'. This resulted in a bilateral trade agreement between Czechoslovakia and the Soviet Union (3 November 1950) giving priority to the production of heavy industrial goods. The pleas of the Czechoslovak negotiators that two thirds of these products 'had never been supplied before' were ignored, and the existing plans had to be revised completely in February 1951. The list of changes included: increased extraction of iron ore; the processing of low quality ores; the building of an aluminium processing plant; the construction of a super-heavy forge; and the development of synthetic rubber so as to avoid dependence on Western supplies. This naturally had an impact on employment as well: 1 530 000 more workers were needed, and 537 000 were to be 'released from farming' for factory jobs. The rate of collectivisation and mechanisation of agriculture would be accelerated accordingly.

In the revised Five Year Plan the target for industrial production was raised from 157 to 198; for metal production from 193 to 267; for the production of the means of production from 170 to 233; the net material product target from 148 to 170. These examples all come from Czechoslovakia. But the same thing happened everywhere else: the planned increase in net material product over five years was raised in Hungary (163 to 230), Poland (170–180 to 212); and Bulgaria (there the five year plan was now to be fulfilled in four years). The producer-goods industry was to be favoured at the expense of agriculture, consumer goods and housing.[32] In Hungary, for example, agriculture's share in investment fell from 15.7 to 12.9 per cent, and that of housing from 10 to 7.6 per cent.[33]

Such a clear establishment of priorities meant suffering for the consumer, which was seen as unavoidable in the interests of long-term progress. But there were problems inherent in the very attempt to plan a whole economy; the economic system was a complex mechanism (especially in industrially advanced countries such as Czechoslovakia), and any alteration in one sphere had an immediate impact on other spheres. One industry's output was another industry's input, and vice versa. If more lorries had to be produced more steel had to be produced to make them; this meant more iron ore; this meant in turn more lorries to carry the iron ore. In the absence of a market, bottlenecks and distortions could only be avoided by planning of the most detailed and delicate kind.

Much could be achieved if priority targets were picked out. In industrial production, even the revised targets of the Five Year Plans were often met. In Czechoslovakia, for example, industrial production went up to a level of 193 instead of the planned 198; the production of the means of production increased to 233, metallurgical production to 323 (an overfulfilment of the plan in this case), and the result was an *annual* increase over the five years of 14.1 per cent in industrial production, and 26.2 per cent in metals alone. The contrast with individual consumption was stark: only a 19 per cent rise over the whole period. Agriculture fell far behind the planned figure: a 3.2 per cent per annum increase from the low level of 1949, amounting to a 13 per cent fall over the pre-war yield.[34] Similar results were achieved elsewhere (percentage annual increases in net material product per capita, 1951–5: Bulgaria 8.1, GDR 13, Hungary 4.6, Poland 6.6, Romania 12.6, Yugoslavia 4.2).[35]

This was the period of 'extensive growth', based on very high investment levels (investment figures for 1953: Czechoslovakia 25%, Poland 28%, Hungary 25%, Romania 32%, GDR 12%), and the use of a whole range of instruments to extract the necessary surplus from the population. The methods of exploitation included compulsory work-brigades ('labour battalions' in Yugoslavia, Bulgaria and Albania, and an organisation entitled 'service to Poland', which was set up there in 1948 for people to do six months' compulsory labour service); overtime (15.5 per cent of Polish miners' work in 1955 was overtime); piece-rate wages (covering 69 per cent of all industrial wages in Czechoslovakia in 1955); 'socialist competition' campaigns of various kinds, such as the Stakhanov movement to achieve higher and better output, and the Ten Minutes Movement, to begin your work ten minutes earlier than necessary; repeated increases in work norms; and a fall in real wages (in Czechoslovakia from 100 in 1950 to 95 in 1953, in Hungary down to 85, in Poland down to 92).[36] Labour discipline was enforced everywhere by severe penalties for the slightest infringement. In Hungary, for example, 15 000 prison sentences were imposed in 1951–2 for breaches of labour discipline.

These forms of exploitation were perhaps paradoxically accompanied by an egalitarian policy towards social differences. The industrial workers were supposed to be the ruling class under socialism, and the lower status of the bourgeoisie was reflected in a narrowing of income differentials. In Hungary office employees and lower-level officials received only 12 per cent higher salaries than skilled workers; high officials and intellectuals only 54 per cent higher. In Poland 33.1 per cent of workers earned over 2000 złotys a month and 52 per cent of intellectual workers earned less than 2000.[37] The overall income spread continued in the post-Stalin era to be far less pronounced than in the West. In Poland in 1972 only four per cent of people 'employed in the socialist sector' (this category covered 64 per cent of the employed population) earned more than double the average income; in Czechoslovakia in 1970 only two per cent (here the socialist sector covered 97 per cent). In comparison, the figure for Great Britain in the late 1960s was six per cent.[38]

This egalitarian approach (much criticised by the economic reformers of the 1960s because of its effect on incentives) was associated with another 'proletarian' feature: upward social mobility for the urban workers. In Czechoslovakia during the 1950s 250 000 communist workers were taken from the factory bench and made into state officials. Conversely, former officials of the bourgeois state were made into workers. The '77 000 for industry' campaign of 1951 was directed at 'cleansing the whole state apparatus of hostile elements' and putting them to work usefully in industry.[39]

Nevertheless, these egalitarian measures did not produce a classless society. The Yugoslav Milovan Djilas was the first to analyse the phenomenon of the 'New Class' in Eastern Europe, i.e. the emergence of a communist élite based in part on higher salaries, but to a much greater extent on non-monetary advantages. The *nomenklatura* system ensured that members of the party had a monopoly of the important jobs. There were special shops for party members, charging lower prices, stocked with goods normally unavailable; there was a special health service, holiday resorts, preferential access to housing, second homes in the countryside, and guaranteed entry to university for children of party members.

THE COMMUNIST PARTIES IN CHARGE

A very important aspect of Stalinism, in Eastern Europe as elsewhere, was absolute party control. This should be taken in the widest possible sense: the communist party ruled over society as the instrument of the 'dictatorship of the proletariat'. The party's aim was complete control of the public sphere. This meant the dissolution of all independent mass organisations. Here we give some examples from Poland; the measures taken in the rest of Eastern Europe hardly differed in essentials. Non-party youth organisations such as the Catholic Youth Movement were banned, and centralised, monopolistic organisations replaced them, e.g. the ZMP (Union of Polish Youth). All young people were pressed to join these party-controlled 'transmission belts'. In fact by 1955 37 per cent of Poles between the ages of 14 and 25 were members of the ZMP; the rest were not in any organisation. The Stalinist ideal was for all identifiable social groups to be gathered together in an organisation subordinate to the party. Hence the writers were formed into the Union of Polish Writers, with its compulsory doctrine of 'socialist realism'; the workers were members of trade unions run by the CRZZ (Central Council of Trade Unions).

In the more narrowly political sphere the party's control was absolute, despite the presence of representatives of the remnants of the non-communist parties in parliament in most cases. The Polish elections of 1952 were held on a single-list basis. The 'National Front for Peace and the Six Year Plan', which was set up and dominated by the PZPR, received 99.8 per cent of the votes cast. In the new *Sejm* (parliament) the PZPR (273 seats) was flanked by obedient satellites from the ZSL or United Peasant Party (90 seats) and the SD or Democratic Party (25). The balance was made up by 37 'independents'. This body simply acted as a rubber stamp for decisions made elsewhere.

This was not all. Under Stalin, 'party control' also meant 'control by a single individual through the mechanism of the party': monarchy rather than oligarchy. Hence every Eastern European country had its own 'little Stalin' in the 1950s. In Bulgaria Chervenkov, in Romania Gheorghiu-Dej, in Poland Bierut, in Czechoslovakia Gottwald, in Hungary Rákosi, in Albania Hoxha, in the GDR Ulbricht all received a level of officially-sponsored adulation second only to that enjoyed by Stalin himself. Party control was secured by various methods. The constitutions of the People's Democracies, adopted in 1948–9, placed authority in the hands of 'workers' and 'peasants'. State officials at the top level were communists. The *nomenklatura* system made certain of that. In Hungary 87 per cent of new top appointees between 1945 and 1948 were party members; this rose to 91 per cent in 1949.[40] Where non-communists survived in office or in the National Front parties, their reliability was ensured by the power of the secret police, and the repeated purges, which hit the non-communists first and then spread to the communists themselves. The purges were such a vital component of the Stalinist system that they deserve separate treatment.

PURGING THE PARTIES

The origins of the purges lie as far back as 1945. The Czech historian Karel Bartošek sees the starting-point of the purges in the brutal expulsion of German minorities from Eastern Europe in 1945 under the principle of collective guilt. This was followed by the action taken against non-communists between 1945 and 1948. The intra-party purge after 1949 was thus a logical extension of the previous measures.[41] Another Czech historian, Karel Kaplan, has examined the purge of non-communists in Czechoslovakia which preceded, but also overlapped, the purge of communists. It began with the setting up of labour camps, action against small traders and farmers, and the removal of reactionary elements from the towns. The Action Committees, which had been so important in February, were reactivated 'so that they can report to us on their enemies'. Čepička recommended casting 'as wide a net as possible'. State security should establish a card index of all those investigated on political grounds. There were 15 camps available, which would hold 30 000 people.

In October 1948 the law on labour camps was put through the National Assembly. A 'black list' of 'anti-state elements' was started, which contained 130 000 names by September 1949. Several thousand families of 'unreliable people' were thrown out of their houses in the major cities of Czechoslovakia. Nor were economic crimes committed by farmers ignored; a Food Commission was set up to punish them for failure to make compulsory deliveries of agricultural produce.[42]

Similar measures were taken elsewhere. In Hungary, for instance, there were 650 000 trials between 1950 and 1953, and over 380 000 convictions, mainly for 'sabotage'. Hankiss lists the major Hungarian trials of political opponents between 1947 and 1951.[43] These measures were followed rapidly by purges of the communist parties themselves. After 1948 the hunt was on for internal heresies, sometimes real but usually imaginary, and the political atmosphere began to resemble that in the Soviet Union in the late 1930s. As in economic policy, the turning-point was the Cominform meeting of June 1948, called to announce the breach between Stalin and Tito. Stalin's reply to Tito, once he had failed to overthrow him directly, was to initiate a hunt for traitors within the communist parties of Eastern Europe. His defiance was an indication that even the most apparently reliable party leader was liable to succumb to the temptation of 'national communism'.

In some countries the accusation of 'Titoism' had a real meaning in terms of policy. In Albania the faction around Koçi Xoxe favoured continued dependence on Yugoslavia. He was in that sense a 'Titoist'. His victorious opponent, Enver Hoxha, wanted independence from Yugoslavia, which implied a closer alignment with the Soviet Union. Xoxe was expelled from the party in November 1948 and executed for treason in June 1949. In Hungary, similarly, the dispute with Tito had an impact on the Yugoslav minority. The general secretary of the Democratic Federation of South Slavs, Anton Rob, opposed the Cominform resolution; his organisation was immediately abolished.[44]

There was no opposition to the anti-Tito resolution elsewhere in Eastern Europe; but it provided the starting-point for an initial round of intra-party purges[45] based on the accusation of 'nationalism'. In Poland Gomułka and his supporters were accused at the CC Plenum of 31 August to 3 September 1948 of 'rightist and nationalist deviation', and dismissed successively from all party and government positions. In Bulgaria, Traicho Kostov was dismissed, as we have seen, for placing his country's national interests above the Soviet Union's. He was also at risk because he had remained in Bulgaria during the war and thereby escaped thorough investigation at that time by the Soviet security services. He was subsequently arrested (June 1949) and hanged in December 1949 after a show trial which had one unusual feature: he retracted his confession in open court, alleging that it had been made under torture. He was persuaded to revert to his original statement, after undergoing further torture during an adjournment.

But the really important show trial of a leading communist happened in Hungary: the trial of László Rajk. Rajk was simply a scapegoat. He was a devoted Hungarian Stalinist who had the misfortune to be a local, not Muscovite, communist excessively popular among younger cadres. Rákosi knew that he himself was disliked by Stalin and he decided that some sacrificial victim must be found. It was better to be the accuser than the accused. Farkas wanted to get rid of a rival and thought Rajk too nationalistic. The head of the ÁVO (the secret police), Gábor Péter, wanted to show his efficiency. So Rajk was chosen to be the victim, and the machinery was set in motion. In the course of 1949 a number of 'experts', including General Belkin, arrived from the Soviet Union under an agreement of February 1949 for close cooperation in security matters. To Rákosi's discomfiture, Belkin reported that the affair was not serious. It was only after Rákosi personally appealed to Stalin in the summer of 1949 that Belkin's team were instructed to work hand in hand with the ÁVO in preparing a case. Rajk was arrested in May, expelled from the party in June, and charged with conspiring with Tito to murder Rákosi, Gerő, and Farkas, spying for the West, and working for the Gestapo and the police of the Horthy regime. A man of great courage, he resisted all tortures but succumbed to the blandishments of Kádár, who offered exile in the Soviet Union provided he sacrificed himself for the good of the party, which had chosen him for the role of traitor.[46]

The show trial of Rajk (September 1949) was the signal for a series of purges and expulsions, which cut a wide swathe through both the pre-1944 members of the party and the former Social Democrats, including those who had guided their party into the merger of 1948. Four thousand former Social Democrats were purged; 350 000 people were expelled from the HWP, 150 000 people were imprisoned, and 2000 executed. A separate wave of purges (1951) removed a further group of communists, including Kádár, Donáth, and Losonczy.

The investigation of the Rajk case sparked off similar investigations in Czechoslovakia, the shocking details of which were uncovered by Czechoslovak historians in the late 1960s and published in the Report of the 1968 Commission of Inquiry (which was immediately suppressed by the post-1968 regime). Although secret police investigations into Noel Field and Gejza Pavlík had long been in progress, the hunt for a 'Czechoslovak Rajk' became urgent after September 1949. In October two Soviet security experts arrived in Prague. They criticised Czechoslovak security for being weak and indecisive. Ironically, Rudolf Slánský, the party General Secretary, was a prime mover in the first purges. He spoke in December of the need for vigilance, 'so that we can unmask the enemies in our own ranks, for they are the most dangerous enemies'.[47]

A special department was set up within the party, independently of the Minister of the Interior, supervised by Slánský himself. A number of less important arrests were made in the autumn of 1949, thereby providing useful material for the preparation of later cases. The first victim of major significance was Vlado Clementis, the Foreign Minister, who was attacked in March 1950 for 'bourgeois nationalism'. He was followed by a number of other Slovaks, such as Ladislav Novomeský and Gustáv Husák (dismissed in May 1950). The actual arrests took place in February 1951. The purge of communists overlapped in Czechoslovakia with a further purge of members of the former parties and 'Vatican agents'. In June 1950 Milada Horáková, an official of the National Socialist Party, was tried and condemned to death for 'leading a subversive conspiracy against the Republic', as were three other people.

The echoes of the Rajk trial also reverberated in the GDR, though more faintly. In August 1950 the CC of the SED expelled Paul Merker, Bruno Goldhammer, Lex Ende, Willi Kreikemeyer, and other 'non-Muscovite' veterans. They were arrested, but no show trials were mounted.[48]

A further wave of purges took place in 1952, but only in Czechoslovakia and Romania. This was a 'purge of the purgers'. The victims were scapegoats for economic difficulties; but the choice of scapegoats was the outcome of factional struggles within the party apparatus. In Czechoslovakia the Slánský group was defeated by Gottwald and Zápotocký; in Romania Gheorghiu-Dej and Bodnăraş were able to purge Luca and Pauker. In both countries increasing food supply difficulties provided one impulse; the other impulse came from the Soviet Union. The anti-Zionist campaign of Stalin's later years was now gathering momentum, and both Slánský and Pauker were Jewish (though hardly Zionist). In November 1951 Mikoyan arrived in Prague with a personal message from Stalin demanding Slánský's immediate arrest.[49]

The required action was taken on 24 November 1951; investigation into the Slánský case set off a wave of further arrests, so that eventually, after a year's preparation, a monster trial could be held (November 1952). Eleven of the fourteen defendants at this trial were of Jewish origin, and Zionism figured strongly in the indictments. Eleven (including Slánský and Clementis) were hanged; three received life imprisonment (including London and Löbl, who both survived to write harrowing accounts of their experience).

The Romanian purge took place in the summer of 1952. Vasile Luca (Minister of Finance) and Teohari Georgescu (Minister of the Interior) were expelled in May, and Ana Pauker was dismissed from the Foreign Ministry in July. Groza ceased to be Prime Minister. Luca was tried and condemned to death in 1954, though Pauker was allowed to retire to private life.

The impact of the purges of 1949 to 1953 varied from country to country. To generalise, one could say that on balance it was helpful to survival at the top to be a 'Muscovite', i.e. to have been in the Soviet Union during the war. It was extremely dangerous to have been in the domestic resistance or the

Spanish Civil War. During the first wave of purges the Muscovites purged the others (in Hungary most strikingly, but also in Poland, Czechoslovakia and Bulgaria). The only exception was Albania, where the resistance leader Hodxa purged the Muscovite Xoxe. The purges of 1952 were on more of an ethnic basis, and they affected both Muscovites and locals.

A NOTE ON NATIONALITIES

The Stalinist attitude to nationalism and nationality problems was ambivalent. In theory Stalin's followers were committed to supporting the aspirations of national minorities. During the early 1930s and again for a brief period after 1939 this was carried very far indeed. The slogan of a separate Slovak state was adopted, for instance. At other times, during the Popular Front period, the unity of states threatened by Fascism was stressed. Once the parties were close to power, after 1945, the latter trend of policy was accentuated. In Czechoslovakia and Poland the communists were in the forefront of the expulsion of the local German minorities. The Germans were punished as a people, not just as Fascists. In Czechoslovakia relative failure in the 1946 elections in Slovakia was followed by a restriction of Slovak autonomy. After the Prague coup centralisation was the order of the day.

But these cases are largely confined to the pre-Stalinist epoch. In general, and once the Germans had been expelled, gaining support by exploiting the national feelings of majority nationalities in a given state was not a feature of the Stalin system at its height. Stalinist demagogy was on a class not a national basis. The multinational states of Eastern Europe were encouraged by the Soviet Union to pay due attention to the needs of their national minorities. The right to education in the minority national language was guaranteed; the distribution of printed matter was permitted; a degree of national autonomy was either allowed to survive (Slovakia) or granted for the first time (the setting up of the Hungarian Autonomous Region of Romania in July 1952).

Stalin's death relaxed many pressures, but it exposed underlying weaknesses in the position of the communist parties, and these often impelled post-Stalinist leaders to play the chauvinist card. Everywhere there was a reversion to assimilationism. The concessions to the minority language and cultures, and the gestures of the Stalin era towards federalism, were replaced by policies aiming at the development of homogeneous national communities. Thus Romania pursued a policy of national oppression towards its Hungarian minority after 1962, not before; Bulgaria took measures against its Turkish population in the 1980s; the national position of the Slovaks in Czechoslovakia actually worsened under Novotný, with the constitution of 1960; the ostensibly anti-Zionist but in reality anti-Jewish campaign in Poland dates from 1967. Even in Yugoslavia, so federal at the outset, an attempt was made, starting in 1953, to promote the assimilation of the constituent nationalities and to establish a new Yugoslav national identity. But the conditions of this experiment were different.

THE YUGOSLAV EXCEPTION

Yugoslavia formed the one Eastern European exception to the blanket imposition of uniformity after 1948. Josip Broz Tito and the Communist Party of Yugoslavia changed after 1948 from being model members of the camp of People's Democracy to outcasts and heretics. Although the quarrel of 1948 came as a surprise to the outside world, the way for it had been prepared by a series of disputes, which went back as far as 1941. The essence of the conflict is easily stated: Tito and the Yugoslav communists were too independent. They had come to power independently, and their ultra-radical policy after 1945 was not the result of obedience to Soviet instructions. On the contrary, Stalin recommended a moderate policy of reconstruction of the economy and a concentration on raw materials and agriculture. This advice was ignored. The first Five Year Plan (1947–52) envisaged a 'great leap forward', with a 223 per cent increase in industrial production and a doubling of national income. Stalin tried to hold the Yugoslavs back by sending as little equipment as possible (a mere million dollars' worth by 1948) and insisting on the delivery of raw materials to the Soviet Union at artificially low prices. Negotiations on the formation of mixed companies, started in August 1946, broke down in February 1947.

There were also foreign policy reasons for the quarrel with Stalin. Tito's Yugoslavia aspired to a role of leadership in the Balkans, thereby encroaching on Soviet prerogatives. The idea of a Balkan Federation was seen by Tito as a way of settling the intractable nationality problems of the area, rather as they had been settled internally by the setting up of a Federal Yugoslavia. The Macedonian question would be solved if Bulgaria and Greece joined a Balkan Federation; the Kosovo question, which had already produced a major rising in March 1945, would be solved by including Albania.[50] Tito and the Bulgarian leader Dimitrov planned to set up a Yugoslav-Bulgarian-Romanian federation. Dimitrov publicly proposed a Bulgarian-Romanian federation as a first stage. Stalin called delegations from the Yugoslav and Bulgarian governments to Moscow ostensibly to discuss this (February 1948). Milovan Djilas has described how Dimitrov was humiliated at this meeting and how instead Stalin proposed the immediate formation of a Yugoslav–Bulgarian federation. Albania would be added later. His aim was probably to dilute the Yugoslav leadership by the addition of loyal Bulgarians. Apart from this, his peremptory tone was seen by the Yugoslavs as a warning sign. A meeting of the Yugoslav CC on 1 March 1948 resolved not to go ahead with the proposed federation. 'For our party and our country, it would be a Trojan horse' commented Tito.[51]

Stalin decided to bring the Yugoslavs to their senses. He used two methods. First, there was an official letter from the Soviet party's Central Committee, signed by himself and Molotov, sent on 27 March. This complained about insults to Soviet military advisers, about the 'undemocratic' character of the Yugoslav Communist Party, about a 'lack of initiative by the party masses', and about the 'excessive role of Yugoslav state security'. The last point referred to the refusal of Ranković to collaborate with Soviet security organs. Stalin also accused the Yugoslavs of Trotskyism, Menshevism, and, for good measure, employing British spies in their government. The Yugoslav CC replied on 13 April, in a letter which rejected all of Stalin's accusations, while stressing the 'unbreakable bond' that linked Yugoslavia with the Soviet Union, and the Yugoslav party's 'fraternal sentiments of loyalty towards the Bolshevik party'. The substance of the disagreement, and the unbridgeable gulf between the two sides, was made clear enough by the Yugoslavs' insistence that 'we are developing socialism in our country in somewhat different forms'. Stalin's rejoinder arrived on 4 May. He added fresh accusations, while upholding the previous ones. Tito had an 'anti-Soviet attitude'; his embassy in London was full of British agents; the failure either to collectivise agriculture or engage in genuine social reform meant the Yugoslav party was a Menshevik party. Finally, and most wounding of all, the Yugoslavs were 'laughably arrogant and childish' in claiming successes for their wartime partisan movement. They were only in power at all thanks to the prowess of the Red Army. The exertions of the partisans had been insignificant. They were invited to submit the dispute to the Cominform. There they would of course be in a minority of one.

Stalin's other method of bringing Yugoslavia to heel was more indirect. This was the secret recruitment of supporters entirely devoted to him, with the aim of fomenting a 'palace revolution' in Belgrade. It didn't work. Out of the top party leaders only Žujović and Hebrang were for Stalin, and the high-ranking generals he relied on, such as Arso Jovanović, were unable to get the support of their officers. Jovanović was shot in August while attempting to escape across the border. Žujović and Hebrang were expelled from the CPY in May, and arrested in June. 12 000 out of the 470 000 party members were arrested along with them and interned on Goli Otok in the Adriatic.

This abject failure forced Stalin to bring the dispute into the open, by having the Cominform meet and pass a resolution against the Titoists. The resolution of 28 June condemned the Yugoslav leaders for 'bourgeois nationalism' and 'currying favour with the imperialist states', and appealed in effect for the 'healthy elements' 'loyal to Marxism-Leninism' to revolt, and replace the present incapable leaders. Yugoslavia was expelled from the Cominform.[52] Even this did not have the desired effect. Tito's reply was to continue to affirm his faithfulness to Marxism-Leninism, and to limit the dispute to one issue: Yugoslav national independence. For several years the internal policy of Yugoslavia hardly differed from that of surrounding communist states. Stalin accused Yugoslavia of failing to collectivise agriculture; Tito replied with the resolution of January 1949 calling for the 'socialist transformation of the village'. Between 1948 and 1950 the area of land covered by collectives grew from 2.4 per cent to 17 per cent. But the step to independence had now been taken, and Yugoslavia thereby passed out of the Stalinist fold. A complete economic blockade ensured by 1949 that Yugoslavia would either have to live in complete isolation or start reaching agreements with the West. She chose the latter course.

This is where Yugoslavia begins to be the exception. She was in fact compelled to trade with the West. 'When we sell copper to buy machines,' said Tito in 1949, 'we do not sell our consciences, only our copper. With the machines from the West we shall continue to construct socialism.' There was already something of a turning-point in September 1950, when Tito decided to condemn the invasion of South Korea by the North, and to accept economic and military aid from the West. In internal policy a number of key shifts took place in 1950. Tito claimed in an address of June to the National Assembly that unlike the Soviet Union Yugoslavia would return to the true Leninist way and allow the state to 'wither away'. State property in the means of production would 'gradually merge into higher forms of socialist property'. This was the theoretical justification for the steps towards de-centralisation already taken (the law of May 1949 on People's Committees) and for the great change in the organisation of production which was impending: the introduction of Workers' Self-Management, by the Basic Law of June 1950. Workers' Councils were to be elected in all enterprises. In theory these Councils had the power of managing 'all state economic enterprises within the framework of the state economic plan'. In practice they had little power over the managers, who were appointees of the relevant industrial ministry until 1953. Moreover, the economy was still planned from the centre, so there was no question of enterprise autonomy at first.

This changed in December 1951 when the Law on the Management of the National Economy was passed restricting central planning to establishing 'basic proportions'. It was a move away from the command economy to 'market socialism'. Collectivisation ceased too in 1951. Two years later the members of the existing collective farms were allowed to vote to dissolve the collective. By the end of the year only 200 000 peasants were still in collectives. In local government, the People's Committees were empowered from 1952 onwards to draw up their own budgets. They were declared 'organs of popular self-government in the communes'. They were given the right to appoint the managers of factories in 1953. A law of 1953 set up two elected representative chambers, one of them a Council of Producers elected directly at the workplace. At its Sixth Congress in 1952 the communist party changed itself into the League of Communists of Yugoslavia. This was intended to symbolise the separation of the party from the state. In all these ways Yugoslavia was moving away from the standard communist pattern.

There were, however, two major obstacles to further progress in this direction in the 1950s: foreign policy and the role of the League. Tito never intended to pursue a foreign policy of alignment with the West. Moreover Stalin's successors in the Kremlin were keen to patch up relations with the Yugoslavs. Hence Yugoslavia pursued a curious zigzag course in foreign policy, sometimes moving closer to the Soviet Union, sometimes further away. This had some effect on what happened within the country. Milovan Djilas was rebuked for criticising Leninism and expelled from the CC in January 1954 when the first moves were being made towards a rapprochement with the Soviet Union. The attempted reconciliation with the Soviet Union after 1957 coincided with Djilas's first imprisonment; and Khrushchev's break with China and consequent moves towards Yugoslavia after the three frosty years of 1958–60 resulted in the return of Djilas to prison, again for public criticism of Stalin (1962). Finally the green light given to economic liberalisation in the Soviet Union with the Kosygin reforms of 1965 allowed the market reformers to win the debate with the centralists in Yugoslavia.

Decisive changes followed, which François Fejtö has exaggeratedly dubbed 'the Second Yugoslav Revolution', or alternatively 'the Great Economic Reform of 1965'. Individual enterprises were now allowed to keep 71 per cent of their net product, instead of 46 per cent as hitherto; the 'political factories', or non-viable enterprises set up in the less developed regions of the country were wound up; permission was given for private firms to be established; the banks were transferred from government to enterprise control (1966); enterprises were given permission to found subsidiaries under their own direct control (1967).

But the reform now met with a further obstacle: the party itself, still led by Tito. He backed up Ranković, who was in charge of both the secret police and the LCY organisation, until the latter made the mistake of attempting a coup (1966). Even after the fall of Ranković Tito warned that he had not 'joined up with any liberals'.[53] As far as he was concerned, the League was needed as an iron band holding together the disparate fragments of Yugoslavia. This was made very clear in the crisis of 1971 over the demands of the Croats for further decentralisation of the country. Tito intervened to dismiss the local Croat communists who had put forward these demands, and had Croat nationalist agitators imprisoned. Certain concessions were made, it is true, in that the 1974 Constitution left great power in the hands of six constituent republics of Yugoslavia, and the two autonomous provinces. But the League of Communists, and its executive arms the bureaucracy and the army centralised on Belgrade, were there to 'hold the ring'.

Hence communism in Yugoslavia continued despite the changes of the 1960s and 1970s to share certain underlying features with the more orthodox communist states further East. The renamed party, the League, still held power in the last resort. No other party was permitted to exist. The League was written permanently into the constitution in 1974. So was Tito himself. Yugoslavia remained an autocracy, under Tito, and when he died in 1980 it became an oligarchy. The cases of Djilas, Mihailov and others demonstrated the limits of press freedom. State control of the economy was retained, though described as 'social ownership'. An employment limit of five workers for private firms was imposed in 1969 and subsequently retained. The trade unions were servile and unresponsive to the workers' needs. Socialist self-management failed to make an impact on the power of the party to make the vital decisions, even at the local level. The party retained a monopoly of all key positions in government, the press and education. Demagogic attempts to preserve this system by calling up the force of Serbian nationalism in fact worsened the situation by exacerbating the national feelings of the Albanians, the Croats and the Slovenes. This eventually led to the disintegration of the LCY into separate national components in the 1980s. Unless these points are borne in mind it is impossible to understand why Yugoslavia, too, foundered in the general wreck of communism. The 'Yugoslav exception', so proudly proclaimed as such since 1950, proved itself no more capable of resisting the process of communist decline than its Eastern neighbours.[54]

5 Eastern Europe after Stalin

The death of Stalin in March 1953 turned out to be an event of tremendous significance for Eastern Europe, because it led to a reorientation of Soviet internal policy. Given the chief features of Eastern European Stalinism, which were imitation of the Soviet model and unquestioning obedience to instructions from Moscow, any reforming impulse would have to come initially from there. In fact during the years between 1953 and 1956 it was often the local communist leaders who were resisting reform (admittedly with some assistance from the Molotov faction in Moscow) and the Kremlin that was pushing for it. The establishment of a collective leadership in Moscow and the separation of party from government set an example that had to be followed. The 'little Stalins' had to be stripped of their autocratic power. Economic concessions had to be made to the people. The worst excesses of police terror had to be brought to an end. This was a minimum programme. Many people wanted to go further. In two countries they came close to succeeding in 1956. We shall look first at Hungary.

THE NEW COURSE IN HUNGARY

A group of Hungarian leaders was invited to Moscow for a meeting a mere three months after Stalin's death (June 1953). The Soviet objective in calling this meeting was to press for the implementation of a 'New Course' and a change of leadership. This was a reaction to the strikes and disturbances in Csepel, Ózd and Diósgyőr earlier that month, which seemed to indicate the impending collapse of the regime. The Stalinist ruler of Hungary, Rákosi, was attacked from all sides by the Soviet Politburo. Khrushchev warned that the Rákosites would be 'booted out summarily by the Hungarian people' if they didn't change their ways. Beria was particularly unpleasant, accusing Rákosi of wanting to become 'the first Jewish king of Hungary', 'which is something we won't allow'.[1]

Imre Nagy (who had specifically been invited to Moscow by the Soviet leaders) was appointed Premier on the spot, though Rákosi was allowed to remain First Secretary of the party. Gerő and Hegedüs were made Nagy's deputies. Farkas and Révai were excluded from the Hungarian politburo. Rákosi had to carry out a self-criticism in which he admitted placing himself above the party, suppressing all advice and criticism and mounting a cult of personality.

But the struggle for reform was by no means won. Rákosi remained First Secretary of the HWP, and he was even able to block the publication in Hungary of the Central Committee's '28 June Resolution' (it only surfaced in 1985, in Paris)[2] which referred directly to his mistakes, and recommended some cautious reforms. They are given here because they are typical of the New Course era: (1) a lower tempo of industrialisation; (2) more stress on light industry; (3) improvements in the standard of living; (4) a reduction in the peasants' taxes and compulsory deliveries of produce; (5) a lower rate of capital investment; (6) slower collectivisation; (7) aid for small farmers; (8) permission for peasants to withdraw from the collective farms and recover their own land; (9) the restoration of collective leadership. Nagy was able to achieve at least the economic reforms. The peasants were given permission to leave the collectives in October 1953; the number of private farms increased by 200 000 between 1953 and 1954; investment in heavy industry fell by 41 per cent; the real wages of the industrial workers increased by 15 per cent. But Rákosi held on as head of the HWP, and the 3rd Party Congress (May 1954) elected a Politburo of nine people, only one of them a reformer (Nagy himself). Although the internment camps were closed in summer 1953 and the 'kulak lists' abolished the former detainees were retried by People's Courts and transferred to ordinary jails. Nagy's opponents were strengthened by developments in the country. A veritable exodus took place from the collective farms, with the result that the proportion of arable land in collectives fell from 26 per cent in 1953 to 18 per cent in 1954; the relaxation of labour discipline led to a fall in productivity in industry; and journalists at the party paper *Szabad Nép* called for democracy within the party and an end to Rákosi's attempts to frustrate the New Course.

He was therefore able to counter-attack with the claim that 'a hostile right-wing wave is sweeping the country'.[3] Moreover, the wind from the East now changed direction. Malenkov's star began to wane, and Khrushchev's to rise. Nagy had been Malenkov's man, following his policies (at least in the sphere of the economy). Although Khrushchev was later to engage in de-Stalinisation himself, he was in alliance at this stage with Molotov and the hardline Stalinists. Hence in January 1955 the Hungarian party leaders were again summoned to the Kremlin. The HWP delegation included Nagy, Rákosi, and three of the latter's supporters. Now Rákosi could take his revenge. Nagy was berated for encouraging factionalism in the party (the activities of the party's reforming journalists), denigrating the party's leading role and denying the class struggle. When he tried to defend himself he was shouted down.[4]

In February 1955 Malenkov was demoted, officially for 'violating the law of the preferential development of Department 1', i.e. the production of the means of production, and in March the CC of the HWP repeated the accusations made in Moscow, adding the charges of 'right opportunist deviation concerning socialist industrialization' and 'rightist views concerning the peasants'. Nagy refused to resign or make a self-criticism, so that the Soviet leaders were obliged to send Mikhail Suslov to Budapest in April to add the weight of his authority. This had the required effect. Nagy was dismissed as prime minister on 14 April and expelled from the party in November. Rákosi, back in power, was able to reverse the New Course. He restored the priority of heavy industry, imposed harsher labour discipline, purged the journalists at *Szabad Nép* (May 1955), pushed the peasants back into their collectives (by 1956 the proportion of arable land under collective cultivation was 22.2 per cent), and called for 'the most Draconian measures' against peasants who failed to fulfil their delivery quotas.[5]

But a return to full Stalinism was impossible, in Hungary as much as elsewhere, because Khrushchev's policy was ambiguous. Having pushed out Malenkov, he proceeded to make peace with the Yugoslav leader Tito (May 1955), who immediately expressed an extreme hostility to Rákosi in particular, denouncing Hungarians who 'have their hands soaked in blood, have staged trials and sentenced innocent men to death', all on the pretext of 'Titoism'. It would be wrong to exaggerate Tito's influence on Khrushchev; it is more likely that after the revelations at the 20th Party Congress (February 1956) Rákosi's uncompromising Stalinism was unacceptable. The final straw was his plan to arrest four hundred of his opponents, including Nagy. Mikoyan stopped off in Budapest on his way to Belgrade in July 1956 and told the Hungarians to get rid of Rákosi, who in astonishment and disbelief telephoned Khrushchev for confirmation. 'If I go, everything will collapse', he pleaded. Khrushchev replied: 'Nothing will collapse. You must resign.' Rákosi was replaced not by Nagy but by another member of his own team, Ernő Gerő, who was equally responsible for the crimes of the previous few years. As Tito later declared, 'Gerő differed in no way from Rákosi'.[6]

The true replacement candidate, the only communist who could stabilise the situation, Imre Nagy, remained out in the cold. He used the time to write a long memorandum in which he justified himself and pointed out the direction the party must follow. 'The party is not a den of criminals, whose unity must be preserved by hiding their crimes,' he wrote.[7] His own programme was one of moderate reform, involving a return to the New Course of 1953–4.

The Gerő leadership of the HWP, unable to revert to Rákosi-style repression, was now forced to preside over the gradual disintegration of its position. The revolt of the press, which began to slip out of the hands of the party leaders in late 1955, and of the intellectuals, who protested in November 1955 to the CC against censorship and 'despotic methods in the cultural field', was strengthened in 1956 by a movement of university students, around the 'Petöfi Circle'. This was set up on 17 March 1956 with the permission of the party, under the aegis of the official youth organisation, DISZ (Federation of Working Youth). Most of the students in the Petöfi Circle were of worker and peasant background. They had benefited from the inbuilt working-class bias characteristic of educational systems under Stalinism[8] but now their bitterness reflected that of the workers and peasants themselves.

A wave of workers' protests and strikes swept Hungary in reaction to the news of the Poznań riots in Poland (June 1956), particularly in Csepel and Budapest. The agitation of the Petöfi Circle ran parallel with the growth of a mood of hatred of the existing regime, so strong that by August and September, party functionaries 'didn't dare walk in the street'.[9] The intellectual ferment among students now started to spark across to the workers. A worker in a telephone factory reported: 'Many workers who attended evening classes at the technical university were put into contact with the debates of the Petöfi Circle. Through them other workers were informed of the debates . . . There was a tense political atmosphere, for a fresh breeze had entered the factory against the suffocating pressure of the party.'[10] Even the official trade unions entered the fray. On 28 September the National Council of Trade Unions (SZOT) demanded more autonomy and welfare for the workers.[11]

The demands of the Petöfi Circle centred around the recent past. They denounced the crimes of the Rákosi leadership and in particular the purges. Survivors, released in 1954 during the short-lived Nagy era, such as Julia Rajk (widow of László Rajk), Ferenc Donáth and Géza Losonczy, added their weight to these denunciations. The party followed helplessly in the wake of the movement of opinion; concessions were wrested from it one by one, but they always came too late. On 3 October, with Gerő on holiday, the CC authorised the solemn reburial of Rajk, the leading communist victim of the post-1948 purges, and the bodies of Rajk and three others were removed from a secret ÁVH burial ground and accompanied by a 200 000-strong funeral procession to their final place of rest (6 October). The agitation only increased; and the mere readmission of Nagy to the party on 13 October was not enough to make any difference: Gerő remained in power.

The party's initial failure to meet the aims of the protest movement meant that it extended much further. Extreme demands started to be raised. In Györ on 16 October the call was raised for 'Soviet forces to leave our homeland'; an editorial by the communist youth paper on 19 October proclaimed: 'we are engaged in a struggle for independence exactly like the one our forebears waged in 1848'; and on 20 October the Writers' Association demanded a 'new, democratically elected party leadership'.[12]

The call for a restoration of national independence was a potent rallying cry; this is why the explosive events of late October were set off by rumours from Poland, which turned out later to be incorrect, that the Soviet Union was preventing the 'national communist' Gomułka from coming to power there (21 October). The Petőfi Circle decided to hold a demonstration in solidarity with Poland, but the movement they had set in motion now went far beyond this. On 22 October the students, who had already separated themselves from the official youth organisation and organised independently as the MEFESZ (Federation of Hungarian University and College Associations), produced a list of sixteen points, many of which were too extreme for the Petőfi Circle to swallow. Demands for the evacuation of Soviet forces, multiparty general elections, restoration of the old Hungarian coat of arms of 1848, publication of foreign trade agreements, especially on the exploitation of Hungarian uranium deposits, and freedom of speech and the press could hardly be accepted by the most liberal communist. Other demands, taken up by the Petőfi Circle as well, fell within the limits of reform communism: a new Central Committee for the HWP, Nagy to be prime minister again, a review of industrial production norms and of the agricultural delivery system, the release of political prisoners, the removal of Stalin's statue, solidarity with Poland, and the convocation of a youth parliament.[13]

The 300 000 demonstrators who besieged the Hungarian Parliament on 23 October, calling for Imre Nagy to speak, made it clear by their slogans that they supported the more extreme of the demands. 'Independence', they shouted. 'Let the Soviet army go home and take Stalin's statue with them'. Nagy failed to grasp the current mood, addressing the crowd as 'Comrades' and holding out the prospect of 'negotiations and the resolution of problems at the centre of the party'. Meanwhile, on the edge of the city park, the offending statue was being torn down by direct action. Another group surrounded the radio building, and demanded that the sixteen points be broadcast. At 8 p.m. Gerő made the provocative announcement that the demonstrators were 'a group of Fascists' misled by enemies of the people. As Tito later commented, this 'insult to a whole nation was enough to put a match to the fire'. Actually it was elements within the ÁVH who set light to this explosive mixture by firing into the crowd. Now the slogan became 'Death to the ÁVH murderers.' By 10 p.m. the radio station was the scene of a full-scale gun battle. The Hungarian revolution was in progress.[14]

The attitude of the army was, as usual, decisive. The soldiers went over to the crowd, handing out their weapons, workers arrived in lorries from the Csepel munitions works with cases of ammunition, and by 1 a.m. on 24 October the radio building was occupied and fighting had spread throughout the capital. It is important to note that these events preceded the first Soviet intervention. When columns of Soviet tanks poured into Budapest in the early hours of 24 October this was a response to a summons from Gerő. After all, the alternative was for the communist party to abdicate. The authorities also decided on a conciliatory move: Nagy would be made prime minister again, and he and four others were added to the CC. Six hardliners were dropped from the Politburo. But Gerő was to remain First Secretary.

The subsequent radicalisation of the revolution was determined by the interaction of three factors: the provocative actions of the ÁVH, the disintegration of communist rule at a local level, and the evolution of the Soviet attitude. A peaceful demonstration in front of the parliament buildings on 25 October, called to protest against the government's description of the previous day's demonstrators as counter-revolutionaries, was marked by fraternisation between the crowd and the Soviet tank crews, many of whom had been told they were there to crush a Fascist uprising and were astonished to see a peaceful and benevolent crowd. But ÁVH machine-gunners opened fire from the roof of the Ministry of Agriculture opposite. They carried on firing until silenced by Soviet tanks. By that time, about a hundred people lay dead, including a number of Soviet soldiers. As Fehér and Heller put it, this event 'can be regarded as an exact replica of the January 1905 salvo' (in St Petersburg).[15]

The incident resulted in an upsurge of revolt throughout the country. A general strike went into effect all over the country on 26 October. Revolutionary councils sprang up everywhere, under a bewildering variety of designations. There were National Councils, Socialist Revolutionary Committees, Municipal Workers' Councils, and plain Workers' Councils. Councils had in fact already been formed on 22 October at the Dimavag Iron Foundry in Miskolc and on 24 October at the United Lamp Factory in Budapest, but it was the conflict with the ÁVH in Budapest on 25–26 October (and many other similar provincial conflicts) which led to their extension to all factories and enterprises. Power passed into the hands of the Councils at a local level, sometimes after bloody battles with the police, sometimes peacefully.

These local workers' and revolutionary councils were initially led by former social democrats or non-party people. Later on communists took some part in them, once the government and the official trade unions had called for their establishment (26 October). After the Hungarian revolution had been put down the supporters of the restored regime were to claim that the workers' councils consisted of reactionaries seeking the restoration of capitalism. But the working-class composition and the programmes of these councils tend to refute this. These were councils of workers, with a programme of workers' control. For instance, on 31 October the Budapest Assembly of Workers' Councils issued a nine-point programme beginning 'The factory belongs to the workers' and continuing 'The supreme controlling body of the factory is the workers' council democratically elected by the workers'. The director of the factory was to be elected by, and responsible to, the workers' council.[16] The programme of the Budapest students remained the basis for the demands of the workers' councils. The Györ National Council added a demand for Hungarian neutrality (26 October). Apart from this, the demands of the workers' councils were related to the immediate military situation. They wanted the disbandment of the ÁVH, the withdrawal of Soviet troops from Hungary, and an end to the fighting.

The other arm of the Hungarian revolution was the military one, the armed fighting groups, which emerged on the 24 October out of the spontaneous resistance to the Soviet intervention. In many cases these groups formed and reformed in response to particular situations. In fact, in the words of a participant: 'Some people got together, fought, went home, then others came and continued the fight. People changed all the time . . . There was no organisation whatsoever.'[17] The numbers involved were fairly small: taken together, the Corvin Alley, Kilián Barracks and Tüzoltó Street groups amounted to between 600 and 1000 people. Molnár gives a total of 1200 to 1800 armed insurgents in the period of the first Soviet intervention.[18]

These fighting groups sometimes provided a refuge for escaped criminals and other people on the margins of society. The so-called Petöfi Brigade, under Peg-Leg Janko, a recidivist with sixteen criminal convictions, was a case in point. Later on, the restored communist government naturally tended to stress the part played by the criminal element. They also exaggerated the role of former fascists and Western agents. The most right wing of the groups was that around József Dudas, which had occupied the offices of *Szabad Nép*, the party's daily newspaper. After being in the communist underground during the war, he joined the Smallholders, and he was imprisoned between 1946 and 1954 on a charge of conspiracy. Now he emerged to demand six ministerial posts for his Hungarian National Revolutionary Council. He appealed to the UN to send troops into Hungary to assist the 'freedom fighters'. But even Dudas thought that 'Fascist and extreme rightwing groups should not be tolerated' and that 'socialism must be preserved'.[19]

Nevertheless, there were certainly people who wanted to take revenge on the ÁVH and on leading communist functionaries. The siege of the Budapest City Party Headquarters, which ended victoriously for the insurgents on 30 October, resulted in the murder of a number of ÁVH men who had already surrendered. The Corvin Alley fighting group tried unsuccessfully to prevent these acts of mob vengeance. 25 of the 100 people in the headquarters lost their lives. Similar incidents took place throughout the country. But the total number of victims claimed by the restored government itself was 234, a figure which includes many ÁVH and party men who died in battle. This contrasts with the estimated 2400 deaths on the other side.[20]

How the situation developed after 25 October was determined in the last resort by the decisions of the Soviet leaders. The fighting groups were capable of dealing with the ÁVH, with some assistance from units of the Hungarian army. But they clearly could not take on the Soviet army, and the reason for their illusory success after 25 October was the curious neutrality of the Soviet troops. The Soviet tank divisions in Budapest limited themselves to patrolling important thoroughfares, and made no attempt to crush the insurrection. Outside Budapest the rebels and the ÁVH were simply left to fight it out. This attitude reflected genuine uncertainty on the part of Khrushchev and his colleagues as to the course to pursue, as well as their wish to proceed in full consultation with the local communists. Mikoyan and Suslov paid no less than three visits to Budapest at this time: 24 October, 27 October, and 30 October.

On their first visit they told the party leaders that Gerö would have to go, and be replaced by Kádár. The news of Kádár's appointment as First Secretary of the HWP was made public on 25 October. He promised negotiations with the Soviet Union 'in a spirit of complete equality' but referred to dangers from anti-democratic and counter-revolutionary elements. A more conciliatory statement was made by Nagy the next day. It endorsed the formation of workers' councils (this was already happening, as we have seen); it proposed a new government on the 'broadest national foundations' which would atone for the 'crimes of the past' and establish a 'free country of prosperity, independence and socialist democracy.' Socialism itself would not be put in question, and the rebels must cease fire. They would receive an amnesty.[21]

A first instalment on these promises was the formation on 27 October of the People's Patriotic Government under Nagy. What Nagy meant by the 'broadest national foundations' was indicated by the inclusion of two non-communist ministers in a cabinet of 26, one of whom (Béla Kovács) stayed at home and did not actually take part in the government. The other was Zoltán Tildy, the former Smallholder Prime Minister. If this was a coalition, it was a coalition of rival communist factions. Kossa represented the Stalinists, Kádár the centre of the party, and Nagy the 'left'.

The views of Imre Nagy had evolved considerably as the October revolt deepened. He refused to describe it as a counter-revolution, and the course of events seemed to confirm precisely a warning he had already given in 1953. 'Today,' he wrote in 1955, 'a return to the policy of the New Course could still check the growing crisis and avert catastrophe. But it is doubtful whether a return to the June principles [of 1953] would suffice as a solution tomorrow . . . If this does not happen soon, there is a danger that the masses . . . will reject both the June way and the Communist Party, and it will become necessary to make a much greater retreat in order to keep the situation under control.'[22] In foreign policy, too, he had already fore-shadowed a situation of Hungarian neutrality in 1955. He demanded 'a new federation of Danubian states . . . which would maintain close relations with the USSR . . . but would remain in every way outside the power blocs'.[23]

So Nagy's policy was to make more and more concessions to the tremendous popular pressure, both in domestic and foreign policy. He used the threat of resignation to prevent the party's Stalinists from mounting a full-scale attack, with Soviet aid, on the main rebel strongholds in the capital early on the 28th October; and he announced instead a series of far-reaching policy changes to take the heat out of the situation. The ÁVH would be dissolved; the Hungarian national emblem would be restored; wages and production norms would be reviewed; the security forces would cease fire; agreement had been reached, he claimed, on the withdrawal of Soviet troops from Budapest.[24]

The policy of the Kremlin in the face of this was still uncertain. In his memoirs Khrushchev asserts that the Soviet leaders changed their minds 'I don't know how many times' about whether to get out of Hungary or 'crush the mutiny'.[25] When Mikoyan and Suslov returned for their third visit, on 30 October, they seem to have agreed to the withdrawal of Soviet troops, negotiations about Hungary's withdrawal from the Warsaw Pact, and the re-establishment of the coalition government, 1945-style. Nagy's extra-ordinary announcement of 30 October abolishing the one-party system and establishing a government of democratic cooperation between the coalition parties of 1945 was made on the understanding that he had Soviet agreement. There was even public evidence to this effect. The Soviet government announced in *Pravda* on 31 October that it was 'ready to review . . . the question of Soviet troops stationed on the territory of the above-mentioned countries [Hungary and Romania]', and that it had 'given instructions to its military command to withdraw the Soviet army from Budapest as soon as this is considered necessary by the Hungarian government'.[26]

If there was hesitation up to 31 October there was duplicity afterwards. At some point during 31 October the decision was taken to crush the revolt. While Soviet tanks were withdrawing from Budapest, fresh divisions were crossing the Hungarian frontier from the Soviet Union. News of this was given to Nagy early on the morning of 1 November. He could get no sense out of the ambassador, Andropov, save the comment that Soviet troops 'were entering to safeguard the withdrawal of the troops that were leaving.' Meanwhile the Soviet leaders were making their political preparations. Secret consultations took place on 1 November between Khrushchev, Molotov and Malenkov on the Soviet side and the Polish leadership; Khrushchev and Malenkov then went to Bucharest, then on to the island of Brioni in Yugoslavia, where they discussed the situation in detail with Tito, Kardelj, Ranković and Veljko Mićunović on the night of 2–3 November. Khrushchev gave his reasons for intervening as the murder of communists in Hungary, the impending restoration of capitalism there, Nagy's declaration of Hungarian neutrality and withdrawal from the Warsaw Pact, and the need to preserve his own authority in Moscow against Stalinist hardliners.[27]

These explanations were not given for public consumption, and so deserve some credence. But equally, they were given to Tito, so they were intended to gain his support. Some of them were clearly inaccurate: no political party was talking of restoring capitalism, and Nagy did not declare Hungarian neutrality until 1 November, in direct response to the threat of intervention, and indeed after the Soviet decision to intervene. There were certainly murders, particularly of members of the state security forces, and the news of the carnage in front of the Budapest Party Headquarters on 30 October may have affected Moscow's views. But the real reason was that Khrushchev was not prepared to take the gamble that Nagy could stabilise the situation by peaceful means, through a compromise with the forces thrown up by the revolution.

Nagy's proposed compromise, which he had described earlier as 'a retreat in order to keep the situation under control', was not given a chance to work. For one thing, he hoped to work through the existing communist party; but it was in an advanced stage of decomposition by the end of October. Many of the rank and file had burned or discarded their party cards. The lower party units, according to a later communist historian 'were paralysed by the revisionist attacks . . . because in a complex situation they became impotent with the disappearance of higher authority.' On 1 November the new communist leader János Kádár concluded that he would have to dissolve the old party and set up a new one, under the title 'Hungarian Socialist Workers' Party'. Its mission, he said, was to represent a 'new type of communism: Hungarian national communism'. Only one section of the former party opposition joined it – including Nagy, Lukács, Kopácsi, Losonczy, and Ferenc Donáth. A rival group – including Miklós Gimes, Peter Kende, and Miklós Molnár – formed around the newspaper *Magyar Szabadság*, with the aim of setting up a 'national, non-communist but socialist revolutionary party'. Lukács, the Marxist philosopher and veteran of 1919, was completely pessimistic about the chances of the refounded party: 'The new party cannot count on any rapid success, because communism is completely compromised in Hungary . . . But the party will exist to safeguard its ideals . . . and in a few years, or a dozen years, who knows?'[28]

This extreme weakness of communism in the context of early November did not mean the approach of anarchy, as the old-guard Stalinists claimed, but rather opened the way to a coalition government, in which the reformed communist party, the HSWP, would share power with the representatives of the Smallholder, National Peasant, and Social Democratic parties. In the next few days, this coalition secured the support of the army and the police. It was even possible to bring over the rebel units. They were placed under the overall command of General Pál Maléter, an officer from the Kilián barracks who had joined the revolution on 26 October, and was now appointed Deputy Minister of Defence.

Meanwhile, the Soviet Union was preparing to attack: militarily, with the gradual advance of its army into Hungary, the surrounding of the provincial towns, and the emplacement of sufficient forces for a frontal attack on Budapest; diplomatically, with the journeys through Eastern Europe we have mentioned, culminating in Tito's (somewhat unwilling) acceptance of the need for military intervention on 3 November; and politically, with the establishment of an alternative government. Kádár and the Stalinist Ferenc Münnich left Budapest on 1 November in a Soviet military aeroplane, which landed that night at Uzhgorod, on Soviet territory. They were followed on 2 November by other leading communists (such as György Marosán and Karoly Kiss). The decision as to who would lead the future Soviet-imposed government was in fact made indirectly by Tito. The Soviet leaders proposed Münnich as Hungarian Prime Minister; but the Yugoslavs expressed a preference for Kádár, because he had suffered at the hands of Rákosi's torturers at a time when Münnich was serving as ambassador to Moscow. The political preparations were completed with the announcement on 4 November of the break with Nagy and the setting up of the 'Hungarian Revolutionary Worker-Peasant Government' under Kádár.

Nagy's supporters within Hungary (though not perhaps Nagy, who displayed a naive faith in Soviet promises analogous to Dubček's in 1968) were aware of the impending catastrophe. Their response was to withdraw from the Warsaw Pact and announce Hungarian neutrality (1 November). For the rest, they decided, in the words of Sándor Kopácsi, the Budapest police chief who went over to the revolution, 'to continue as if nothing were wrong', to organise a return to work, the dissolution of the fighting groups, and the return of weapons into the hands of a new force of order, this time dedicated to upholding neutral and democratic Hungary, the National Militia.[29]

A new government of 'democratic national unity' was now set up (3 November). In this coalition the communists were in a distinct minority (only Nagy himself and Géza Losonczy were members; Kádár was appointed *in absentia*). There were three Smallholders (Zoltán Tildy, Béla Kovács and István Szabó), three Social Democrats (Anna Kethly, Gyula Kelemen, and József Fischer), and two representatives of the National Peasant Party, now renamed the Petöfi party, (István Bíbó and Ferenc Farkas). Pál Maléter became Minister of Defence. The new Nagy government stressed its commitment to socialism; and the members of other parties equally stressed their hostility to a return to capitalism.

At the same time, the situation of political pluralism, freedom of the press and liberal democracy opened the way to changes in the system if the population should wish it. A number of small parties did emerge on the right of the political spectrum. The Democratic People's Party, the Hungarian Independence Party, the Hungarian Radical Party, the Christian Democratic Party, and the Catholic People's Party all had a relatively conservative standpoint. There were even people who wanted to restore the Horthy regime. But it proved impossible to reconstitute the former fascist party, the Arrow Cross. The one man who could have united all these disparate forces, and provided a focal point for the reaction was Cardinal József Mindszenty, Primate of the Hungarian Catholic Church, who was released from prison on 31 October. But his only public intervention was an ambiguous speech, delivered rather late in the day (3 November). Some commentators have described it as 'very aggressive and menacing'[30] and Isaac Deutscher called it 'the climax of anti-communism'[31] but in fact it was chiefly notable for disclaiming a wish to interfere in politics. The Cardinal called for the 'restitution of the institutions and societies of the Catholic Church' and affirmed his belief in 'private ownership rightly and justly limited by social interests'. He cautioned his hearers against taking vengeance on the adherents of the 'fallen regime'.[32]

The situation could certainly have evolved in various directions, but the Soviet intervention on 4 November cut off these possibilities. Trends towards a restoration of capitalism did not emerge in any strength during the short, hectic period of the Hungarian revolution. If anything, the programme of the revolution was neutralism, a multiparty system, and the retention of the socialist foundations of economy and society, with the exception of collective farms, which the peasantry were rapidly abandoning in November (they continued to leave even after the defeat of the revolution, with the result that by the end of January 1957 only nine per cent of the arable land was held by producers' cooperatives.) This was not so unusual for the epoch. It had already happened in Yugoslavia, it was happening in Poland, and even where no dramatic events took place the mid-1950s were a period of deceleration in the collectivisation process in Eastern Europe.

On the morning of 4 November 2000 Soviet tanks, supported by 150 000 soldiers, went into action against Budapest. At dawn, Imre Nagy broadcast to the nation: 'Today at daybreak Soviet troops attacked our capital with the obvious intention of overthrowing the legal Hungarian government. Our troops are in combat. The government is at its post. I notify the people of our country and the entire world of this fact.' But this unequal contest could only end in defeat. Nagy had in any case been taken by surprise. Up to the last moment he had rejected suggestions for the organisation of resistance. His radio broadcast did not call for resistance, though it admitted the fact of resistance. Coordination was not assisted by the springing of a KGB trap the previous night on unwary Hungarian negotiators led by the Minister of Defence, Maléter.

Scattered fighting did occur, however, for the next five days (longer outside the capital). The participants were first and foremost the workers of Budapest and the industrial towns of the provinces. The greatest damage to buildings and the largest number of deaths took place in the predominantly working-class districts of Budapest. Once the centre of the city had been reduced (this took three days) the tanks and troops could move on the outlying districts of Újpest to the north and Csepel to the south. The workers of the Csepel Munitions Factory held out longest, until 11 November. But military defeat was not the end of the matter. The workers (with considerable encouragement from young intellectuals) now set up revolutionary councils to act as centres of opposition to the new regime. Unlike the workers' councils of late October, whose main thrust had been towards workers' self-management, these new councils were on a district rather than a factory basis and their aim was to preserve the achievements of the revolution by using the weapon of the general strike. This fight, which went on until the beginning of December, was a remarkably valiant rearguard skirmish; but in the nature of things it could be nothing more.

It did, however, have a temporary effect on the policy of the Kádár government. Kádár agreed to meet a delegation from the Central Workers' Council of Greater Budapest soon after it was established on 14 November. He agreed in principle with most of their demands, such as the inclusion of Imre Nagy in the government, the holding of democratic elections and the withdrawal of Soviet troops. But he wanted the general strike ended first, and offered no guarantee that the demands would be implemented. No agreement could be reached under these conditions. But the workers' councils had no reserves to draw upon to enable them to conduct a long strike, and they simply had to return to work a few days later (19 November). Even so, two further 48-hour strikes were called, the first on 21 November, in protest against the sending of Soviet tanks to prevent the establishment of a National Workers' Council, the second on 8 December in protest against the shooting of demonstrating miners by Soviet troops in the provincial centre of Salgótarján.

The Kádár government now decided to act against the Central Workers' Council, decreeing its dissolution on 9 December. Martial law was proclaimed, all the remaining workers' councils above the local level were dissolved and public gatherings were prohibited for one month. The Central Workers' Council replied by organising a general strike on 9 and 10 December, but with the arrest of most of its members, including Sándor Rácz, the chairman, and Sándor Bali, the secretary, the backbone of resistance was broken. Local workers' councils survived, their powers highly reduced by the decree of 5 January, until their final abolition on 17 November 1957. But with the dispersal of the Central Workers' Council the government had broken the last obstacle to its power. Many of the other workers' councils followed the example of the one in Csepel, which announced its self-dissolution on 8 January.

Now that he was firmly in control of the country, Kádár endeavoured to steer a middle course between the 'revisionists' of the Nagy-Losonczy group and the Stalinists of the Rákosi–Gerő clique. The CC of the new party attempted to distinguish between the 'counter-revolutionaries' and the 'majority of the masses who participated in the events' who were 'good patriots and honest workers' (Resolution of 5 December). Kádár made sure that the old Stalinists were not restored to leading positions. Twelve former members of the CC, including Gerő and Hegedűs, were deprived of party or state office (14 November). That did not mean there would be no repression, but at first even the repression was limited. It is possible that

Kádár was acting in good faith when he offered a safe-conduct out of the Yugoslav Embassy to the Nagy group, who had taken refuge there in the aftermath of the overthrow of their government. They were unfortunately kidnapped by a Soviet military detachment on leaving the embassy, and taken to Romania (22 November). But a tougher line was soon taken, on Soviet insistence. Khrushchev and Malenkov arrived in Budapest early in January and impressed on Kádár that more forceful action was needed. Soon afterwards the death penalty was imposed for striking or incitement to strikes (15 January); the writers' and journalists' associations were suspended (17 January); a number of leading revisionist intellectuals were placed under arrest (they eventually received sentences varying from death to long prison terms); the Workers' Guards set up in the factories during the revolution were disbanded (February 1957); the 'mistakes' of Nagy were now redefined as the 'treason' of Nagy; 45 per cent of the lawyers in Budapest were disbarred; and severe purges were put in hand in the public services, the army, and the Frontier Guards. The electric fences and minefields on the border with Austria were restored (not before two hundred thousand Hungarians had fled). In the year between November 1956 and November 1957 20 000 people were arrested, 2000 executed, and some thousands deported to the Soviet Union.[33]

Nevertheless, Kádár was able in the long run to pursue the middle course for which he has become famous. He continued to reject Stalinism, and was able to fend off a dangerous attack by Révai, the only leading Stalinist to return from Soviet exile. Révai made a severe onslaught on Kádár's moderate policies in the party paper, *Népszabadság*, in March 1957. 'Anti-Stalinism,' he said, 'was only the mask of anti-communism.' Whereas Imre Nagy 'should be condemned without reservation or appeal', Rákosi and Gerő deserved approval for 'never betraying the dictatorship of the pro-letariat by allying themselves with the counter-revolution'. 'The balance-sheet of the last twelve years was largely positive,' he added.[34]

Révai's attack was especially dangerous because of his links with the hard-line faction of Molotov, Malenkov and Kaganovich in Moscow. Hence Khrushchev's victory over this group in June was a relief to Kádár. Révai's influence declined rapidly after that. The HSWP party conference in late June 1957 did not accept his criticisms, and confirmed that, although an ideological battle had to be waged against revisionism, the party should call on the cooperation of non-party people wherever possible. The Kádár regime was thus able to establish itself as a regime of compromise, pursuing a course of consolidation.

The Hungarian uprising of 1956 indicated one of the paths a country emerging from Stalinism could take: an uncompromising stress on national independence, a full restoration of democracy, and a disintegration of the leading position of the communist party, leading towards catastrophe. There were two others. The ruling party could choose to retain a large part of the Stalinist system, limiting changes to the absolute minimum. In the absence of popular pressure this was the natural course to take, and it was taken in the rest of Eastern Europe. There is one exception. In Poland it proved to be possible to follow a path of compromise and party-led reform, avoiding the catastrophe of foreign invasion by preserving enough of the previous system to reassure the Soviet Union; and it is to Poland that we now turn.

THE POLISH ROAD FROM STALINISM

The Polish situation after the death of Stalin was marked by a number of peculiarities which enabled the authorities there both to undertake far-reaching changes in policy and to avoid the catastrophe which occurred in Hungary. Firstly, there is the character of the party leadership of the PZPR. Whereas in every other country of Eastern Europe there was a strong Stalinist faction in place in 1953, which was concerned to resist, or at the very least to sabotage, the moves towards liberalisation introduced by Malenkov under the slogan of the 'New Course', it was the former Stalinist leaders themselves who introduced the New Course in Poland. Bierut announced it at the Ninth CC Plenum in October 1953. It was confirmed at the Second Party Congress in March 1954, which promised a 20 per cent increase in the standard of living. This meant that the fall of Malenkov (February 1955) did not have the devastating impact that it had in Hungary: in fact it was scarcely noticed in Poland.

There was no one capable of reversing the New Course (though Minc and Nowak would have liked to), so that it simply continued up to 1956, whereas in Hungary Rákosi, in Czechoslovakia Novotný, and in the GDR Ulbricht, all had that capacity, and all brought the New Course to an end after a short factional struggle. When Bierut died (March 1956) his long-time associate and fellow-Muscovite Edward Ochab simply took over and pushed things along, announcing (April 1956) that the party would be democratised, and that Gomułka had been cleared of unjust allegations of subversive activity. And eventually, when things become too hot for him, in October, he withdrew gracefully and allowed Gomułka to take over.

Secondly, the role of the party intelligentsia was greater in Poland than elsewhere, because there was a group within the leadership which had already started to evolve towards greater liberalisation and independence of the Soviet Union. The first people to advocate liberal reforms were the CC secretaries Morawski, Matwin and Albrecht. By the summer of 1956 such top leaders as Ochab, Cyrankiewicz, Zambrowski and Staszewski had come round to the same point of view.[35]

The comparatively mild application of Stalinist terror in the early 1950s to Poland was a further, uniquely Polish feature. The PZPR was not cowed or demoralised by Stalinism, because the purges of Gomułka and his associates had been conducted half-heartedly and unwillingly. Hence it was possible to clip the wings of the secret police early on, in 1954.

Nevertheless, the situation in 1955 was marked by an awkward balance between two party factions, neither of which had the upper hand yet. Hence contradictory moves were made. On the one hand, Leon Kruczkowski could call in *Nowe Drogi*, the party's theoretical journal, for 'a great candid discussion which goes right down to fundamentals' (March 1955); on the other hand the head of the Writers' Association, Jerzy Putrament, proclaimed at roughly the same time that 'bourgeois recidivism must be repulsed' adding 'any weakness in the understanding of socialist realism must be removed' (June 1955). This balancing act ended in March 1956 with the arrival from Moscow of the details of Khrushchev's secret speech against Stalin.

Thirdly, the explosion of working-class discontent (at Poznań) came at the right time (June 1956). If it had happened any sooner it would have forced a reversal of the reforming course; but now the international auspices were favourable again (after Khrushchev's reconciliation with Tito, and above all his secret speech at the Twentieth Party Congress of the CPSU). The Poznań riots gave a powerful forward push, adding momentum to the reform pressures.

Hence it was not necessary for the Soviet leaders to intervene directly (as they did in Hungary) to secure a local party leadership genuinely committed to reform. In this sense it is hard to agree with Brus[36] when he says that 'the initial impetus for change came from the Soviet rather than from the national side'. In fact in Poland the reverse was the case. Soviet leaders came to Poland in person at least three times in order to hold back a movement that appeared to be getting out of control (Khrushchev in March 1956;[37] Bulganin and Zhukov, July 1956; the whole Soviet leadership, October 1956). Whether these interventions succeeded or not is hard to say. Complete failure would have necessitated military intervention, and that didn't happen; but a partial failure, in the sense of enforced concessions to determined Polish interlocutors, cannot be ruled out. Ochab later commented: 'I did take into account the possibility of intervention: never before or since has anyone played the kinds on tricks of our Soviet friends that they put up with from us.'[38]

This brings us to the fourth peculiarity of the Polish situation, namely the strongly nationalist element in all these transactions. Whereas in Hungary the nationalist element was frustrated for so long that it overflowed the bounds of reason – or at least reason of state – in Poland the readiness of all leaders, whether Stalinist or not, to extract the maximum possible autonomy for their country was remarkable. Konstantin Rokossowski, the Minister of Defence, was perhaps the leading exception, but he had spent most of his life in the Soviet Union, rising to become a Soviet marshal; hence the Poles regarded him as a Russian.

Let us now look at the course of events in detail. The initial stage was that of partial reforms from above, without any change in leadership. Bierut announced a copy of Malenkov's New Course in October 1953, which was confirmed at the Second Congress of the PZPR in March 1954. He admitted failures in agriculture, claiming that they resulted from an excessive pace of collectivisation. His answer was to slow it down. Actually collectivisation had never been very rapid in Poland: seven per cent of the arable land was collectivised between 1950 and 1953, and a further four per cent was added in the next two years. Investments, Bierut added, would be directed away from heavy industry towards consumer goods, housing and agriculture. The standard of living would rise by 20 per cent in the next two years.

This last promise was very unrealistic, given that the Six Year Plan was still in force. Still, industrial growth was adjusted downwards from 1953 onwards, with the percentage of the net material product devoted to accumulation falling from 28 per cent (higher than anywhere else except Romania) in 1953 to 23 per cent in 1954, 22 per cent in 1955 and 21 per cent in 1956. The level of real wages, having reached its lowest point at 84 in 1953, rose to 94.8 in 1954, 100 (the baseline index of this series) in 1955, and 111.5 in 1956. The rate of house construction was also increased (dwellings built per 1000 inhabitants in 1950 = 2.7, 1955 = 3.3, 1956 = 3.3).[39]

The reform process was now given a further impetus by the breaking of a major political scandal. Colonel Józef Światło, a high official in State Security, who had defected to the West, made a number of highly damaging revelations in September 1954 in broadcasts transmitted from Munich by Radio Free Europe. Since he had been in charge of the secret personnel files of the Politburo, he was in a position to reveal both secret police methods and party corruption, real or alleged. It proved impossible to ignore these broadcasts (the jamming seems to have been inadequate). The party leaders, after claiming there was no truth in his allegations, decided even so to remove the main people involved, such as Radkiewicz, the Minister of Public Security (December 1954), and his deputy Roman Romkowski, and to sentence one of the culprits, Jacek Rozański, to five years in prison (January 1955). The Ministry itself was abolished, and questions of state security were entrusted to a Committee for State Security responsible to the Council of Ministers. At the Third Plenum, in January 1955 Bierut admitted that State Security had been 'a state within the state' and that the party had failed to exercise adequate control over it.

The freer atmosphere now allowed the intellectuals to raise their heads. Adam Ważyk, who had been a leading exponent of socialist realism in the early 1950s and had published a sycophantic poem on Stalin, now published his 'Poem for Adults', which contrasted official claims with the reality of life in Poland (August 1955), and demanded a new policy of 'clear truth' and 'burning reason'. It was perhaps a little too early for this. Ważyk was sharply reprimanded, and those who had published his poem (the editors of the review *Nowa kultura*) were dismissed.

The real turning-point as far as freedom of dissent was concerned was the Twentieth Party Congress, and particularly the publication in March 1956 (not quite legally) of the text of Khrushchev's secret speech attacking Stalin. This was 'the large stone which sets an avalanche in motion' (Mond).[40] Gomułka subsequently said that thanks to the Twentieth Congress 'an electrifying, healthy current went through the mass of Party people'. The reality was less romantic. Certain middle-ranking leaders of the PZPR (Staszewski, Morawski, Matwin), less compromised by Stalinism than their elders, decided to sacrifice a couple of prominent leaders of the early fifties (Berman, followed by Minc) and to use their control of the press to influence public opinion. So the party intellectuals were let off the leash, which allowed an upsurge of free expression among young people in particular, with the Union of Polish Youth (ZMP) in the forefront. The ZMP's journal, *Po Prostu* (Plain Speaking), became the liveliest and most outspoken paper in Poland, with an eventual circulation of 200 000 copies. In March 1956 it printed a letter asking 'What about the Central Committee? To whom is it responsible?' Blind faith, they said, must be replaced by a world outlook worked out by the individual person. They did not restrict themselves to theory, either, but pointed out the contrast between the privileges of the ruling group and the difficult living conditions of the masses.

The writers also returned to the attack after the Twentieth Congress. At the Council of Culture and Art in March 1956, Antoni Słonimski attacked the doctrine of socialist realism, under which 'writers were haunted by the positive hero and typicality'. He demanded that the Writers' Union 're-nounce its drum-beating and public confessions', and called for a 'true democratisation of public life . . . and a return to rational and unfettered thought.' We must 'clear the road,' he said, 'of the whole of the mythology of the era of fear'.[41] With the removal in April of the Minister of Culture, Włodzimierz Sokorski, the way was open for the blossoming of a Polish press and literature which was witty, lively and highly adventurous.

Polish economists made a central contribution in this respect. In June 1956 the Second Congress of Economists was the scene of a 'more merciless and thorough scrutiny of the economic system than anywhere else in the East, even including possibly Yugoslavia'.[42] Oskar Lange complained that 'the oppressive rule of dogma is killing off Polish economic thought'; Fabierkiewicz said 'the Soviet system suits a country with immense natural resources but is harmful when applied elsewhere'; Kurowski called for the introduction of free, market-determined prices; Brus wanted a combination of decentralisation and directive planning; others called for foreign (Western) investment and the restoration of private industry (the so-called 'third sector'). These were merely recommendations; whether they would be put into practice would depend on political events.

The temperature was raised further by the rebellious attitude of the industrial workers. Fifteen thousand people employed in the Stalin Works in Poznań, the largest industrial enterprise in Poland, were up in arms about an increase in production norms, tantamount to a fall of 3.5 per cent in wages since 1954, and a deduction of a total of eleven million złotys in taxes from their overtime pay. The refusal of the Minister for the Motor Industry, Julian Tokarski, to make the key concession of a 20 per cent wage increase, combined with fears for the safety of the workers' delegation sent to Warsaw to negotiate this, led to explosive demonstrations on 28 June. The city jail was seized, the UB (state security) building was attacked, and the slogans raised were more political than economic. They included 'Down with the Russians', 'We want freedom', 'Down with Soviet occupation', and 'Down with false communism'. The local troops were not capable of dealing with the situation (in fact some soldiers refused to fire) and reinforcements were sent from Warsaw. By the time the fighting ended, the official casualty figures were 53 dead and 300 wounded. This was an underestimate. According to figures published in 1981 there were actually 75 dead and 900 wounded.[43]

These events were a severe shock to the party, and the initial attempt to blame the affair on enemy agents quickly gave place to a wave of official self-criticism. The party's daily newspaper, *Trybuna Ludu*, admitted on 6 July that 'the strike action of the Poznań workers was to a considerable extent caused by bureaucratic distortions of the proletarian state.' At the Seventh CC Plenum, in July 1956, Edward Ochab, First Secretary of the

PZPR since March, took up the theme of 'bureaucratic distortions' and 'loss of contact with the masses', and Cyrankiewicz announced a 'two year emergency programme to remove the most painful grievances of the working masses'.

Opposition to this change of line was led by the so-called Natolin faction of the party, formed around the Soviet ambassador Ponomarenko, and consisting of older 'Muscovites' such as Zenon Nowak, Jóźwiak, Matuszewski, the Minister of Defence Marshal Rokossowski, and the head of the official trade unions, the CRZZ, Wiktor Kłosiewicz. The Seventh CC Plenum, in July 1956, demonstrated the relative weakness of this conservative faction of the party, despite the Soviet support that propped it up. Bulganin, the Soviet Prime Minister, came to Warsaw in an attempt to overawe the leaders of the Polish party. He warned them that 'the policy of liberalization and self-criticism has been pushed too far',[44] and he later publicly attacked 'hostile and opportunist elements' (22 July).

Despite Bulganin's pressure the Seventh Plenum charted a course towards further liberalisation and 'democratisation', in both political and economic affairs. Independent farmers and artisans would be encouraged; 'excessive centralisation of planning and management' would be liquidated; 'the prerogatives of socialist enterprises would be widened'; the real wage would be raised by 30 per cent; the revision of work norms was declared unacceptable if this caused a drop in wages. The political programme of the Seventh Plenum was less dramatic. The role of the *Sejm* (Polish Parliament) was to be enhanced; Gomułka had his party rights restored; Rapacki and Gierek were elected to the Politburo; Tokarski was sacked. That was all. The Natolin group remained in place, and were able to resist 'the consistent implementation of the decisions of the Seventh Plenum' thereby 'paralysing the party's work'.[45]

In this situation the initiative passed to the lower levels of the party, particularly in the Warsaw City Party Committee, where the 'revisionist' or 'progressive' current was entrenched. Lechosław Goździk, party secretary at the Żerań Automobile Works, later recalled: 'We decided that it would not be a bad thing if a Workers' Council was set up in the factory to administer it.'[46] The role of party activists at this time was stressed by *Po Prostu* (5 August): 'The most active elements in the movement of the masses in the last few months have unquestionably been the communists, ideologically armed.'[47]

There was spontaneity as well, but it was not limited to the Workers' Councils. A broad front for independence, democratisation, and improvement of living conditions was formed out of a large number of currents of Polish life: Catholics (the one and a half million people who made the pilgrimage to Częstochowa on 26 August despite the complete silence observed about this by the official press); former Social Democrats; former Home Army men; the peasants who had been forcibly enrolled in the collective farms; members of the hitherto tame non-communist parties in the National Front; the trade unions under pressure from the workers. It was an alliance between these diverse elements which brought Gomułka to power in October 1956.

By 9 October the progressives were strong enough in the Politburo to force the resignation of Minc, and on 15 October the Politburo agreed to appoint Gomułka, remove Rokossowski, and recommend the next Plenum to elect a new Politburo from which the Natolinites would be completely excluded. The progressives also refused an invitation from Khrushchev to visit Moscow, feeling that they would be stronger on home ground. The Soviet leaders were worried by these developments, particularly by the proposed removal of Rokossowski. The Natolin faction envisaged mounting a coup at this stage, and they got as far drawing up a list of seven hundred people to be arrested by the army on the eve of the Eighth Plenum.

They were frustrated in part by General Komar, an old associate of Gomułka's who had been appointed head of the Internal Security Corps in August. He ordered his forces to occupy key buildings in Warsaw. But the population of Warsaw played a part too. Mond refers to the 'quasi-revolutionary activity of Stefan Staszewski and the Warsaw City Party Committee', who organised the workers of the big factories (particularly Żerań, where Goździk had been active since May), the university students, and the journalists and formed them into an instrument of political pressure.[48] During the night of 18–19 October 'working Warsaw mounted guard, convinced that its voice would be heard in the CC Plenum'[49] although the rest of the country watched events passively, and apprehensively.

The critical point was the opening of the Eighth Plenum on 19 October. The official task of the Plenum was to give effect to the changes already decided by the Politburo. But it was immediately interrupted by the unexpected arrival of a top level delegation of Soviet leaders, including Khrushchev and Molotov. They were backed up by a simultaneous advance of Soviet troops towards Warsaw. Discussions with the Soviet leaders went on throughout the day. Tense discussions with the Soviet leaders now took place. Gomułka later claimed that his intransigence saved the day ('If your tanks don't stop immediately I shall tell the whole truth to the Polish people') but the reality was that he was able to convince the Soviet leaders that he was a suitable replacement for Ochab, and that he would not undermine the foundations of communist rule, or friendship with the Soviet

Union. The Chinese also put in a word for him. As Ochab later recounted: 'The Soviet leaders presumably thought that Gomułka would put the country in order, and he was the one to stake their bets on.'[50] The appointment of Gomułka was hardly a Soviet 'success' (Sakwa) but it was not a failure. He offered a guarantee that the party would be able to ride out the wave of democratisation and new thinking sweeping the country.

The Eighth Plenum reassembled on the 20th October. It elected a new Politburo headed by Gomułka and excluding Rokossowski and the other Natolinites. The new leadership quickly announced a series of reforming measures. The Soviet troops left the outskirts of Warsaw and returned to their bases on 23 October; the electoral law was revised to allow choice between candidates; Kłosiewicz resigned as head of the trade unions (26 October); special shops for party functionaries were abolished (27 October); Cardinal Wyszyński, the Roman Catholic Primate, was freed from the prison in which he had been held since 1953 (28 October); Rokossowski was replaced as head of the armed forces by General Spychalski (28 October); all Soviet advisers attached to the Polish army and police returned home (30 October). These measures were taken against a background of continuous street demonstrations, often shouting anti-Soviet slogans, which the government contained by persuasion rather than force. The Żerań factory workers and the party journalists played an important part in this self-limitation of the Polish revolution of October 1956. The decisive factor here was the news from Hungary, which was seen as an omen of what could happen in Poland. This did not imply any lack of sympathy with the Hungarians, but it strengthened the argument of 'Polish *raison d'état*', which meant that Poland could not afford to quarrel with the Soviet Union, ostensibly because of the 'threat from West German revanchism', really because of the danger of Soviet invasion. As the CC put it on 2 November: 'Here and there voices can be heard demanding the withdrawal of Soviet army units from Poland . . . Such demands in the present international situation are contrary to the most vital interests of our nation and the Polish *raison d'état*.'[51]

Gomułka saw his main task as to restore the power of the party. This meant restricting concessions to a minimum. There was a danger that the spontaneous pressure from the party's rank and file against former Stalinists, which forced the resignation of eleven out of the nineteen Provincial Party Committees in October 1956, would lead to the complete disintegration of the party, as had happened in Hungary. Gomułka put a stop to this, saying in November: 'I doubt whether it would be possible to find activists . . . who cannot be accused of doing something wrong if their past work is now evaluated.'[52]

There would be no large-scale purge of Stalinists. The enthusiasm with which most Poles greeted Gomułka's appointment was based on a misunderstanding. The illusion that the Polish party could be reformed from inside lasted until the mid-1960s; it was gradually destroyed by the progressive dismantling of the liberalising achievements of October 1956. But there were some important exceptions to this: Polish–Soviet relations, agriculture, and, to some extent, religious affairs. Concessions in these spheres were essential if stable party rule was to be restored.

Gomułka was able to achieve a favourable settlement of Polish–Soviet relations with the Declaration of 18 November 1956, which came at the end of five days of talks in Moscow. By this declaration, the Soviet Union affirmed the equality of rights between the two countries; cancelled Poland's debts in compensation for the excessively low price it had paid for the coal deliveries of 1948–53; donated 1.4 million tons of grain; provided 700 million roubles of credit for Polish purchases within the Soviet Union; began again with the repatriation of Poles still held there; and ordered Soviet army officers and security advisers to return home. Subsequently (18 December) movements of the Soviet army within Poland without prior Polish consent were prohibited. It should be added that Gomułka considered that full Polish independence was impossible. His answer to foreign policy problems was to maintain a close friendship with Khrushchev and rely on Moscow's support against West German claims to the Western Provinces.

In agriculture, the attempt of the early 1950s to stamp out private cultivation was abandoned. The collective farms were allowed to dissolve quietly. By March 1957 83 per cent of them had vanished. By 1959 they covered only one per cent of the arable land (an area of 222 000 hectares). Collectivisation remained the ultimate aim. As Ochab, now Minister of Agriculture, said at the 3rd Party Congress (March 1959), 'the future belongs to the producers' cooperatives alone, but the voluntary principle will be maintained.' The state farms (PGRs) were retained, however, and the proportion of arable land cultivated in this fashion remained roughly constant (13 per cent in 1955, 12 per cent in 1960). They were reorganised and put directly under the Ministry of Agriculture (instead of, as heretofore, the Ministry of State Farms); detailed planning of output was abolished and the system was decentralised. By 1960 their economic performance equalled that of private farms. This may have impressed economists but it did not impress the peasants.[53]

The communist party's policy continued to be marked by a suspicion of private farming. Instead of the stick, Gomułka hoped to use the carrot to induce the farmers to rejoin the collectives. The few surviving collectives received tax concessions and benefited by a 25 per cent reduction in the rent paid for machinery from the state machine and tractor stations (POMs), which were retained to service the collectives when the GOMs (communal machine and tractor stations) were dissolved in October 1956. When this inducement proved ineffective the party tried another tack: it set up Agricultural Circles (*kółka rolnicze*). The machinery was handed over to these Circles where they existed. Non-members could rent it, but at 20 per cent extra. Furthermore, the Circles received almost all the 25 billion złoty 'Fund for Agricultural Development' created in June 1959 and financed from the obligatory deliveries of the peasants themselves. The peasants were not impressed by the Circles, either, although the party saw them as 'guiding the village towards socialist development'. By 1960 only 600 000 people had joined the Circles: roughly 15 per cent of all private farmers. Polish agriculture continued to suffer from the inability of the party to accept the predominance of private farming with a good grace.

In religious affairs too there was a definite change of policy after 1956. The release of Cardinal Wyszyński was followed by an agreement between the government and the episcopate (8 December 1956) which provided for the lifting of the decree of 9 February 1953 and the consequent reintroduction of religious instruction into schools, the recognition of the Church's jurisdiction over the appointment of bishops and other clergy, the return of priests and nuns to the Western Territories, and the appointment by the Pope of five resident bishops in the Western Territories. Bolesław Piasecki's *Pax* organisation lost its monopoly over the Catholic laity, and control of the Cracow weekly *Tygodnik Powszechny* reverted from Piasecki to a group of Catholic intellectuals led by Stanisław Stomma, who were close to the hierarchy but prepared to reach a *modus vivendi* with Gomułka. The government promised that it would 'remove the obstacles that existed in the previous period to the realization of the principle of full freedom for religious life'.[54]

Despite all this, the relationship between church and state continued to have its ups and downs. In 1958 the police raided the Jasna Góra monastery in Częstochowa, the shrine of the Black Madonna, and confiscated printing equipment and pamphlets. In 1959 taxation of church property was resumed, and in April 1960 there was a violent riot at Nowa Huta, the steel town, where the authorities persistently refused to allow a new church to be built. But these were relatively minor upsets. Until 1965 there was uneasy coexistence rather than conflict between church and state.

The picture was different in other spheres of policy. Gomułka had already laid down the limits of reform in his speech of 29 November 1956. No opposition parties would be permitted to exist, he said. He justified this by hinting at a Soviet veto: 'People who criticise us for not including the freedom of all parties in our programme would perhaps suggest that we should shift the geopolitical situation of Poland, moving it to another part of the globe, or even to another planet?'[55] Moreover 'the extent of democratic liberties would be determined by the conditions which accompany the construction of socialism'.

In the eyes of Gomułka, the period 1956–7 was one of partial and temporary retreat by the party. He meant to make up lost ground when it became convenient. The history of the workers' control movement demonstrates this. Workers' control had spread rapidly in October 1956, spurred on by the journalists of *Po Prostu*. The Ninth Plenum of the Central Council of Trade Unions (CRZZ), held between 16 and 18 November, demanded the introduction of workers' self-management into economic and social life. Self-management through workers' councils was also advocated by the economists Oscar Lange and Włodzimierz Brus, who drew up the first comprehensive plan of economic reform, under the aegis of an Economic Council, set up by the government as an advisory body in December 1956. According to their proposals, central planning would be implemented through market mechanisms and direct industrial democracy.

This, the first comprehensive economic reform plan in Eastern Europe, was presented in April 1957. It was ignored. Although Gomułka proclaimed in May 1957, at the Ninth Plenum, that the specifically Polish road to socialism was characterised by Workers' Councils, he attacked the 'anarchist utopia' of using them 'to replace centralised administration', and he underlined that 'the party organisation in the factories must remain as before the leading political force'. The law of December 1957 provided that the trade unions would collaborate in preparing and conducting elections to the workers' councils, and 'if the plan is not fulfilled, and there is inadequate productivity, the workers' council can be dissolved by the competent ministry in agreement with the appropriate trade union presidium'.[56] Thus the Workers' Councils had already lost much of their autonomy when in 1958 they were incorporated (alongside factory party and trade union committees, the youth organisation, and the technical staff organisation) into quarterly Conferences of Workers' Self-Management (KSR). This was tantamount to abolishing them.[57]

The reform of the political system was also strictly limited in scope, as displayed in the elections of January 1957 for the *Sejm*. Although more candidates could stand than there were seats, unlike in 1952, and this opened the possibility of competition between the ZSL, the SD and the PZPR, this was cancelled out by the single list system. The electors could, however, affect the place of candidates within the unified list of the Front of National Unity (FJN) by judicious deletions. Hence Gomułka's dramatic speech of 19 January 1957: 'To cross out the candidates of our party means to cross out the independence of our country, to cross out Poland from the map of European states.'[58]

At this stage, he still enjoyed considerable prestige among the Poles. The voters responded by exercising great self-restraint. Only one party candidate was defeated by the crossing out of his name. The results (largely determined in advance, through the single list system) were: PZPR 52%, ZSL 26% and SD 9%. The other successful candidates were independents. The composition of the new government, however, was overwhelmingly communist. Zenon Nowak, one of the chief supporters of the Natolin faction, was made Deputy Prime Minister. The ex-Socialist Cyrankiewicz became Prime Minister.

There was a rapid return to conservatism in the cultural sphere too. The year 1957 saw the sacking of the editorial board of the party's daily newspaper, *Trybuna Ludu*, and the gradual obliteration of *Po Prostu*, first by the removal in April of its editor, Eligius Lasota, then by its suspension during the summer of 1957. The journal was finally closed down in October and ten of its editors were expelled from the party for 'spreading disbelief in socialist construction' and taking an 'unfruitful and negative standpoint'. What they had done in fact was point to the prosperity of capitalist Europe, and ask, in their issue of 30 September 1957: 'How did it happen that in spite of our expectations the capitalist countries have been able to avoid an economic crisis?'[59]

The hopes of the leading Polish writers Adam Ważyk, Jerzy Andrzejewski and Jan Kott that they could build a bridge between Polish and general European culture by their proposed journal *Europa* were frustrated. Permission for this was refused in November 1957, and they all left the party. They would have been thrown out anyway, in the mass purge, or 'verification', instituted by the PZPR in October 1957. By the end of 1958 28 000 members had been expelled either for 'revisionism' or 'dogmatism'. Gomułka always placed greater stress on the fight against revisionism. 'The revisionist wing must be cut off from the party', he told the Tenth Plenum in October 1957. 'Dogmatists' were a danger, but not such a serious one. Revisionists, he said, were 'tuberculosis' for the party; dogmatists merely 'influenza'. Among the revisionists, Professor Kołakowski was his *bête noire*. The latter's 'revisionist longings' had won the attention of 'the bourgeois and Trotskyite press'. Kołakowski was not deterred by these attacks, becoming if anything more audacious, challenging historical determinism and insisting on the superior role of the moral judgement of the autonomous individual. In 1959 he was dismissed from the chief editorship of *Studia Filozoficzne*, the Polish philosophical journal, for playing off the 'liberalism' of the younger Marx against orthodox communist interpretations of his work. Further acts of cultural repression followed. Literary journals such as *Nowa Kultura* and *Przegląd Kulturalny* were subjected to censorship from the autumn of 1957 onwards; *Nowa Kultura* lost most of its editorial board in May 1958.[60] Writers who had tasted freedom of expression in 1956 now had to take care not to go too far. Dissidents in general had to take note of the reorganisation of the security police in 1959 under General Mieczysław Moczar, a former communist partisan 'with a reputation for toughness'.[61]

The years that followed saw a progressive narrowing of the freedom of action of Polish intellectuals. In 1962 the authorities closed the Crooked Circle Club, centre of revisionist discussions for the past seven years. In 1963 *Przegląd Kulturalny* was forced to cease publication because it 'was causing ideological confusion'. In July 1963 Gomułka justified the harsher course at a CC Plenum on the grounds that artists and writers had become 'corrupted by bourgeois ideology'. 'The party,' he added, 'would never permit the propagation of anti-socialist views uncritically imported from the capitalist world.'[62]

The dissidents did not give way without a fight; hence Gomułka's actions actually increased the ferment in intellectual circles, given that he was still trying to pursue a middle course and avoid a return to the fiercely repressive measures of the Stalin era. Hence in 1964 the Letter of the Thirty-Four, a protest against press censorship signed by leading members of the academic and cultural élite, resulted in loss of privileges and publication opportunities for the signatories, but not expulsion from the party, and only one of the thirty four was actually brought to trial. Harsher measures were taken in 1965 against Jacek Kuroń and Karol Modzelewski, but their offence was greater. They had presented an *Open Letter to the Party* to their local party organisation, in which, after a devastating analysis of the current Polish situation, they concluded that the only possible solution was 'the overthrow of the prevailing system. Revolution is a necessity for development.' It would inevitably be a proletarian revolution. The working class would not necessarily have to take up arms, however, since the apparatus of coercion would be weakened by its minority position. In July 1965 they were convicted of advocating the 'forcible overthrow of the political and socio-economic system of the People's Republic of Poland'. Kuroń was given three years, Modzelewski three years and six months.[63]

The gloom this trial created was deepened in 1966 by, first, the expulsion of Leszek Kołakowski from the party for a speech at Warsaw University in which he pointed out all the ways in which the rulers of Poland had retreated from the promises of October 1956, and, second, the expulsion of twenty-two leading Polish writers from the party for protesting to the Central Committee about Kołakowski's treatment. There was little left of Poland's 'intellectual October' by 1966.

In the economy, too, the reforming impulse of 1956 ran into the sand rather rapidly. The strong position of the workers after October 1956 was reflected at first in an annual rate of increase in real wages of 15 per cent in 1956 and 12 per cent in 1957. This was partly a result of the retention of the 1953 work norms when they had long become out of date owing to the introduction of more efficient machinery, partly of the tendency of managers of industrial associations, given that there was a labour shortage, to hand out higher wages than provided for in the plan. In addition, the inadequate performance of agriculture, resulting from a drought in 1958, led to a severe meat shortage. So the government raised meat prices by 25 per cent in 1959. It also increased work norms. There were some strikes against this, but Gomułka still enjoyed sufficient support to carry through his harsher policy.

After 1959 economic policy returned in many ways to the centralised and production-oriented system of the early 1950s. Eugeniusz Szyr and Julian Tokarski, two members of the Stalinist old guard removed in 1956, were reappointed in November 1959, as Deputy Prime Ministers; the number of obligatory targets to be met by enterprises was increased from six or eight to nineteen; a sharp increase in investment was made (17.2 per cent in 1959). There was a fall in real wages in 1959–60, which brought the average for the first Five Year Plan period down to 5.1 per cent; during the next five years (1961–65) real wages only increased by 1.5 per cent per annum, while the net material product increased by 6.2 per cent per annum. This is a measure of the change in policy since 1956.[64]

Thus by the mid-1960s Gomułka had successfully accomplished what was dubbed the 'small stabilisation'. Poland had slipped back, with the exceptions we have noted, to the level of Czechoslovakia, Bulgaria and the rest. As in the case of Hungary, the divergent development which seemed to have been initiated by the events of 1956 was beginning to converge again. In the Soviet Union, the hesitations and uncertainties of the mid-1950s gave way to a definite decision to coordinate and integrate the policies of the bloc, militarily through the Warsaw Pact, economically through Comecon and politically through successive conferences attended by the member states of the 'socialist community'. Clear signs of this were the common decision to undertake a 'great leap forward' economically after 1958, the increasing integration of the Eastern European economies, the greater role of intra-bloc planning through Comecon, the common setback to optimistic plans for expansion in the early 1960s, and finally the common response to failure which allowed the green light to be given for economic reforms in the later 1960s.

6 The Quiet Years, 1957–68

With the vast socio-political movements which had stirred Hungary and Poland to their roots in 1956 now laid to rest, there begins a period of calm and surface stability for Eastern Europe. The rulers rule; the ruled obey and carry on working. The economy continues its planned advance towards the goal of 'developed socialism'; full collectivisation of agriculture brings most sectors of the economy under state control; moves towards the economic integration of the member countries of the CMEA are set afoot. Political events do occur, certainly, but none of any significance. This period lasts for four or five years. At the end of that time, clouds begin to form on the horizon. At the economic level, the 'extensive' development of the whole period after 1948 (which can be seen as relatively homogeneous, given the absence of any real economic reforms after 1956) was nearing the end of its effectiveness. Ever-increasing inputs of capital and labour were sufficient until the early 1970s to guarantee continued industrial advance. But 'as the potential for further increases in the output of labour declined, the growth rates of output and output per worker also declined'.[1] The rate of growth of Net Material Product, at constant prices, on official statistics, fell from 7.0% p.a. in Czechoslovakia in 1956/60 to 1.9% in 1961/65; corresponding figures for the GDR are 7.1 and 3.4, Hungary 6.0 and 4.1, Poland 6.5 and 6.2.[2]

This point applied far less to the Balkan countries, so that the historic division we noted earlier between the formerly backward south east and the already developed centre and north was accentuated rather than reduced by economic development. Romania's average annual rate of growth of NMP between 1956 and 1960 was 6.6%; between 1961 and 1965 it rose to 9.1%. Corresponding figures for Bulgaria are 9.6% and 6.6%, for Albania 7.0% and 5.8%. Here the Stalin model of extensive economic growth continued to look appropriate, and seemed to be continuously successful. Elsewhere, the economic difficulties of the early 1960s told their own story, and were indeed a predisposing factor in the attempt to mount a renewed attack on the problem of economic reform after 1962.

It would be wrong to exaggerate the difficulties facing the centrally planned economies in the 1960s. Apart from Czechoslovakia, where the performance of the economy was highly inadequate in terms of growth for several years (NMP growth of 1.4% in 1962, decline of 2.2% in 1963, growth of 0.6% in 1964)[3] they continued to grow at respectable rates, and consumption levels continued to rise. But the signs of stagnation or at least reduced growth combined with the arguments of the economists and the comparison with the West to produce a feeling at the top of the communist parties that some reform are now necessary.

As usual, Soviet permission for economic reform was a prerequisite to putting it into effect elsewhere. This appeared to be given implicitly by the publication in the Moscow *Pravda* in September 1962 of a pro-reform article by the leading Soviet economist Professor Yevsai Liberman. This allowed the GDR government to set off a 'second wave of economic reform' in 1963. In July the 'Guidelines for the New Economic System' were approved by the SED. Czechoslovakia followed in January 1965, and Hungary started to prepare a reform which eventuated in 1968. The reforms comprised the following key elements: (1) a reduction in the number of centrally planned, mandatory output targets. In Czechoslovakia, for example, they were reduced from 1300 to 52; (2) greater emphasis on income and profit as criteria for judging success; (3) a strengthening of economic incentives, with employees paid more in more efficient enterprises; (4) price reforms, dividing prices into the three categories of fixed, controlled and free. In Czechoslovakia seven per cent of prices were to be free, 29 per cent were to fluctuate within a centrally determined band, 64 per cent remained fixed; (5) the concentration of enterprises into larger units. In the GDR there were to be 90 'associations of publicly owned enterprises', or VVBs. Finally, (6) decentralisation of economic decision-making to these larger units.

There were many weaknesses both in the reforms themselves and in their setting. They did not meet the real problems of a low rate of technological progress, and the absence of a rational price structure. They were largely irrelevant to agriculture, now completely collectivised, except in so far as state farms benefited from points 2 and 3 on financial incentives. The physical allocation of producer goods was continued. The reforms met with sabotage from an entrenched bureaucracy, since the functionaries carrying out the changes were those who had run the old system. They were implemented half-heartedly because the party apparatus in fact opposed reform. They were an attempt to solve the economic problem without touching on politics. They differed from the first wave of reform in 1956–7 in that the workers themselves were not given a role. Workers' councils, which had figured in reform blueprints of an earlier era, were now excluded.

Finally, in each case the reforms were only implemented for a short period, before recentralisation set in. In the GDR the New Economic System lasted from 1963 to 1968 or at the latest December 1970 (the 14th CC Plenum of the SED decided to restrict the powers of the VVBs and increase the number of prescribed plan indicators); in Czechoslovakia from 1965 to July 1969; in Hungary from 1968 to 1972; in Poland the first set of reforms was thwarted by the workers' revolt of 1970 and the second set of 1972 was ended in 1975 with the withdrawal of the elements of autonomy granted to the 'Large Economic Organisations' or WOGs. Reasons for failure included the political obstacle of the resistance of the ruling élite; adverse economic conditions which strengthened the hand of opponents of reform; and above all the technical difficulty, perhaps even the contradiction, involved in retaining central control of the economy and building a market mechanism into it.[4]

Politically, the restoration of many aspects of the Stalin model in the late 1950s seemed initially to be successful. The rule of a single party leader was restored after the interval of uncertainty which had lasted until 1957. Gomułka in Poland, Kádár in Hungary, Novotný in Czechoslovakia. Zhivkov in Bulgaria, Gheorghiu-Dej in Romania, and Ulbricht in the GDR were all able to ride out challenges to their authority and exert similar sway to their predecessors although they depended more than before on the consent of their colleagues; while Enver Hoxha in Albania remained unchallenged throughout the vicissitudes of the post-Stalin era and the break with the Soviet Union. In order to stay in power, these rulers often had to resort to demagogic nationalist manoeuvres, since full-scale Stalinist terror was no longer appropriate. This resulted either in discrediting the government itself (the Polish anti-Zionist campaign of 1967–8 for example) or in arousing dormant nationalist feelings among the ethnic minorities, which stored up much trouble for the future (the Hungarians reacted in this way in Romania and Czechoslovakia, the Turks in Bulgaria, the Albanians in Yugoslavia, and the Slovaks in Czechoslovakia).

In the cultural and intellectual spheres there were two insoluble problems. First, the ending of Stalinist methods of retaining control meant that party tutelage was seen more as an irritant than an overpowering, all-dominating presence requiring absolute submission (Romania, Bulgaria and Albania are again exceptions); second, the penetration of Western ideas could no longer completely be prevented, given the increased sophistication of the economy, the need for the transfer of advanced Western technology, and the consequent lowering of the barriers to the flow of information. Comparisons were inevitable. Some degree of satisfaction of the people's material needs might have made the situation tolerable. But, as Matejko concluded in 1974, in a comment as judicious as it was prophetic, 'the progressive disparity between the aspirations of the masses and their modest satisfaction . . . leads to an imbalance that will probably influence to a large extent the future of Eastern Europe'.[5]

Finally, the growth of an educated and urbanised public, working class and otherwise, which was a success for communist policy, had paradoxical results. It undermined the very foundations of communist rule because it strengthened the tendency to question its justification. The quiet decade of the 1960s is therefore marked by a building up of pressure of various kinds; and in two countries where different pressures coincided the result at the end of the decade was a deep-going political crisis. In the Polish case there was renewed intellectual ferment followed by an explosion of working-class discontent (1968–71); in the Czechoslovak case the rulers themselves instituted a broad, but essentially prophylactic movement of reform (1968) which was, however, nipped in the bud by a Soviet invasion. But let us first consider the countries which avoided severe crisis at the end of the 1960s.

The German Democratic Republic seems. at first sight to be just as subject as Poland and Czechoslovakia to the pressures mentioned above. It is sometimes claimed that ease of emigration was a safety-valve for dis-contented people. This does not explain the absence of crisis after the building of the Berlin Wall in 1961 made it impossible to leave the country without permission, although it does explain the lack of any substantial opposition to Walter Ulbricht in the 1950s. Ulbricht's political skill and his determination to 'construct socialism' in the GDR is an important personal factor here. He purged the party from top to bottom after the riots of 17–18 June 1953 (62.2 per cent of SED District Committee members were replaced between 1952 and 1954); he gave lip-service to the 'New Course' just long enough, and then announced its abrupt end, asserting in 1955: 'it was never our intention to choose such a false course and we shall never choose it'. He carefully avoided any discussion of Stalin's errors in 1956, despite Khrushchev's secret speech; he chose the right moment (just after the Hungarian uprising of 1956) to strike against the 'revision-ists', ignoring the advice of 'softer' members of the leadership like Schirdewan, Wollweber and Oelssner. Wolfgang Harich was jailed for ten years; Ernst Bloch was pushed out of his Leipzig University lectures (1957). Furthermore, Ulbricht overruled the objections of his colleagues Selbmann, Oelssner and Leuschner when at the 35th CC Plenum in February 1958 he launched a renewed drive for the collectivisation of agriculture, the abolition of private trade and commerce, and rapid indus-trial growth. The result was success in physical terms (an 11 per cent rise in industrial production 1958, 12 per cent in 1959) and an increasing outflow of refugees, from the low point of 144 000 in 1959 to 199 000 in 1960 and 155 000 in the first half of 1961 alone. If this went on the GDR would be bled white. The flood of refugees had to be damned.

Ulbricht's answer to the problem was to build the Berlin Wall. The SED had been pressing for such a solution since November 1960; at the beginning of August 1961 the party secretaries of the Warsaw Pact countries finally gave their consent to the idea, despite the clear loss of prestige that would result for the whole of the 'socialist camp'. On 13 August 1961 the 'anti-Fascist protection wall', as it was called officially, was erected in Berlin. The SED could now continue building its version of socialism behind secure barriers; it continued to do so until the Hungarian communists in their reforming enthusiasm started to leave the door to the West ajar (September 1989). In the meantime the GDR had become the most industrially developed member of the CMEA, with the highest standard of living and the highest level of productivity. It ranked ninth in the world as an economic power by 1970, and enjoyed an average annual rate of growth of industrial production of 5.8% between 1960 and 1964, and 6.4% between 1964 and 1970. The per capita rate of growth of the standard of living between 1970 and 1975 was 4.9% – the highest in the 'socialist bloc'. The citizens of the GDR were able to buy television sets (69% of households in 1970), refrigerators (56%), washing machines (54%). Many even had motor cars (16%). Wages rose from 555 marks a month in 1960 to 755 marks in 1970, while prices fell by 0.1% during that period.[6]

In fact the GDR was so evidently stable and effective as a political formation that Walter Ulbricht succumbed to a kind of 'dizziness with success' in 1967. Socialism had already been built, he said. The task was now the 'completion of socialism'. The 'developed socialist society' would be based on the 'scientific-technical revolution'.[7] This attempt to strike out on a different path from the Soviet Union (at least in theory) gave rise to complaints from Moscow, and the SED Politburo decided that Ulbricht could no longer continue as First Secretary (May 1971). He was replaced by the sober and cautious Erich Honecker, who acted more as the captain of a team than as a powerful single leader of the traditional type. The 'developed socialist society' idea was dropped, and from 1973 onwards the GDR was referred to more modestly as a country of 'real, existing socialism'. The message was clear: the GDR was not to pursue a separate ideological development but to follow faithfully behind Soviet thinking. The Eighth SED Congress, held in June 1971, proclaimed that the party's task was: 'to raise the material and cultural level of the people on the basis of a high tempo of development of socialist production and growth in the productivity of labour.'[8]

The economic ideas of the reformers of the 1960s were also rejected. We have already mentioned the decision of December 1970 to move back towards centralism and strengthen direct state control over the VVBs.

Günter Mittag, the chief proponent of the New Economic System, was removed from the Council of State (1971) and the CC Secretariat (1973). He was replaced as Secretary for the Economy by Werner Krolikowski, a man without economic training. Instead of allowing prices to rise to reflect costs a hand-to-mouth policy of extra subsidies, savings (e.g. on streetlighting) and intensification of labour was adopted. The oil price rise of 1973 resulted in a 170 per cent increase in raw material import prices between 1970 and 1974. This was not reflected in price-increases within the GDR.

The SED leadership had decided that the only way to stay in power was to ensure a rising level of material prosperity. Hence the principal task of the five-year plan for 1971–75 was described as 'the further raising of the material and cultural living standard of the people'. High growth rates were secondary, and were to be achieved not through investment but through 'intensification of production'. The quality and quantity of consumer goods were to be improved. A generous social policy was outlined as well.[9] If the masses were satisfied, the intellectuals could be permitted a certain degree of freedom. Hence in 1972 Honecker introduced a 'literary spring' by declaring 'there can be no taboos in the field of art and literature'. This did not last. In 1976 the folk singer Wolf Biermann was deprived of his GDR citizenship; writers who protested against this were disciplined in various ways. The limits on free expression remained narrow, but the development of a dissident movement was prevented partly by the network of informers for the *Stasi*, and partly by the safety-valve of emigration. Many writers left to continue their work in West Germany. The fact remained that party congress followed party congress in the GDR with no sign of crisis and every appearance of stability, founded on economic success. The cracks that developed in this imposing edifice in the 1980s will be considered in our final chapter.

For Hungary, too, the 1960s and 1970s were quiet years. Kádár pursued a course of compromise after a period of hesitation between 1957 and 1962 which was caused largely by external pressures. The resurgence of dogmatism in the Soviet Union after 1957, conditioned by Khrushchev's need to fend off Chinese criticisms of his 'revisionism', led in Hungary to a return to rapid collectivisation of agriculture, a reimposition of orthodoxy in the cultural sphere, and a rejection of economic reform.

Let us look first at the renewal of collectivisation. The 1956 exodus from the collective farms was arrested in 1957, but the new regime was initially in no hurry to complete the 'socialist transformation of agriculture'. However, on his return from a visit to Moscow in January 1959 Kádár announced that the great lesson of the recent 21st Congress of the Soviet party was Hungary's need to catch up on collectivisation. She was falling seriously behind Czechoslovakia (75 per cent by 1959) and Bulgaria (92 per cent). A Central Committee resolution of March 1959 accordingly relaunched collectivisation, which was pushed forward rapidly, so that by 1962 75 per cent of working peasants were in the collectives, and 18 per cent employed on the state farms. Second, culture. In July 1958 the CC issued cultural guidelines calling for 'party-mindedness' and 'the efficient dissemination of the Marxist-Leninist world view and the defeat and displacement of bourgeois views.' Later in the year György Lukács was criticised sharply for 'idealism and revisionism' and prevented from publishing until 1964. In 1959 the Office of Church Affairs was revived, as part of a drive to recover control of believers and discourage religious practices. Third, economic reform. In 1957 the report of the Varga Commission, which had recommended decentralisation, was rejected, and no further attempts at economic reform were made for the next five years.

The turning-point came in November 1962, at the 8th Congress of the HSWP. Changes in the Soviet Union were a vital factor in altering the political atmosphere. Khrushchev had launched a second wave of de-Stalinisation at the 22nd Party Congress of the CPSU in October 1961, and Kádár was able to take advantage of this. In November 1962 he announced a series of steps to win over those Hungarians, the vast majority, who remained outside the party. Party membership, standing at 499 000, had failed to return to the level of the early 1950s. It would never in fact do so. So Kádár proclaimed an opening to the rest of society. The keynote of his speech, and also the slogan that sums up Kádárism, was 'those who are not against us are for us'. Technical expertise instead of party membership would henceforth be the criterion for occupying key positions; candidates for higher education would be judged by ability not by class criteria; the party itself was slightly democratised: party members could present dissenting views in their own organisations. Two of the most notorious veterans of the Rákosi era, György Marosán and Karoly Kiss, were removed from the Politburo, while the economic reformer Rezső Nyers was brought into it.[10]

Kádár's objective was to turn himself into a 'benevolent monarch rather than a domineering despot' (Hankiss).[11] This did not mean the abandonment of single-party rule. It did mean a reduction in censorship, especially for economic writings, and above all a return to economic reform. In 1966 the CC approved the Nyers model of economic reform, and in 1968 it was launched, under the title of the New Economic Mechanism. The delay in implementation can be explained partly by resistance from dogmatists

1. The atmosphere of the 1947 elections in Poland. The headquarters of the Warsaw Committee of the Polish Workers' Party, guarded by submachine guns

2. The seizure of power in Prague, February 1948. Two lorry-loads of People's Militia disembarking

3. Hungarian insurgents on the way to Budapest at the end of October 1956

4. A triumphant Dubček arrives at Košice after his meeting with Brezhnev, 2 August 1968

5. The limits of modernisation. An ox-drawn cart still in use in Moravia in the 1960s

6. The new urban landscape. High-rise flats in Warsaw

7. The continuing backwardness of agriculture in Poland. Farmer ploughing near Lublin in 1980

8. The face of dissent. Jacek Kuroń in full flow at Warsaw University, 1976

9. The Ursus Tractor Factory near Warsaw at a standstill during the strike over free Saturdays, January 1981

10. The mysterious General Jaruzelski, sandwiched between his allies. *Right*: General Hoffman, GDR, *Left*: General Kulikov, USSR

11. Presiding over decline: A Warsaw Pact meeting of 1986. *Left to right:* Zhivkov (Bulgaria), Ceauşescu (Romania), Husák (Czechoslovakia), Gorbachev (USSR), Kádár (Hungary), Jaruzelski (Poland), Honecker (GDR)

within the HSWP, especially the trade union representatives, and partly by uncertainty about the Soviet attitude after the fall of Khrushchev. In fact Brezhnev refrained from supporting Kádár's domestic opponents, and allowed the reform to go ahead. It involved the elements mentioned above: a relaxation in central planning, autonomy for the enterprises, repeated adjustment of prices to bring them into line with those prevailing on the world market, abandonment of the traditional emphasis on promoting heavy industry, encouragement of private farming.[12] It proceeded smoothly for four years, but then ran into the twin obstacles of an entrenched state bureaucracy, which was threatened by loss of its monopoly power over the economy, and increasing economic difficulties. We shall examine later the question of whether the Hungarian economic reform survived in the harsher climate of the 1970s. It is in any case certain that Hungary remained the most liberalised of the Eastern European communist countries, if one excludes Yugoslavia. It was also the most stable.

Further south, the Balkan countries of Romania, Bulgaria and Albania also seemed to be immune from political or economic crisis after 1956. Their development proceeded smoothly along well-worn tracks after the initial impetus of de-Stalinisation had died out. In fact the story is a twofold one, of continuing economic growth under a modified command economy, and of successful manipulations by the top party leaders to ensure their retention of personal power. The control exercised by the party, the power of the police, and the uniformity of cultural and intellectual life remained permanent features of the situation. In Bulgaria the BCP's First Secretary, Todor Zhivkov, removed his rivals Chervenkov (1961) and Yugov (1962), to ensure that he remained sole ruler for the next two decades. In Romania Gheorghiu-Dej had no rivals, because Pauker, Luca and Georgescu had already been purged in 1952. With breathtaking hypocrisy he claimed that they had been purged for their Stalinism: hence Romania had no need for any further de-Stalinisation. In 1956 the Chişinevski-Constantinescu faction in the party leadership tried to use the 20th Party Congress revelations to get rid of Dej, but he succeeded in purging these new opponents at a party plenum in June 1957. He was able to transfer power smoothly to his successor, Nicolae Ceauşescu in the course of the 1960s. The latter became party leader in 1965, and head of state in 1967. Romania thus followed the standard pattern of Balkan communism. It did however possess two highly distinctive features which deserve a brief examination: an extreme nationalism, and an independent foreign policy.

Gheorghiu-Dej's nationalism was displayed in the destruction of the Hungarian minority's autonomy in Transylvania and an increased stress on

Romanian cultural hegemony there. Moreover, Russian-language teaching was quietly eliminated from the schools, and the diffusion of Soviet culture was brought to a halt in the 1960s. Independence in foreign policy was made easier by the withdrawal of the Soviet garrison in 1958. This was perhaps a gesture of gratitude by Khrushchev for Dej's staunch support in 1956 over the Soviet intervention in Hungary. The first truly independent stand made by Romania was in 1962 when Gheorghiu-Dej resisted Khrushchev's attempt to make the CMEA a genuine instrument of economic integration. Under the proposed 'international socialist division of labour' Romania was to be locked into the position of supplying agricultural products to the more advanced members of the CMEA. This would mean abandoning the programme of developing heavy industry. This Dej would not do. He defied Soviet pressure openly at the CMEA session held in March 1963. The other CMEA members were not in sympathy with this approach and Romania did not secure any assistance in developing its economy. Instead, Dej hoped to secure the machinery and equipment that was needed from countries outside the Eastern bloc. The share of the non-communist world in Romania's foreign trade grew from 20 per cent in 1955 to 33 per cent in 1964.[13] By 1970 it was 55 per cent.[14] In 1972 Romania joined the IMF and the World Bank. It was the first communist country to do so.

Economic independence went hand in hand with political independence. In 1964 Romania took a resolutely neutral stance on the Sino-Soviet dispute, and the RWP proclaimed 'the exclusive right of every party to set its own political line'.[15] This approach was developed further by Ceauşescu, who refused to break with Israel in 1967, entered diplomatic relations with West Germany, and in August 1968 denounced the Warsaw Pact invasion of Czechoslovakia in uncompromising terms: 'It is inconceivable that a socialist country . . . should trample the freedom and independence of another state under foot.'[16]

Within Romania the picture was completely different. In the political sphere both Dej and Ceauşescu insisted on maintaining absolute personal control, through the Romanian Communist Party (as the Romanian Workers' Party was renamed in 1965). The practical absence of a Romanian dissident movement made this easier. Ceauşescu moved in an increasingly authoritarian direction after 1971, endeavouring to establish a dynastic form of socialism through a policy of extreme nepotism. His wife, Elena, (CC member since 1973) his son, Nicu, (CC member since 1982), and other relatives, were placed in positions of power, and a 'cult of personality' was developed around him. At the November 1971 CC Plenum liberalism was attacked and the doctrine of 'socialist realism' in culture was rehabilitated. Ceauşescu thus returned to the method of rule characteristic of Stalinism at its height. But there was also an atavistic element in this situation. Ceauşescu was described as 'the embodiment of the spirit of the Romanian people' in 1974, at the 11th Party Congress, and in the 1980s he began to adopt the title 'conducător', in obvious imitation of the pre-war Romanian dictator General Antonescu. He was compared with Julius Caesar, Peter the Great, and Napolean Bonaparte. The establishment of the Ceauşescu dynasty was a truly unique development in Eastern European communism.

In the economic sphere no substantial changes were made in the Stalinist command system. In fact the state plan was meant to be more comprehensive, not less, under the Directives of 1967. It was maintained that 'any tendency to exclude any branch of the economy from planning is injurious . . . and introduces anarchistic market elements into production, sales and distribution'.[17]

Insistence on an autarchic development of heavy industry, particularly steel and machine tools, meant tremendous concentration of investment in those branches, and in industry generally, at the expense of agriculture. The share of agriculture in total investments fluctuated around 14 per cent in the late 1970s, whereas 35 per cent of the labour force was employed in that branch. The stagnation of agriculture was a serious problem the Romanian government took no steps to solve. Romania was untouched by economic reform. Even the Machine Tractor Stations, set up everywhere on the Soviet model in the 1950s in Eastern Europe and dismantled following the Soviet example in the 1960s, were left in existence and simply renamed 'agricultural mechanization enterprises'.[18] The collective and state farms remained at 92 per cent of the total land area the overwhelmingly dominant form of agricultural enterprise.

As a result of a combination of neglect and inherited backwardness, the share of agriculture in national income in 1979 was a mere 16 per cent. Mechanisation was less developed than anywhere else in Eastern Europe except Albania. There was one tractor per 102 hectares in Romania; one per 50 hectares in Czechoslovakia. 170kw of electricity were available per hectare in Romania, 381kw in Czechoslovakia. The wheat yield per hectare was 2.8 tonnes in Romania, compared with 4.0 tonnes in Bulgaria. The figures for other agricultural products display a similar picture.[19]

Romania was a disaster waiting to happen; but in the 1960s and 1970s it seemed a model of stability. The same can be said of Bulgaria and Albania. All three countries were characterised by a weak or non-existent dissident movement; rule by a single person; rejection of economic reform; maintenance of a pattern of rapid industrial growth with priority to heavy industry; continuation of high growth rates into the late 1970s, but not beyond. As we shall show later, the 1980s, the last decade of communism in Eastern Europe, were universally a turning-point as regards growth. There were also major differences between the three countries. In foreign policy there was a whole spectrum in the Balkans from Bulgaria's close identification with the Soviet Union, through Romania's independent position, to Albania's complete break with the Soviet Union and orientation towards China (late 1960s) followed by a break with China (1979) and total isolation under the slogan of 'self-reliance'.

In economics Bulgaria was more of a success in real terms throughout the 1960s and 1970s (Romanian growth figures are considered to be rather inflated), thanks to its readiness to move towards economic integration with the other CMEA countries (unlike Romania or Albania). A pattern developed whereby Bulgaria received supplies of raw materials and energy predominantly from the Soviet Union and exported mainly machinery, electrical equipment and processed food. In line with the continued stress on developing the Bulgarian machine-building industry, the proportion of food processing in Bulgarian industrial production fell progressively from 34 per cent in 1960 to 23 per cent in 1977, while machine-building rose from 12 per cent to 28 per cent. Nevertheless, food remained an important component of exports, to East and West alike. Success in agriculture was helped by flexibility towards private farming. Although Bulgaria moved rapidly towards full collectivisation between 1956 and 1958, collective farmers were allowed to hold up to 0.5 of a hectare each in individual ownership. A mixed system prevailed after 1970, in which gigantic 'agro-industrial complexes' over 10 000 hectares in area coexisted with small private plots. The latter covered 13 per cent of the arable land in 1975 and produced 25 per cent of agricultural output, including 53 per cent of the potatoes and 41 per cent of the fruit.[20]

In politics Bulgaria fitted the Balkan pattern. Todor Zhivkov was able to emerge unscathed from the factional disputes of the period after 1956. The demotion of the arch-Stalinist Chervenkov in 1956 was followed by a power struggle between Zhivkov and Anton Yugov, who took over as premier from Chèrvenkov in 1956 but was eventually dismissed in November 1962 for allegedly 'undermining the unity of the party' and 'violating socialist legality'. This confused and self-contradictory indictment barely hid the essentially personal nature of the conflict. Yugov was also a scapegoat for the partial failure and abandonment of the 'Great Leap Forward' in industry in 1960. Zhivkov had claimed in 1959 that national income would be doubled in three years. The target was clearly unrealistic. One of the charges against Yugov in 1962 was that he had expressed doubts about the Great Leap Forward.

After 1962 Zhivkov's position was unchallenged, and he presided over a closed society based on restriction of information to a minimum, with severe measures taken against the few dissidents who dared to speak. The most notorious case was the murder of the writer George Markov while in emigration in 1977. In economic policy it was the mixture as before. Not until 1979 (1982 in industry) was a start made with economic reform, with the introduction of a New Economic Mechanism which was cautious in the extreme.

In summary, one may say that the post-Stalin years saw the development of a considerable differentiation and diversity among the countries of Eastern Europe, based on geographical position, inherited resource base, and cultural traditions, but also on specific political trends within the ruling communist parties. The attempt to combine economic reform with the maintenance of full control by the communist party in a political sense had resulted in evident contradictions in the northern tier of countries. These were to burst forth in Czechoslovakia in 1968 and in Poland in 1970 and 1980, while in the southern tier the issue was hardly even raised as yet. We shall now look at the attempt to secure a much more thorough-going and wide-ranging transformation of the communist system from above in Czechoslovakia, which was thwarted rapidly by Soviet intervention.

7 Czechoslovakia in 1968: Climax and Defeat of Reform Communism

The attempt made to reform the communist system from above in Czechoslovakia was more far-reaching, and had a better prospect of success, than anywhere else in Eastern Europe either before or since. In order to explain the depth of the movement towards change within the party itself, one must bear in mind that Czechoslovakia had hardly undertaken any de-Stalinising reforms at all in the late 1950s. The thorough and dramatic character of the changes of the Dubček era resulted from their belatedness.

The lack of reform after 1953 can partly be explained in personal terms. Of the rival claimants to the mantle of Klement Gottwald, who died in 1953, the more liberal Antonín Zápotocký was defeated by the Stalinist apparatchik Antonín Novotný. There were of course deeper reasons as well. The purges lasted longer in Czechoslovakia, and they were more severe. While Osvald Závodský was being hanged and Gustáv Husák receiving a life sentence (1954) protest was bound to be muffled by fear. Moreover, Czechoslovaks did not generally feel that Stalinism was an alien imposition, so that nationalism could not come into play as it would in Hungary and Poland. The CPCz had after all secured 43.3 per cent of the vote in Bohemia in 1946. Communism had not been imposed by the Red Army.

Material factors also played a part. Despite Novotný's determination to continue the traditional Stalinist stress on heavy industry and armaments production (the rate of growth of heavy industry rose from 4% in 1954 to 10% in 1957 and 13% in 1959) it proved possible to combine guns with butter at this stage. Personal consumption went up 6% in 1955, 8% in 1956, and 8% in 1957. The strikes of May 1953 were not repeated. The workers remained passive because their material situation was constantly improving after the low point of 1953. Real wages went up 9% in 1954, 11% in 1955, and by an average 4.6% per annum between 1956 and 1960. No doubt the return to rapid collectivisation after 1953 upset farmers, but their only recourse was to go to the towns, which they did in large numbers. Agriculture lost 40% of its labour force between 1948 and 1960. Output stagnated, with a 1.7% annual growth rate in the period 1956–60. But there was no resistance.

The intellectuals were kept firmly in their place by Novotný. The writers, who had declared in 1956 that they were 'the conscience of the nation', were rebuked in June 1957 for this 'imperialist propaganda'. A full-scale 'fight against revisionism' mounted by Novotný in 1958 resulted in the sacking of 8000 'unreliable officials'. In 1962 Rudolf Barák, the Minister of the Interior, was tried and convicted ostensibly for embezzlement, but in fact because he had tried to take advantage of the de-Stalinising measures of the 22nd CPSU Congress to remove Novotný from office. A tentative economic reform in 1958 was abandoned a year later because it was accompanied by a slight decline in the rate of economic growth (from 8 to 6 per cent). The promulgation of the 1960 Constitution, which declared Czechoslovakia a 'socialist republic' and no longer a mere 'people's democracy', crowned this edifice composed of quantitative economic growth, and political and cultural stagnation. When change came, under the carapace of Novotný's autocracy, it ripened gradually and at first imperceptibly in the early 1960s.

In general the forces operating in favour of change were the same as elsewhere in Eastern Europe: the impulse provided by the second wave of Khrushchev's de-Stalinisation in the Soviet Union (proclaimed at the 22nd Congress of the CPSU in 1961); the psychological need to uncover the miserable truth about the repressions and purges of the early 1950s; the evident limits to economic growth under the command economy, revealed by the stagnation of the early 1960s; the increasing self-confidence and independence of the cultural intelligentsia. One extra factor in Czechoslovakia was the Slovak question,[1] which had a twofold bearing in the 1960s.

The centralising policy of Antonín Novotný, culminating in the abolition of the Slovak Board of Commissioners in 1960, had the effect of increasing Slovak resentment against dictation from Prague; and the purges of the early 1950s had affected a number of leading Slovak members of the communist party, who were condemned for their 'bourgeois nationalism', i.e. their attempts to defend Slovak autonomy. Hence demands were raised for both the restoration of Slovak autonomy, a long-term goal, since it would need a revision of the 1960 Constitution, and an immediate investigation into the purge trials. The latter demand was partially satisfied by the Kolder Commission. Appointed in September 1962, this commission reported in April 1963. Although the Kolder Report was not made public by the party authorities they did act on it. Vladimír Clementis was rehabilitated posthumously; and Gustáv Husák was readmitted to the party, alongside roughly 400 lesser functionaries.

Before this the 12th Party Congress (December 1962) had made certain terminological changes, modifying Marxism-Leninism in line with the reforming message from the Soviet Union. The class struggle was no longer the main driving force of social development, it was declared. Hence the dictatorship of the proletariat needed to be converted into a 'state of all the people'. This certainly allowed some freedom of movement in theory, but it would be wrong to exaggerate its significance. Czechoslovak reformers writing in 1968 saw the 12th Congress differently: as the zenith of a 'merger between party and state', involving a 'narrow centralization of the direction of the party and society'.[2] There is no doubt, however, that a qualitatively new phase begins some time after this.

Two events in 1963 mark the start of the new phase: the election of Alexander Dubček as First Secretary of the Slovak Communist Party in succession to the discredited Stalinist Karol Bacílek; and the Kafka Conference at Liblice. The coming to power of Dubček in Slovakia meant that ideas still too advanced for Prague could be published in Bratislava. During 1963–4 the weekly of the Slovak Writers' Union, *Kultúrny život* was the only public tribune for Czech and Slovak writers and historians who otherwise had no chance of publishing critical articles: Evžen Löbl wrote on economics, Pavol Štefček on literature, Miroslav Kusý on social philosophy, and Gustáv Husák on the Slovak national problem. The Prague spring was thus preceded by a Bratislava spring, and when in 1967 Novotný took *Literární noviny* away from the Czech writers, *Kultúrny život* opened its pages to them.

The Kafka conference of 1963, with its implication that his exploration of the life of an imaginary citizen caught in the toils of bureaucracy could now be discussed openly, was of symbolic significance. It marked the abandonment of the attempt to control literature, and beginning of a considerable loosening of censorship, which permitted unorthodox ideas to be expressed openly in both the cultural and scientific fields. The golden age of Czechoslovak theatre, cinema, literature and historiography begins in 1963. The next four years saw the emergence of the novelists Mňačko, Škvorecký and Kundera, the film directors Forman and Menzel, the dramatists Pavlíček and Havel. Philosophers (Kosík's *Dialectic of the Concrete* came out in 1963); legal theorists (Mlynář published *The State and the Individual* in 1964); sociologists (Radovan Richta's team published *Civilisation at the Crossroads* in 1964); and economists (Šik and Selucký), all probed the boundaries set by the censors. But the conceptual framework of these theorists was always Marxist, and the aim was not to tear down the structure erected in 1948 but to cleanse it of Stalinist distortions. The leaders of the reform tendency were mainly repentant Stalinists, who had themselves been closely involved in setting up the system of People's Democracy.

Theoretical discussions were one thing. Would action follow? That depended on the course of the intra-party struggle between the entrenched supporters of Novotný and the advocates of reform. This was nowhere truer than in the economic sphere. Šik's reform plan had already been put forward in 1964; and it was a response to a crisis in the economy which had already made itself felt in 1962. Yet it was not put into effect until January 1967. Šik himself explained why in 1966: economic reform, he said, could not be carried out without a democratisation of the political system. This was what Novotný could not accept. His attitude was clearly expressed in a statement of October 1965: 'No, comrades, we shall not allow liberalising, let alone capitalist, influences in our economy.'[3]

Although the failure and abandonment of the Third Five Year Plan in 1962 was the starting-point for the reforming endeavours of the economists, it should be noted that the economic crisis itself had apparently been overcome by 1966. The Czechoslovak economy resumed its upward trend after the four lean years of 1962–5 (when the rate of growth of the national income was respectively 1%, –2%, 1%, 3%). National income increased by 5.7% in 1966, and by 7.5% in 1967. Even agriculture improved. Between 1961 and 1965 it had registered a negative rate of growth, at –0.6% per annum. Now it suddenly leapt forward, with an 18% rise in gross agricultural output in 1966. The net material product, which had grown by only 1.9% per annum over the years 1961–65, increased its growth rate to an average of 6.9% over the years 1966–70.[4]

The tension within the party did not arise from an acute crisis in the economic system, but from a chronic malaise, which was partly psychological. The administrators and technicians were tired of uninformed bureaucratic interventions into their activities; they wanted to be paid according to their achievements and therefore opposed the egalitarianism that characterised the wage structure in the early 1960s; the intellectuals wanted the removal of censorship and a thorough investigation into the crimes of the Stalin era; and the Slovaks had their own specific reasons for discontent, which were partly of a long-term historical character.

The reform of January 1967 was stymied by the bureaucrats who were in charge of economic management. The result was that what was intended as a technical economic reform became politicised. A sharp conflict developed between the spokesmen of bureaucratic vested interests, such as Novotný, Hendrých, Kolder, and Lenárt, who still dominated the Presidium, and a heterogeneous coalition of reforming economists (Šik, Selucký), aggrieved Slovaks and Moravians (Dubček, Černík, Špaček) and returned rehabilitees

(Husák, Smrkovský, Pavel). Various events of 1967 sharpened the conflict between the factions. The Six Day War of June 1967 led to a polarisation between progressive opinion, which favoured Israel, and official policy, which followed the pro-Arab line set by the Soviet Union. The Fourth Congress of the Czechoslovak Writers' Union was the scene of tense clashes over this issue, and over a resolution by the Union's Presidium which condemned censorship and criticised the party's continuing interference in art and literature. While party conservatives criticised this document, radicals such as Václav Havel and Ludvík Vaculík wanted to go much further and fight for a democratic society and the elimination of the communist party's monopoly of power. The congress itself tended to follow the radicals, nominating Havel and Vaculík to the union's central committee. The party leaders refused to accept these nominations.

Disciplinary measures were taken against the writers after the congress. Vaculík, Antonín Liehm and Ivan Klíma were expelled from the party, and the journal *Literární noviny* was removed from the control of the Writers' Union and placed under the Ministry of Culture and Information. The writers were not at all cowed. This indicates the weakness of Novotný's position; he could not carry his colleagues with him on any more severe measures. Moreover, the brutal police beatings of students protesting against bad living conditions in hostels in Strahov (31 October 1967) met with criticism within the Central Committee. But the fear of what Novotný *might* do also strengthened opposition to him at this time. Smrkovský (a victim of the 1950s, now rehabilitated) told the December CC Plenum: 'Many comrades fear – and not without reason – that it might come to a relapse into the 1950s, to severe measures against the opposition in the party, and that the logic of such a struggle might lead again to the use of the security organs to solve intra-party problems.'

Novotný endeavoured to use all the classic instruments of power, but they broke in his hands. He appealed to Brezhnev in Moscow; the latter did indeed visit Prague (8 December), but only to say 'It's your affair'. There were also personal reasons for this: Novotný had always been Khrushchev's man and he had failed to congratulate Brezhnev on deposing him in 1964. He tried to get the support of the army, but General Václav Prchlík, head of its Main Political Directorate, successfully obstructed the preparations for a coup which were made by Generals Šejna and Janko and Miroslav Mamula the party's security chief.

The climax came in January 1968, when the Central Committee resumed a plenary meeting which had been adjourned in December. The CC Plenum was the scene of 'a criticism of party policy such as no Central Committee had ever seen in the past or would ever see in the future.' (Tigrid)[5]. Largely under the impact of powerful speeches by Šik and Smrkovský against the 'cumulation of functions' (i.e. Novotný's position as simultaneously head of state and head of the CPCz), by Dubček on the disadvantages suffered by Slovakia, and by the Moravian Josef Špaček on the need for reform of the political system, Novotný was forced to resign as First Secretary of the party, though he stayed on as President of the republic. Who was to succeed him? Smrkovský and Šik were unacceptable to the conservatives; Lenárt and Martin Vaculík were unacceptable to Novotný's opponents. Alexander Dubček emerged as a compromise candidate, proposed by Novotný himself and approved unanimously (5 January 1968). These discussions were kept secret, hence the replacement of Novotný by Dubček looked like a mere change of personnel. Smrkovský was dissatisfied with the refusal of the other party leaders to make any public statement on the issues.[6]

The impression which began to emerge from Dubček's speeches of January and February was that he was a restrained and moderate reformer. While proposing an 'action programme' which would express 'the progressive forces of our society' he insisted that the general line remained correct and would not be changed (speech of 1 February). Mlynář later noted that three months went by 'without any clearly conceived policy declarations from the CPCz leadership'.[7] Not until March 1968 did the party's organisational journal, *Život strany*, begin to advocate more active participation by party members in the making of policy.[8]

Behind the scenes, the promised 'Action Programme' was slowly taking shape, put together by almost a hundred party officials and academics. But the atmosphere of public discussion began to change in February, owing to the relaxation of the censorship. By the beginning of March the censors had ceased to exercise effective control over the press. The organ of the Writers' Union was allowed to reappear on 1 March, and many other papers (including purely party organs) began to publish daring articles. The most outspoken of all was *Student*: in this journal the philosopher Ivan Sviták and his colleagues wrote exactly as they pleased. Sviták uncovered awkward memories about the communist seizure of power, even suggesting that the death of Foreign Minister Jan Masaryk in 1948, commonly considered suicide, might well have been a murder committed by members of the Soviet security organs.[9] This brought an official protest from Moscow.

In the middle of March public meetings began to take place, attended by thousands of people, at which freedom of speech was called for and exercised. New organisations came into existence, such as the Academic Council of Students in Prague, K231 (for ex-prisoners arrested under Paragraph 231 of the law of 1948 for the Defence of the State), and the KAN (The Club of Committed Non-Party People), which was founded by the radical intellectuals Sviták, Havel, and Černý. The Socialist and People's parties, tame survivals of the pre-1948 political system which were still permitted to exist within the National Front framework, began to show signs of life. Finally, critical voices began to be raised at district party conferences of the party itself (in mid-March). There were some conservative voices from the rank-and-file, but they were very much in the minority.

By the time that the Action Programme appeared (10 April 1968) it had become more of a 'reaction programme', expressing the views of the top party leadership on the process of renewal that was occurring in the country at large. The issuing of the Programme was accompanied by the complete capitulation of Novotný and his supporters. At the April Plenum of the CC he was removed from all his positions (he had already been replaced as President in March by General Svoboda), four of his closest associates were dropped from the Presidium, and three (Hendrých, Štrougal and Koucký) were removed from the Secretariat. The radical reformers Smrkovský and Kriegel were brought in for the first time. But in general the Dubček team consisted of people who embodied continuity with the moderate reforms of 1966 onwards. They mistrusted the radical forces which had emerged with the abolition of censorship and the media explosion; but they remained committed to freedom of the press. It was typical of the new atmosphere that the debates at the Central Committee Plenum of April were published in full in the party organ, *Rudé právo*.

The CPCz's Action Programme was a rather moderate and harmless document, full of vague and cloudy formulations.[10] Ivan Sviták commented at the time: 'Their maximum programme is our minimum programme'. Radoslav Selucký added that it was the maximum that could be expected from the existing Central Committee.[11] The Action Programme covered many areas, but these can be boiled down to six: the role of the party, the non-party organisations, the rights of individuals, relations between Czechs and Slovaks, economic policy, and foreign policy.

The programme proposed, not the abandonment of the party's leading role, but a different way of implementing it. Here are some choice extracts: 'The party cannot enforce its authority. Authority must be won again and again by party activity. The party cannot force its line through directives.' The 'false thesis' that the party was the instrument of the dictatorship of the proletariat was rejected. 'The party's goal,' according to the programme, was 'not to become a universal caretaker of society . . . [but] to arouse socialist initiative and win over all the workers to communism through systematic persuasion and personal example.' This was highly unrealistic as an objective. Once the people were given the chance to defy the party they might well do so. The forces of repression would then have to be brought into play to maintain the party's leading role. The alternative would be abdication. The authors of the programme were unwilling to face this bitter conclusion.

Instead, in the section on non-party organisations, they excluded free competition between political parties in favour of a kind of overall tutelage to be exercised by the communist party over the respectable little parties of the National Front. The statement 'socialist state power cannot be monopolised by a single party' was either hypocrisy or self-deception. In actual fact, power would continue to be monopolised by the CPCz, but 'the National Front . . . and the social organisations' (e.g. the trade unions and the League of Youth) would 'take part in the creation of policy'.

The programme was stronger on the rights of individuals. There were guarantees of freedom of assembly, expression, and association. There would be no preliminary censorship of publications. There would be political and civil rehabilitation of both communist and non-communist victims of the purges of the fifties. The role of state security would not be to solve internal political questions but to defend the state against external enemies.

There was to be full equality between Czechs and Slovaks, expressed in' a new constitutional law which would establish 'symmetrical arrangements' between the two nations. Slovakia would have its own executive and legislature in Bratislava, and the Slovaks would have equality of rights in the central government organs in Prague.

The section on economic policy contained a retrospective criticism of 'the precipitate expansion of heavy industry, costly investments and excessive demand for labour-power and raw materials' but stressed that 'this one-sided development cannot be changed overnight'. Democratisation, already stated not very originally to be the key to improving intra-party life, was also to apply in economic affairs. Enterprises 'must be allowed to react in a creative way to the needs of the market. Economic competition must be the basic stimulus for improving production and lowering costs.' Partial workers' control was envisaged, hedged round by careful restrictions. There would be 'democratic organs' in the enterprises, and the enterprise director would be responsible to them. But 'the indivisible authority and competence' of the leading officials would not be altered.

Finally, the foreign policy of the Czechoslovak Socialist Republic would not be changed. The alliance with the Soviet Union and other socialist states would remain 'fundamental'. Nevertheless, Czechoslovakia would henceforth play 'a more active role' in foreign affairs. What that meant was not specified.

The moderation of the Action Programme reflected both differences of opinion within the CPCz and considerations of prudence towards the Soviet

Union. The former anti-Novotný coalition became sharply divided once Novotný himself had left the scene: some party leaders saw his removal as a mere change of personnel requiring only slight corrections to the course hitherto pursued. Conservatives like Indra, Bil'ak and Jakeš began to look to Moscow for protection. Their opposition was one reason why very little was done between April and June to put the programme into effect.

The economic reforms envisaged in the Action Programme and outlined in more detail in the government programme presented by Černík to the National Assembly on 24 April faced three obstacles. The first was the ingrained conservatism of what Šik called 'left-wing sectarian forces which still believe in the return of the bureaucratic centralistic socialist system'.[12] The second was the inherent difficulty of the economic situation. The trend towards greater democracy encouraged by the reformers meant that workers were now free to demand wage increases of up to 20 per cent and sometimes enforce these demands by striking;[13] the further freeing of prices (13 per cent of prices were freed or partially freed in 1967; 28 per cent in 1968)[14] resulted in a 25 per cent increase in enterprise incomes in the first quarter of 1968, while industrial output only rose by 6.2 per cent. Conservatives argued that the centre must be strengthened in the name of economic discipline; reformers countered that if the enterprise were freed of the dead weight of administrative indicators the market would force them to exercise economic discipline themselves.

The third obstacle was the lack of any driving force towards economic reform from the workers themselves. They continued to the sceptical about the impact of economic reform on their standard of living and general situation; conservatives such as Novotný and Oldřich Švestka made demagogic use of these fears. 'If to be a conservative means to oppose the lowering of the workers' standard of living, I am proud to be a conservative' said Novotný in February. Many workers reacted favourably to this argument. They had got into the habit in the previous twenty years of seeing the state as 'a benevolent uncle'. The writer Ludvík Vaculík found that a 'typical' working-class response was 'The intellectuals are swine because they were the ones who contributed towards the losses. The so-called new economic system is a swindle, which is based on the assumption that the same people will stay on top.'[15]

The result of these obstacles was that the Enterprise Statute, which was supposed to establish enterprise autonomy, to allow the formation of small new private businesses, and to bring workers' representatives into management through Workers' Councils, was not placed before the National Assembly until January 1969, after the Soviet invasion. Immediately, afterwards the whole idea was shelved.[16]

Nor could it be said that progress was made in other spheres covered by the Action Programme. The result was that the Dubček leadership increasingly fell behind the movement of popular opinion, or at least the group of journalists and intellectuals who had appointed themselves representatives of that opinion. Dubček was still in a minority in the party leadership.

Skilling estimates that as late as June the top party leadership (defining this as the Presidium plus the Secretariat) consisted of eleven 'conservatives' (Lenárt, Kolder, Kapek, Bil'ak, Piller, Rigo, Barbírek, Švestka, Sádovský, Indra and Voleník) seven 'moderate reformers' (Dubček, Černík, Šimon, Císař, Mlynář, Erban and Slavík) and three 'more vigorous reformers' (Špaček, Kriegel and Smrkovský). Dubček gave clear expression to his moderate line in April in *Rudé právo*: 'Democracy includes discipline. A situation where everyone speaks about everything and does as he wishes – that is something which has nothing in common with democracy.'[17]

The moderates were fighting on two fronts – or three if you count Moscow. Dubček was subjected to severe criticism when he went there on 4 May; six days later there were reports of Soviet troop movements towards the Czechoslovak border and rumours of forthcoming intervention; at home the party's Presidium supported Švestka, conservative editor of *Rudé právo*, against his opponents on the paper, and called on the press to 'oppose anti-socialist forces'; meanwhile the new Minister of the Interior, Josef Pavel, claimed on 8 May that 'Western espionage centres' were increasing their activities in Czechoslovakia. The moderates on the other hand tried to rebut these claims and fears, but responded to the increasing pressure from forces outside the party by stressing their dedication to maintaining the socialist system. Even the distinctly radical reformer Smrkovský wrote in May: 'Let no one think we shall give up what we have fought to attain, and that we are abandoning everything for which we made the revolution. Certainly not.'[18] He backed this up by intervening personally in Ostrava on 12 May to restrain an attempt by local progressives to 'go it alone' and set up a separate CPCz of Bohemia and Moravia. Gustáv Husák, who was still in the moderate camp at this stage, condemned 'opposition for the sake of opposition' (9 May).

The moderate course triumphed at the CC Plenum of 29 May to 1 June. Here Dubček pushed through a resolution that the party would 'mobilise all the forces of our people and the socialist state' to suppress 'an attack on the historic reality' of the CPCz's domination over society. This was the 'conservative' part of the resolution. But at the same time a party congress was called for 9 September, a month earlier than planned, with the obvious purpose of voting the conservatives off the CC sooner rather than later. Novotný's party membership was suspended (partly on Husák's insistence, though the latter was still kept out of the CC), Martin Vaculík, who had supported Novotný, was removed from the Presidium, Zdeněk Mlynář was made head of the Legal Commission of the CC, and the setting up of Enterprise Councils as organs of workers' self-management was accepted in principle.

The first reform measures followed at the end of June. The National Assembly enacted a limited number of laws, covering the rehabilitation of victims of the 1950s, the punishment of guilty officials, the ending of censorship from above (though retaining self-censorship by editors), and the creation of Czech and Slovak National Councils, which were together to work out a law converting the country into a federation. Other important measures (such as the introduction of enterprise councils) were merely 'under discussion' at this stage.

The victory of the moderates at the May–June Plenum did not end the political ferment in the country. Despite the reform measures of June, many progressives felt that there were certain straws in the wind pointing in a quite different direction. Švestka, still editor of *Rudé právo*, made a strong attack on 'anti-socialist efforts' on 23 June, and endeavoured to interpret the post-January movement as a 'rebirth of the socialist revolution achieved from the positions of Marxism-Leninism'; anonymous abusive letters, sometimes anti-Semitic in tone, were received by leading progressives such as Edward Goldstücker, Ludvík Vaculík, and Pavel Kohout; finally Soviet press polemics began again. On 20 June Warsaw Pact manoeuvres began on Czechoslovak territory. This was not unusual given Czechoslovakia's membership of that organisation, but many people within the country thought the timing was suspicious.

The response of the progressives to these developments was the counter-offensive known as the Two Thousand Words, a statement drawn up by Ludvík Vaculík, signed by some sixty people, mainly scientists and artists, with a sprinkling of ČKD workers, and published on 27 June. Its content reflected the combination of fears of Soviet interference and domestic conservatism which had sparked it off. Reference was made to the twin dangers facing the country. First there were 'foreign forces' threatening to 'intervene in our development'. The people would stand behind the government 'if necessary with arms' in the fight against this. Second, there was domestic conservatism, which was preventing further democratisation; this would be countered by the weight of public opinion. People who had abused their positions of power would be forced out by 'public criticism, resolutions, demonstrations, demonstrative work brigades . . . a strike, or a boycott of their doors'. In short, the manifesto called for the people to take the initiative themselves, at a local level.[19]

The Two Thousand Words was an exclusively Czech manifesto: Slovaks had not been asked for advice or signatures, and Novomeský later expressed his anger about this.[20] But the Slovaks had not been ignored deliberately, and the criticisms from Bratislava were actually a sign of the demagogic use of Slovak nationalism by more conservative elements (Novomeský and Husák) who wanted to portray the Czechs as dragging their feet over federalisation.

The Two Thousand Words Manifesto produced an immense reaction. Progressives generally welcomed it, but the moderates were horrified by what they saw as an irresponsible act. Dubček condemned it implicitly by denying that 'strikes and demonstrations' could deal with unsolved problems; Císař and Šik condemned it explicitly. Smrkovský described it as an act of 'political romanticism'; according to Pithart he 'became hysterical and threatened tanks'. Both Czechoslovak conservatives and Soviet commentators seized on the Manifesto as a proof that the CPCz was no longer the leading force in society. An article in the Moscow communist daily *Pravda* referred to it as 'an organisational preparation of the counter-revolution'.[21]

The controversy stirred up by the Two Thousand Words gradually died down within Czechoslovakia, but it was a different matter elsewhere in Eastern Europe and in the Soviet Union. The Kremlin and its conservative allies, particularly Ulbricht and Gomułka, were now convinced that a dangerous situation had developed, requiring some form of intervention, not necessarily military, but backed by the threat of force. Brezhnev decided that the Czechoslovak party leaders should be invited to a joint meeting of all the Soviet bloc states in Warsaw; in this way very strong pressure could be applied. The CPCz Presidium, following Dubček's advice, refused to go to Warsaw (12 July), in spite of the theoretical majority enjoyed by the conservatives on the party's supreme policy-making body. Kolder wanted to appeal to the CC against this decision, but was voted down. Hence the Warsaw Meeting of the five parties (East German, Polish, Hungarian, Bulgarian and Soviet) went ahead without Czechoslovak participation, and duly produced the minatory Warsaw Letter of 15 July.

Essentially the letter contained two complaints and one promise. The complaints were, first, that 'hostile forces' within the country were 'creating the threat that Czechoslovakia may break away from the socialist commonwealth', and, second, that 'the CPCz was losing control over the course of events and retreating more and more under the pressure of anti-communist forces' such as the agitation around the Two Thousand Words, which were a 'platform of counter-revolution'. The first complaint was about the foreign policy potential of the situation; the second about the alleged collapse of communist authority within the country, and in particular the increased independence of the media from party control. The 'promise' was in fact a threat. There *are* forces in Czechoslovakia, the Warsaw Letter said, that can uphold the socialist system and defeat anti-socialist elements, and the Czechoslovak party should rally these 'healthy forces'. In doing so 'it can count on the solidarity and general assistance of the parties of the fraternal socialist countries.' Thus the ideological foundation was being laid for Warsaw Pact intervention against the Dubček leadership.

This was a well-thought out programme, and only one thing was lacking: a determined conservative faction within the CPCz sufficiently strong to provide an alternative party leadership. The impact of the Warsaw Letter disappointed its authors' expectations. There was a closing of the ranks around Dubček and the moderate course pursued hitherto. The CPCz Presidium immediately rebutted the Warsaw allegations, denying any change in Czechoslovak foreign policy, pointing to the Warsaw Pact manoeuvres themselves as 'concrete proof of our faithful fulfilment of our alliance commitments', and rejecting the accusation that 'the political role of the CPCz' was under threat by 'reactionary, counter-revolutionary forces'. The Presidium's statement of 18 July did concede that there were certain 'negative aspects' and 'extremist tendencies', but saw the decisions of the May–June Plenum as a way of overcoming them politically. It pointed out that it had condemned the Two Thousand Words Manifesto at the time, and added the telling point that, despite its appeals to the people to 'engage in anarchist acts' 'campaigns of this kind did not in fact occur in our country'.[22]

In conclusion, the Presidium conceded that the 'advice of the five parties was no doubt sincerely intended', but made it clear that it was inappropriate since it failed to take into account 'the entire intricacy of the dynamic social movement . . . or the complexity of the conclusions adopted by the May Plenum'.

Immediately after this meeting, Dubček called a plenum of the CC (19 July), to confirm and strengthen the impact of the Presidium's statement. The lack of a strong conservative faction, even on this more conservative body, was shown by the unanimous vote in favour of Dubček's resolution. Only 88 of the 107 members turned up. As Hejzlar pointed out 'the conservatives simply stayed away'.[23] The Slovak CC had already approved the attitude of the Presidium (18 July).

But it was not just the party that united around Dubček. It was the whole population. The Warsaw Letter opens a period when the natural development of events was distorted by the pressure from abroad. This is why one cannot draw on evidence from the July–August period, as Hejzlar does, to show that the process of social rebirth in Czechoslovakia would have followed the moderate, gradualist path marked out for it by Dubček and his colleagues. The Warsaw Letter had a twofold impact. It lent the CPCz a reserve of credit among the population at large, as shown by a public opinion survey of July, which indicated that 57 per cent of the population had confidence in the party, and only 16 per cent had no confidence. It also gave Dubček an effective argument with which to restrain the radicals. The political clubs KAN and K231 ceased their activities voluntarily in August; the Social Democrats were dissuaded from attempting to set up a separate political party. A resounding manifestation of support for the Dubček leadership was organised by the radicals of the Writers' Union journal, *Literární listy* on 26 July. This was the Message from the Citizens to the Presidium, thanking the Presidium for its fortitude, and expressing the aims of the people in four words: Socialism, Alliance, Sovereignty, Freedom. The Message was subsequently signed by over a million people.

Dubček tried to combine firmness with readiness to negotiate, and he made a number of concessions on personnel matters to the conservatives to demonstrate this. General Prchlík was dismissed on 25 July for allegedly 'disclosing military secrets about the Warsaw Pact' (in fact he had simply criticised Soviet hegemony over the Warsaw Pact forces); the state security service was removed from the control of the Minister of the Interior Josef Pavel and placed under Viliam Šalgovič, a conservative who later collaborated with the Warsaw Pact invasion.

This combination appeared at first to be effective. The Soviet leaders agreed to a bilateral meeting on Czechoslovak territory, thus conceding the two points on which Dubček had insisted. The discussions, held between 29 July and 1 August at Čierna nad Tisou, were long and stormy, but they resulted in apparent agreement. A bland communiqué was issued, concealing the extent of the outstanding disagreements. According to the communiqué, 'a broad, comradely exchange of opinions on questions of interest to both sides took place at the meeting'. In form at least, the Czechoslovak delegation conceded a great deal: they agreed to take part in a meeting of the Five at Bratislava the next day. Yet they were not put in the dock at Bratislava, perhaps because they accepted a highly orthodox declaration presented by the Soviet side (4 August). The Bratislava Statement referred to 'unshakeable fidelity to Marxism-Leninism', 'indoctrination of the masses in the spirit of proletarian internationalism', the 'implacable struggle against bourgeois ideology', and 'unswerving determination to develop and defend socialist gains'. It also evoked 'the common international duty of all socialist countries to support, defend and consolidate these achievements'. A Czechoslovak attempt to add a clause about 'respecting the sovereignty and national independence of each country' was defeated.[24] It is hard to see why Dubček regarded this declaration as a success. Perhaps he thought that the phraseology presented here was meaningless and could be ignored. In fact the Bratislava Statement opened the way to criticism from the Soviet side on the grounds that the Czechoslovaks had taken no steps to implement it. This was true. The Czechoslovak leaders thought they could simply go ahead with preparations for the 14th. Party Congress as if nothing had happened. This was despite the clear warning given on 17 August by the Hungarian party leader Kádár on a visit to Prague that Moscow would take 'extreme measures' if the Bratislava agreements were not carried out at once.[25]

There was no sign in August that the CPCz leaders were prepared to moderate their course any further. A proposal presented by Mlynář for a three-month ban on any publication that issued material damaging to Prague's foreign relations was rejected by the Presidium. New party statutes, issued on 10 August, made considerable inroads into the Leninist principle of democratic centralism. The 'minority has the right to formulate its standpoints and request that they be recorded, and to persist in its view and request from the relevant Party organisation a repeated evaluation of its, the minority's, standpoints on the basis of new information.' This did not amount to a complete renunciation of the 1921 ban on factions, since it was described as 'inadmissible to organise minority supporters outside the framework of the statutes or to set up groupings of party members with their own fractional discipline.[26]

But it did mean considerable freedom of dissent and criticism. Moreover, all party organs were to be elected by secret ballot, and officials were only allowed a limited term of office.[27] The disturbing impression created in the Soviet Union by these changes in organisation was strengthened yet further by the results of the first tier of elections to the 14th CPCz Congress. Only 10 per cent of the elected delegates belonged to the conservative wing of the party, while 10 per cent were radicals, and 80 per cent favoured the Dubček line. It was clear that four fifths of the old CC would not be re-elected at the forthcoming congress.[28] The conservatives had to act now or they would be finished.

The Soviet decision to intervene was made some time in the middle of August, perhaps at a meeting of the CPSU politburo on 17 August, perhaps before. It has sometimes been asserted that the Čierna nad Tisou and Bratislava meetings were merely a cover for invasion preparations, but Mlynář, Tigrid, Golan, Skilling, and Dawisha all concur in the view that the final decision to invade was made at very short notice. The Soviet side hoped to coordinate its military moves with a political offensive by an alternative party leadership within the country (as had happened in 1956 in Hungary), and the highly pessimistic 'Report on the Present Political Situation in the ČSSR', laid before the presidium on 20 August by Kolder and Indra, was part of a plan to prepare politically for the invasion by bringing about a last-minute overthrow of Dubček's team. A secret meeting between Indra, Kolder, Kapek and other conservatives in mid-August drew up a list of people who could be relied on to outvote Dubček. This potential majority consisted of Bil´ak, Kolder, Švestka, Rigo, Barbírek and Piller. But things went wrong. Barbírek and Piller failed to support Kolder, and a bitter argument was still going on within the presidium when the news arrived that the troops of five Warsaw Pact countries had crossed the borders of Czechoslovakia and were advancing towards Prague (11.40 p.m.).

This was a great shock, not least to Dubček, who commented: 'On my honour as a communist, I declare that I did not have the slightest idea . . . that anyone proposed taking such measures against us . . . I, who have devoted my whole life to cooperation with the Soviet Union, now they do this to me! This is the tragedy of my life!'. Why did the invasion take place? The question still cannot be answered definitively. Galia Golan gives a succinct statement of one view: 'It was the democratic nature and content of the Czechoslovak experiment, rather than some fabricated "danger" of neutralism or pro-Western tendencies which precipitated the invasion.'[29]

One reservation needs to be made here. Golan stresses the impending abdication of the party from its 'leading role'. But in view of what we know of the new party statutes, the operative phrase is rather 'fears of abdication'. The leading role of the party was not about to be abandoned, but the Soviet leaders feared that this would be the logical culmination of the reform process. The communist party would lose power eventually. On that point they were probably right.

Roughly two hours after receiving the news of the invasion (at 1 a.m., 21 August) the CPCz Presidium issued a statement condemning it as 'contrary to the fundamental principles of relations between socialist states and a denial of the basic norms of international law'. There were only four votes against this, cast by Bil´ak, Kolder, Rigo and Švestka. Moreover, the minority were curiously hesitant and indecisive, despite the assurance of Soviet support. The idea of a 'Workers' and Peasants' Government', modelled on the one set up under Kádár in Hungary in 1956, was allowed to drop once President Svoboda had made it clear that he would refuse to cooperate with such a body. The only decisive action taken on the conservative side was the arrest of Dubček and others by the StB, on the instructions of Šalgovič, its head since June, in the early hours of 21 August. Even then, most of the arrests were carried out by Soviet rather than Czechoslovak security organs. The conservatives in the Czechoslovak security services had already been considerably weakened by the Minister of the Interior, Josef Pavel, who had removed one hundred and fifty of those most closely associated with the Soviet organs by retiring them on full pay.[30]

The events of 21 August opened a seven day period during which practically the whole of the Czechoslovak population stood on one side in support of Dubček and his team, with the Warsaw Pact forces and a small number of conservatives in the other side. Militarily, no doubt, the operation was a success. There was no resistance by force (Dubček had explicitly ruled this out) but a combination of unofficial and official resistance which consisted largely in ignoring the invaders and continuing life as if nothing had happened. The official resistance started at the top, with President Svoboda, the head of state, and continued down through the National Assembly, the government, the Party Presidium, the National Front, and above all the Party Congress.

The 14th Party Congress, originally set for September, was pushed forward to 22 August and held in secret at the ČKD-Sokolovo factory in the Prague suburb of Vysočany. Most of the Czech delegates (about 1150) were able to get there; but only 50 Slovaks turned up, allegedly because Gustáv Husák persuaded the rest to stay in Bratislava and hold their own Slovak Congress.[31] After some hesitation, the delegates rejected the idea of calling themselves the 'Czech Communist Party' and instead declared unanimously that they were the 14th Congress of the Communist Party of Czechoslovakia (CPCz). They then proceeded to elect a new Central Committee without a single conservative member, but with an appropriate number of Slovaks, including Dubček and Husák. The 14th Congress went on to condemn the Soviet intervention as a breach of Czechoslovak sovereignty, demand the withdrawal of foreign troops, and defend the reforming policies hitherto pursued by the CPCz. A proposal for an indefinite general strike was rejected, but they did call for a one-hour general strike in protest against the occupation (23 August).

While the communist delegates to the 14th Congress were meeting behind closed doors, the population of the country threw itself into an extremely effective campaign of passive resistance. The occupying forces were disorganised by the removal of street signs, house numbers, and plaques; the walls and pavements were covered with graffiti; the mass media (radio, television, newspapers) continued to function underground;

all the mass organisations condemned the invasion (although the Slovak communist response was somewhat ambiguous).[32] The stalemate between occupiers and resisters was broken by the news of the Moscow compromise of 27 August. Immediately after the invasion the reformers on the Presidium had been arrested and transported to Soviet territory. On President Svoboda's refusal to negotiate without them they were brought to Moscow, where they met the Soviet negotiators as well as a number of moderates and conservatives on the Presidium who had been invited to Moscow without being arrested. After several days of tough negotiations in Moscow with almost the whole of the CPCz Presidium (only Kolder and Kriegel were missing, for very different reasons), the Soviet leaders decided after all to permit the reformers to remain in formal control of their country. For their part, Dubček, Černík and Smrkovský conceded restrictions on the freedom of expression enjoyed hitherto by the media, a ban on attempts to set up political parties outside the National Front, personnel changes to remove individual progressives particularly abhorrent to the Soviet side, the invalidation of the 14th Party Congress, and the gradual withdrawal of occupation troops 'as the situation normalised'.[33]

It was somewhat difficult to sell this compromise to the people of Czechoslovakia, who were inclined to regard it as a surrender. But the efforts of Dubček and his colleagues, combined with the readiness of communist leaders within the country to accept their arguments, were crowned with success. For instance, whereas on 27 August the Prague weekly *Student* had described the agreement as 'a capitulation equivalent to high treason', by 31 August the editorial board had disavowed this position.

The Moscow Protocol was certainly a surrender on the part of Dubček and his colleagues; but the relevant institutions were brought round one after another to recognising its necessity and taking the first steps towards fulfilment of the Soviet desiderata. It must not be thought that the conservatives were riding high at this time. They kept rather quiet, concentrating on defending their conduct in the days immediately after the invasion. At the CC Plenum of 31 August only one voice, that of General Rytíř, was raised against the post-January reforms. Moreover, only one radical voice was raised against accepting the Moscow compromise: that of Jaroslav Šabata, Brno Party Secretary, who neatly reversed the Moscow position that 'normalisation is the prerequisite for the withdrawal of the troops'. On the contrary, he said, 'withdrawal of the troops is the prerequisite for normalisation.' Gustáv Husák made the obvious reply: 'If this is what you think, go to our partners and negotiate it. But if you recognise that we are not strong enough, spare us these adventurist solutions.'

The line eventually accepted unanimously by the CC was put by Dubček: the Moscow Protocol would be accepted, 'normalisation' would take place, but the party would proceed further along the path of the socialist reforms started in January and outlined in the Action Programme. The 14th Congress would neither be annulled nor confirmed, but the old CC would be expanded by coopting some of those elected to the CC at that congress.[34]

There now began a transitional period, which lasted from September 1968 to April 1969. During this time the reform communists tried to preserve the essence of the Action Programme in domestic affairs, while repeating assurances of their loyalty towards the Soviet Union and the Warsaw Pact. The unrealistic character of this course of action became more and more evident. One of the earliest people to realise this was Zdeněk Mlynář, who resigned all his party functions in November 1968 and withdrew into private life. The mass support of the population for the reform programme made things more difficult for Dubček now. Mass social mobilisation, largely absent until the Soviet invasion, was a product of the seven days after 21 August. Now every step backwards taken by the Dubček leadership under Soviet pressure was accompanied by a popular protest, which in turn increased that pressure (the anti-normalisation demonstrations of 28 October and 7 November; the protest strike of Czech university students, 18–21 November; the suicide of Jan Palach on 16 January 1969 in protest against the continuing censorship; the subsequent mass demonstrations of 18–20 January).

The situation was made more complicated by the drawing out of new implications from the Action Programme, which continued even after August. Work on the Czechoslovak Constitution was still in progress, and on 28 October the establishment of a federal system was announced, to take effect from 1 January 1969; rehabilitations continued; the formation of interest groups continued (excluding K231 and KAN, which were now in effect banned); Workers' Councils were set up in many enterprises, despite a government instruction of 24 October prohibiting the formation of any new ones.

The militancy displayed by the industrial workers in defence of the reform programme was remarkable, given their initial lack of interest. It found an outlet both officially, through the party-run trade union structure, the Revolutionary Trade Union Movement (ROH), and unofficially, through the Workers' Councils which sprang up after the invasion. The ROH Central Council provided itself with new statutes in September 1968 stressing its right to defend the 'political and economic interests of its members' and to pursue 'a policy independent of the state and the political parties'. It also allowed the formation of autonomous trade unions for the first time.

As a result an intermediate tier of craft unions was created, such as the 900 000 strong Czech Metal Workers' Union, led by the radical Vlastimil Toman. The ROH and its now autonomous individual affiliates waged a series of campaigns against 'normalisation'. Under its chairman Karel Poláček it protested against the ban on forming new Workers' Councils, and in fact these councils continued to be formed after the ban (113 existed on 24 October; 500 in March 1969); it campaigned against the 1969 price rises; it demanded that Smrkovský be retained as chairman of the Federal Assembly (the Metal Workers went further and threatened a strike over the issue); there was a spontaneous stoppage in support of the student strike of November 1968. Finally, the Seventh Congress of the ROH, held in March 1969, selected its delegates by secret ballot, and supported the economic and political use of the strike weapon. Poláček gave a surprisingly forthright speech, given his promotion by Husák to the Presidium a month later. He was evidently reflecting the views of the Congress, not his own, when he announced that the ROH would never again accept a role subsidiary to the party; defended the 'post-January spirit'; and stressed the 'right to self-determination and sovereignty of the socialist countries', thus implicitly rejecting the doctrine of limited sovereignty.

The reaction of the Czech workers to invasion in 1968 was analogous to that of the Hungarian workers twelve years earlier. In both cases, radicalisation was a product of the Soviet intervention, and reflected a combination of national objectives and specifically class aims. Yet the Czech movement differed in being less militant, in its reliance on resolutions and protests rather than the weapon of an all-out general strike. It never escaped from its defensive role of endeavouring to stiffen the backbone of the Dubček leadership against Soviet pressure. This is why it could make no effective response when Dubček pulled the rug from under the resistance movement by successive surrenders.[35]

The phenomena we have described were bound to be short-lived, given the steady pressure from the Soviet Union, exerted both through Soviet envoys, such as First Deputy Foreign Minister V. V. Kuznetsov, who spent much of his time in Prague between September and January, and through frequent visits by Czechoslovak party leaders to Moscow. A particularly flagrant example of this pressure was the dressing-down Brezhnev gave to a three-member delegation (consisting of Dubček, Černík, and Husák) which visited Moscow on 4 October: the CPCz had utterly failed to carry out the Moscow Protocol, he said. The Czechoslovaks should 'learn to do as they are told'. In particular they had left notorious revisionists in the party leadership.[36] The three men capitulated in face of this onslaught, with Černík leading the way. They conceded the continuing presence of Soviet troops in the country with no time-limit; the postponement of the party congress; and the disavowal in effect of the Action Programme. In this way, Dubček's position in the country was gradually undermined. He was forced to sacrifice his political friends one by one. Mlynář, Prchlík, Pavel, Špaček, L. Vaculík, and Goldstücker all fell victim to the vain chase after the mirage of 'normalisation'. The abandonment of Smrkovský, on 4 January, was a severe blow both to Dubček's position and his popularity. The campaign to defend Smrkovský was an issue over which tremendous trade union support had been mobilised. But the CPCz Presidium condemned the strike threat (3 January), and Smrkovský himself begged the workers not to come out in his support (5 January). Dubček was subsequently criticised for failing to make use of the popular support that was available to him. Ivan Sviták, for instance, wrote: 'The actions of Dubček after August 1968 were a skilfully executed betrayal of the confidence of the population.'[37] And Jan Kavan later recalled that 'the party leaders were more afraid of the consequences of resistance than of capitulation'.[38]

Did Dubček have an alternative? He had devoted his life to cooperation with the Soviet Union, and he rejected a policy of confrontation with it. The only other option was to resign, giving up hopes which had indeed already proved nugatory. The final nail in his political coffin was the 'ice-hockey crisis' of March 1969. On two successive weekends Czechoslovaks sought vicarious satisfaction by celebrating their ice-hockey team's two successive victories over the Soviet Union; the second of these demonstrations led to the destruction of the Prague office of the Soviet airline Aeroflot (28 March). This was the opportunity Dubček's opponents had been waiting for. A Soviet ultimatum was presented by Marshal Grechko and Deputy Foreign Minister Vladimir Semyonov, demanding the immediate restoration of order, on pain of a renewed Warsaw Pact intervention. This was all nonsense. Order had already been restored. In any case, the failure of the police to defend the Aeroflot offices was probably a provocation by the security services themselves. The real objective was to secure the removal of Dubček and the promotion of the 'realist' wing of the party, led by Husák and Lubomír Štrougal, who used the argument that 'either we do something immediately or the Soviet comrades will do it for us.' In 'realistic' terms it was hard to refute this. On 17 April a CC Plenum accepted Dubček's resignation, elected Husák First Secretary of the CPCz, and set up a new Presidium from which all moderate reformers except Dubček were excluded.[39]

The Czechoslovak Communist Party was henceforth directed by a group consisting of 'realists', i.e. former moderate reformers who had decided to abandon the reform course altogether, and 'conservatives' such as Bil'ak, who had never supported reform anyway. The 'long, painful road of compromises and retreats'[40] had come to an end. Now Husák would advance in the same direction, but willingly and with enthusiasm. A cascade of measures after April clearly indicated the changed atmosphere. They affected economics, culture, personnel policy, and other areas of Czechoslovak life. A feeling of depression descended on people. The Enterprise Statute, centrepiece of the microeconomic reform, was buried in April by the Czech National Council; the idea of workers' councils was officially repudiated in May; obligatory planning targets for 1970 were introduced, and central wage controls were reimposed, in July. In May the reformist journals *Listy* and *Reportér* were banned; in July a new minister of culture, the conservative Miroslav Brůžek, was appointed, followed in August by a new minister of education (Jaromír Hrbek). The May Plenum of the CC removed Šik, Kriegel and Vodsloň, and Kriegel was expelled from the party. Further street demonstrations took place on 20 August 1969, the anniversary of the Soviet invasion, which the clandestine opposition declared a 'day of shame'. A highly effective boycott of all public institutions and transport was carried through as well. A Ten Point Manifesto, signed by a number of leading intellectuals, among them Šik, Havel, Kohout, L. Vaculík, and the chess grandmaster Luděk Pachmann, was also circulated at this time. In summary, it condemned the dismantling of the Action Programme that had taken place, and called on the workers to refuse their support to the new regime. This led Husák to mount a further campaign against the ideas and the supporters of the Prague Spring. Dubček was removed from the Presidium in September 1969. Seven people were expelled from the CC, and the conservatives Švestka, Kolder and Kapek were promoted. The Soviet intervention was proclaimed to be 'fraternal assistance', the 14th Party Congress was declared illegal and anti-party.

The way was now clear for a thorough purge of party and state organs. In January 1970 the CC initiated a mass 'verification' of party members with the aim of removing 'rightists'. The screening process proceeded throughout 1970, and was naturally accompanied by a thorough purge of representative bodies and state institutions. 82 members of the Czech National Council had to go; 25 000 local councillors; 20 per cent of the Central Council of the Trade Unions (ÚRO); 40 per cent of all managers; 900 university teachers, including 65 per cent of all members of Departments of Marxism-Leninism; 40 per cent of all journalists; a third of the officers in the army and the police.

The purge was comparable in its dimensions with the purge of non-communists in 1948.[41] By December 1970 the screening of party members had resulted in the removal of 387 000 people, or 22 per cent; a further six per cent left of their own accord. This left roughly 1 200 000 people, or 72 per cent of the former total, who remained in the party.[42] The membership figures soon recovered; there were strong opportunistic reasons for joining, and by the end of 1971 the CPCz, with 2 320 000 members, was bigger than ever before. The following description of the screening process is drawn from the recollections of Milan Šimečka.[43]

Three categories were established: the 'healthy core', the 'right-wingers', and the 'dupes of the right-wingers'. The job of the healthy core was to get those who had been duped to admit it; then 'party intuition' would decide who should be re-admitted. This intuition infallibly recognised who was suitable, largely by disqualifying those who showed 'independence of mind, generosity, tolerance, excessive education, high moral principles, courage and so on'. Many members did not even reach this hurdle; all they had to do was stand by what they had said and done in 1968 and they were automatically expelled. The result of this procedure was a party which consisted of obedient mediocrities.

Why did the Czechoslovak experiment come to grief? The reform communists (e.g. Hejzlar and Mlynář) considered at the time, and subsequently, that the sole obstacle to their success was the attitude of the Soviet Union and its allies, which resulted in the intervention of August 1968. Gordon Skilling, in his very thorough study entitled 'Czechoslovakia's Interrupted Revolution', also adopted this view. 'The experience of 1968,' he wrote in 1976, 'demonstrated all too clearly the narrow limits to reform and independence set by Moscow.'[44]

It is hard to disagree. There is, however, a certain narrowness in a view which makes the international framework the sole and determining factor in 1968. Many subsequent writers, after examining the internal difficulties involved in the reform of a communist system, have concluded that the experiment would have failed in any case. The reform communists condemned the invasion and proclaimed that it was literally unnecessary because communism was not in danger in Czechoslovakia in 1968. In saying this they differed both from the 'dogmatists' of the Husák epoch and the non-communist current of writers such as Tigrid, Pithart and Ostrý, who are much more sceptical about the chances that the CPCz might have been able to preside over an orderly transition to 'socialism with a human face'.

The reform communists tended in retrospect to underplay the internal dynamic of the situation, the way the CPCz was being outflanked by the movement of society as a whole. As we have shown, it was precisely the threat of the Soviet invasion (a threat only Dubček seemed unaware of) which led the radical reformers to moderate their activity after July. If the Soviet invasion is taken out of the picture for the purposes of analysis, as the reform communists would advocate, the threat of invasion must by the same token be removed as a factor in the situation. We are then left with the atmosphere of spring 1968: a spontaneous explosion of demands from all sectors of Czechoslovak society, which could only result in the disintegration of the communist system.

The reform communists suffered from many illusions; but one should not paint their intentions in excessively dark colours, as Tigrid and Pithart tend to do. Pithart claimed in 1987 that the reform communists never genuinely intended to respect the wishes of the rest of Czechoslovak society, that even without the Soviet intervention they would have intervened to put the brakes on a process whose inexorable development would have deprived them of power.[45] The conservative faction would certainly have done this; but by July 1968 they were powerless anyway, and they admitted as much by failing to turn up to support the Warsaw Letter on 19 July. The reform communists would perhaps have behaved like those later reformers, the Hungarian communists of the late 1980s, who waited until Kádár was safely out of the way and then started voluntarily dismantling their own power in the hope that the public would turn back to them in gratitude. But this is mere speculation.

One thing is certain: the invasion of the Five put a stop to any future developments of this nature. There was no possibility that the reform communists could return to the leadership of the party, and even if they had done they would never have been tolerated by the public as they had been in 1968. As Jiří Pelikan wrote in exile, 'The very term "communist" has been discredited among the peoples of Eastern Europe. They associate it with the idea of one-party rule and dictatorship of the apparatus, relying on the hegemony of the Soviet Union.'[46] When the movement of dissidence revived in the late 1970s, to arrive after many vicissitudes at its triumphant conclusion, the former reform communists in it, like Zdeněk Mlynář, were political ghosts, people who through an understandable atavism were still fighting a battle that had already been lost. In the meantime, the terms of the political debate had altered. History had moved on towards new tasks.

8 The Brezhnev Years: Dithering at the Top and Revolt from Below

The invasion of Czechoslovakia meant that the Soviet Union had imposed a veto on radical reform anywhere in Eastern Europe. The limits of the Eastern European countries' sovereignty were now clearly spelled out. On 26 September 1968 *Pravda* carried an official statement on the 'Sovereignty and International Obligations of the Socialist Countries'. This attacked the doctrine of non-intervention into the internal affairs of other states as 'legalistic formalism', and added that 'sovereignty should not be understood abstractly'. The independence of the People's Democracies did not include the right to get rid of socialism; every communist party was responsible before its own people and the whole communist movement for the maintenance of the achievements of socialism. 'The weakening of any member of the world socialist system . . . would strike directly at all the socialist countries, and they could not stand by indifferently in this situation.'[1]

Put more briefly, this was the 'Brezhnev Doctrine' of the limited sovereignty of the socialist countries. The Soviet leader explained in November 1968 that the intervention in Czechoslovakia was not an exception but followed from general principles and might well be repeated elsewhere: 'If forces hostile to socialism attempt to distort the development of a socialist country and press for the restoration of capitalism, if the cause of socialism is in serious danger in one country, this becomes a problem not just for that country but for all socialist countries.' Brezhnev himself later denied that a doctrine of 'limited sovereignty' existed, calling it 'an invention of our enemies' (1971), but repeated references to 'the international duty' of communists and the celebration of the intervention in Czechoslovakia in the Soviet press as a 'triumph of the principles of proletarian internationalism' made it clear that a right to intervene in countries where socialism was 'in danger' was now a fixed principle of Soviet policy.[2]

For the last time, as it turned out, Marxist-Leninist orthodoxy was reimposed in Eastern Europe. In economic policy these were years of caution, described by Brus as 'the collapse of the second wave of economic reform'.[3] In Czechoslovakia and the GDR, there was a retreat from reform back to central planning. As we noted in Chapter 6, the decision to change

142

course and abandon the reforms of previous years was made in December 1970 in the GDR. The Eighth Party Congress of the SED (June 1971) reintroduced central decision-making and controls, and in 1972 the remaining mixed enterprises were nationalised. In Czechoslovakia, the reimposition of obligatory plan targets in July 1969 was followed by a decree outlawing all retail price increases from 1 January 1970. The Fourteenth Party Congress (May 1971) condemned the price reform of 1968.[4]

In Hungary, the picture was more mixed. The freer years before 1968 had seen the careful preparation of a model of economic reform, which was approved in 1966 by the CC by a narrow majority and launched on 1 January 1968 as the New Economic Mechanism. The events of 1968 placed Kádár in a difficult position, but he was able to preserve Hungary's economic reforms by giving the necessary guarantees of subservience to the Soviet Union in foreign policy. Hungarian troops took part in the intervention of August 1968, 'in fulfilment of their international duty' and 'to protect the Hungarian minority in Slovakia'. The USSR was certainly concerned about the dangers inherent in the Hungarian reforms, but the reformers could point to the immediate success of the NEM (an increase in the rate of growth of national income from 4.5 per cent in 1968 to six per cent in 1969 and a 14 per cent increase in the volume of foreign trade), and Soviet warnings were only issued in private discussions with Hungarian party leaders. Kádár was able to persuade Brezhnev to come to the Tenth Congress of the HSWP in November 1970 and express his approval for the measures taken by the Hungarian party 'to solve the most important problems of the development of socialist society.'[5] Strengthened by this, the Hungarian government extended its policies of liberalisation into other spheres. An electoral reform allowed more than one candidate to stand in most of the constituencies (though in the 1971 elections 98.8 per cent of the votes were cast for the National Front); steps were taken towards a reconciliation with the Roman Catholic church (Cardinal Mindszenty was allowed to leave the US embassy, his place of refuge since November 1956, and go abroad); restrictions on foreign travel were eased; there were substantial imports of Western technology and consumer goods to satisfy the people and improve the quality of production.

These measures led however to a deterioration in the balance of trade, and in November 1972 a CC Plenum voted a package of 'extraordinary measures' to put right the 'difficulties of reform'. Fifty one large enterprises, which together accounted for 55 per cent of the country's industrial output, were returned to direct ministerial control. Stricter controls were imposed on incomes, prices and foreign trade. This was the more necessary in that the world oil price rises of October 1973 were used by the Soviet

Union in 1975 as a justification for doubling its own oil prices to CMEA customers. Hungary suffered severely in view of its dependence on imports. The enterprises were shielded from the resultant inflation by the use of budget subsidies. Domestic prices were held down and state control was reintroduced. Rezső Nyers, the 'father of the economic reform', was dismissed in March 1974 and removed from the Politburo in 1975. Jenő Fock, the prime minister since 1967, another strong supporter of reform, was dismissed in 1975 for his 'failure to get people to realize their responsibilities for the economy as a whole.' Even so, some of the features of the New Economic Mechanism were retained.[6] The 11th Party Congress, meeting in 1975, reaffirmed the 'right of artisans and shopkeepers to private property and the acquisition of wealth . . . within limits'.[7]

In Poland an attempt was made to continue with economic reform after 1968, but this ran up against fierce resistance from the Polish workers, rather than a Soviet veto. In general, the kind of reforms of the communist economic system that were indicated could only be implemented with the acquiescence of the working classes, who would initially be the main sufferers. In Poland this was not forthcoming, and the resultant crisis, which we now turn to examine, was just as decisive in its consequences for Eastern Europe as the failure of the Czechoslovak reform experiment.

THE SECOND POLISH CRISIS

The Polish events of December 1970, which led to the replacement of Władysław Gomułka as First Secretary of the PZPR by Edward Gierek, should not be viewed solely as a case-study in party factionalism, though that was certainly a factor. They were first and foremost a working-class protest against Gomułka's policies. This protest was preceded by the gradual accumulation of a series of deep fissures in his position, which weakened him *vis-à-vis* society as a whole, and within the ruling party in particular.

His successor represented a genuinely different policy, one of technocracy, import-based economic progress, and a simultaneous growth of consumption. Gierek stored up trouble for the future but kept everyone happy for the moment. Gomułka had favoured economic growth, but he was determined to provide the resources for this by a policy of austerity and restrictions on mass consumption, whereas Gierek thought that both a high level of investment and growth and higher living standards and personal consumption could be achieved simultaneously, by using long-term credits from abroad to purchase advanced Western machinery. The difference between Gomułka's policy and Gierek's was implied by the retrospective analysis of the former's faults made at the 8th CC Plenum in February 1971 and published subsequently in a special limited edition of the party journal *Nowe Drogi.*

Professor Pajestka, vice-chairman of the Planning Commission, said at that meeting that Gomułka had been wrong to think that 'the problem of progress can be solved by increasing society's burden'. 'The restriction of consumption growth,' he added, 'does not always assist economic progress and under certain conditions it can hinder it.'[8] A similar point was made by another member of the CC, the editor of *Polityka*, Mieczysław Rakowski. He described the December 1970 decision to raise prices as 'the apogee of the puritanical concept of socialism' held by the Gomułka leadership.[9]

Thus there were some real differences between the pre-1970 and post-1970 regimes. There were factional conflicts too. A competition for the succession to Gomułka had been in progress since 1965, on the assumption that he could be forced into retirement. Initially the fight was between the partisans and the technocrats. Mieczysław Moczar, Minister of the Interior, head of the veterans' association ZBoViD, was the leader of the 'partisan' faction, so named because of their stress on the Polish resistance struggle of the Second World War, which involved a more favourable evaluation than hitherto of the Home Army resistance fighters of the wartime period. The party boss of Katowice in Silesia, Edward Gierek, a practical, pragmatic, hard-boiled technocrat, was Moczar's chief opponent.

Moczar favoured a demagogic Polish nationalism, as a way of dealing with the increasingly powerful dissenting movement. His was a safe kind of nationalism, however. It glorified the Polish past, but avoided any criticism of the Soviet Union. A scapegoat for Poland's difficulties was available in the shape of the Jewish minority; a suitable opportunity appeared for the 'partisans' in 1967, when the outbreak of the Six Day War compelled Gomułka, for reasons of foreign policy, to line up with the Soviet Union in support of the Arab countries. He also decided to mount an anti-Zionist campaign within the country, warning Jewish citizens of Polish descent on 19 June 1967 against forming a 'fifth column' of Zionists in Poland. This anti-Zionist agitation led to a 'verification drive' in November and December 1967 as a result of which many Jews were purged from the PZPR. They were usually charged with making pro-Israeli statements, and 'unmasked' as Zionists.[10]

This campaign coincided with an upsurge in the movement of dissidence in Poland, stimulated in part by the news of the fall of Novotný in Czechoslovakia. The initial issue was censorship. In January 1968 the play 'Forefathers' Eve', by the nineteenth-century Polish playwright Mickiewicz, was taken off the stage. 'Forefathers' Eve' portrayed the struggle of Polish patriots against Tsarist occupation, and it naturally contained anti-Russian lines, which the audience applauded vigorously. Although the play had been banned under Stalin, it had been performed repeatedly since 1955 with no untoward consequences. That is why some people regarded the decision to ban it in 1968 as a provocation by Moczar's supporters. Several months of student protest began, culminating in March 1968 when students and police fought on the streets of Warsaw. An intensified ideological onslaught was mounted in the press against both Zionism and the economic reformers in the party, some of whom were Jewish. Many of those who had survived earlier attacks on dissent were now forced out of their jobs, and usually out of the country as well. Professor Brus, for example, was denounced as the 'principal carrier of the deadly bacilli of economic revisionism', and dismissed. The philosopher Leszek Kołakowski, the sociologist Zygmunt Bauman, and many others were dismissed at the same time (March–April 1968). Whole university departments were disbanded. The Warsaw City Party Secretary, Kępa, blamed the student disturbances on Jewish students manipulated by Jews in the party leadership like Zambrowski and Staszewski. Gomułka distanced himself from these extreme views in July, preferring to blame that old standby, 'revisionism', but the damage had been done. Two thirds of the 30 000 Jews still living in Poland had left by the end of the year, taking advantage of emigration permits offered by Gomułka himself.

At this point, Moczar seemed close to victory, but the hidden weakness in his position was its very dependence on nationalist demagogy. The Kremlin saw dangers in Moczar's 'national communism', and Gomułka was able to call on Brezhnev's backing to defeat him. Poland's participation in the Warsaw Pact invasion of Czechoslovakia in August 1968 also strengthened the First Secretary's position. At the Fifth Party Congress in November 1968 Moczar was stopped in his tracks. He remained a mere candidate member of the Politburo, although his supporter Stefan Olszowski was elected to the Secretariat. The other main result of the Fifth Congress was the removal of Jews, 'liberals' (27 of them), and former socialists from the Central Committee. Only 52 out of the 91 members of the new CC had belonged to it previously.[11]

This purge did not end the conflict between rival party factions. A row blew up between Gierek and Bolesław Jaszczuk, whom Gomułka had appointed as Chairman of the State Planning Commission. Gierek's proposals for a considerable increase in investment in the highly industrialised regions and the extractive industries were rejected. The Congress adopted instead the Jaszczuk proposals for a concentration of investment on more modern branches such as machine building, electricals and chemicals. The

Jaszczuk plan also involved a new system of premiums and bonuses to give incentives to productivity, and a break with the extensive method of economic development. This came to be described as the strategy of 'selective growth', because Jaszczuk intended to favour some industries and run down others. He wanted to cut back on investment in traditional heavy industries, particularly shipbuilding and aircraft construction. In fact he thought they should stop building aircraft altogether 'because it is absurd in a small country like Poland'.[12]

The implementation of this plan weakened the ageing party leader in two ways. Firstly, it angered the Soviet Union, because it implied an attack on industries traditionally linked with the latter; Gomułka failed in his attempt to persuade the CMEA that Poland was simply changing its specialisation and could perfectly well integrate with the rest of the bloc on the basis of more modern industries (April 1969). From then onwards Brezhnev regarded him with suspicion, despite his loyalty to the 'socialist camp' in 1968. Secondly, it had internal consequences, which were more serious. The move to 'selective growth' meant laying off surplus workers. A decree of 1970 laid off 200 000. A wage freeze was also imposed in 1970. The terrain was being prepared for an explosion of working-class discontent. It was brought to a head by the Politburo's decision of 9 December 1970 to increase as from 13 December the prices of certain essential foodstuffs, despite the opposition of Gierek.

The background to the price rise lay rather in agriculture than industry. Agricultural production had fallen by 5.5 per cent in 1969 and by 4.1 per cent in 1970. The wheat harvest in particular fell by 22 per cent in 1970. The overall performance of agriculture during the six years between 1965 and 1970 was very bad: the rate of growth of production was negative (–0.3 per cent).[13] The weather was partly to blame for this. The winter of 1969–70 was exceptionally severe. There were also long-term structural factors: the continuing fragmentation of holdings, and, partly as a result of that phenomenon, the peasants' continuing fear that their land would be recollectivised. Few peasants had large holdings, because if they did they were treated as kulaks, i.e. subjected to steeply progressive taxation and high levels of compulsory crop deliveries. Moreover, at its Fifth Congress in 1968 the party began to make noises about a restoration of cooperative agriculture. Perhaps this was a reflection of Gomułka's own intellectual sclerosis in his later years. But there was no sign of any party opposition to the idea. The Minister of Agriculture, Jagielski, said the progress of mechanisation could only be secured by the social ownership of agricultural machinery, and he reasserted the government's commitment to

Agricultural Circles as the 'germ cells of socialism in the countryside'. The shortfall in agricultural production in 1969–70 was in part a peasant reaction to this threat of further party intervention in the countryside. An extra 3.5 million tonnes of wheat were needed in 1970; Gomułka did not want to buy it from the West, because this would have meant sacrificing 15 per cent of Poland's machinery imports. Nor did he want to cut down on the export of meat, which was a valuable source of foreign exchange. The alternative was to reduce demand by increasing prices.

The price increase of 13 December 1970 was 17.6% overall, and within that 33.4% for lard, 36.8% for jam, 92% for coffee, 16% for flour, and 38% for the cheaper cuts of beef. An attempt was made to soften the blow by lowering the prices of luxury goods. Television sets went down 13%, refrigerators 16%, nylons 41%, tape-recorders 21%, if you could find these products. The verdict of Eugeniusz Szyr (later deputy Prime Minister) is worth recalling: 'Universal indignation was aroused by the fact that the price reductions on industrial goods affected products either not available on the market at all, or already withdrawn from production . . . The aim of the price rises was supposed to be to alter the structure of consumption. But in fact they led . . . to a reduction of real incomes, particularly among the worst paid families.'[14]

The price rise was also announced at the worst possible moment, just before Christmas. The party was admittedly in a difficult situation, and all economic reformers agreed that a rise in prices was necessary. But December was not the right moment for action. In fact the decision had been made the previous January, but implementation was postponed for a series of frivolous reasons, such as the need to draw up the treaty with West Germany, the need to work out the new Five Year Plan, the summer holidays, and finally the festival of the Silesian miners. The December price rise was a result of sheer incompetence, not deliberate provocation.

The workers' reaction was fierce and immediate. On 14 December 3000 people marched on the administration building of the Gdańsk shipyards, and clashed with the militia. On 15 December there was a general strike in Gdańsk; Zenon Kliszko ordered the police to fire on the workers, and a crowd attacked and burned down the Gdańsk party headquarters. Battles raged throughout the city. On 16 December troops entered the city, and workers' committees drew up a list of demands, including a pay rise of 30 per cent, lower taxes, a price freeze, the withdrawal of the army, and the punishment of those responsible for the state of the economy. These demands were refused. On 18 December Gomułka asked for Soviet aid in re-establishing order. Brezhnev refused, advising instead that a 'political solution' be sought to the conflict. There were already 46 people dead and

1165 wounded; this made a political solution more difficult. From that time onwards, Gomułka was finished. On 19 December he was asked to resign, and he did so the next day from his hospital bed, having suffered a stroke while attempting to defend his policies. His successor, Edward Gierek, promptly announced that the 'working class' had been 'provoked beyond endurance', and promised higher wages. A number of Gomułka's supporters were removed from the Politburo and the Secretariat, including Jaszczuk, who was the scapegoat for economic failure.

The scope and depth of the explosion of December 1970 is shown by the events of January. Gierek's first moves were a series of economic concessions: he froze work norms for two years, he suspended the wage freeze, he raised the minimum wage by 17.6 per cent and family allowances by 25 per cent. This was not enough to stem the wave of discontent. Spontaneous mass meetings discussed the events, and raised demands which went beyond the economic sphere. Workers now called for the punishment of those who had given the orders to shoot in December, for the release of arrested demonstrators, and for the conversion of the trade unions and workers' councils into organs capable of genuinely expressing the workers' needs.

A series of strikes in January 1971 underlined these points. On 5 January the Gdańsk shipyard workers struck, demanding that Gierek come in person to meet them. On 18 January they struck again and issued a comprehensive list of demands, including the dismissal of people like Cyrankiewicz, Kociołek, and Moczar, all thought to be too closely associated with the old regime. On 23 January there was a general strike in Szczecin, and a strike committee took over the city for three days; during this time (24 January) Gierek, Jaruzelski (the Minister of Defence) and Jaroszewicz (the Prime Minister) actually came to Szczecin to hold discussions with the strikers. The chairman of the strike committee, Edmund Bałuka, who foreshadowed the later tactics of Lech Wałęsa by persuading the workers to occupy the shipyard, read out twelve demands, the most important of which were as follows:

(1) restoration of food prices to the pre-13 December level; (2) immediate, legal and democratic elections to trade unions, workers' councils and party and government organisations; (3) workers to receive full pay for the strike period; (4) no reprisals; (11) guarantees of personal safety for the strike committee; (12) no more harassment of workers by the security services; (6) honest information to be given on the political and economic situation in the shipyards and the country as a whole.[15]

For nine hours Gierek's delegation argued with the workers on these points. It must be accounted a great personal success that the new party leader was able to give away practically nothing and gain the workers' support. His phrase 'Will you help us?' and the workers' reply 'Yes we will' became the underlying slogan of the Gierek regime. In effect the wool was pulled over their eyes. The demand for honest information brought the reply 'There has been too much of that recently.' It was 'out of the question to encourage agitation among the workers by publishing these demands'. There was 'no possible way of going back to the pre-December prices'. 'Don't demand from us a democracy for all.' 'The only solution is that you work harder and still harder, so that our economy produces its maximum.' All Gierek offered was moral exhortation and dark hints about the 'dangers of anti-Sovietism'. Although one delegate expressed indignation at 'the new aristocracy that is going to steal everything' (a true prediction, given the corruption of the Gierek years), the sense of the meeting was summed up by a worker who said 'We all know how to work . . . Comrade Edward [Gierek] is the right kind of man. Let's give him at least a year or two and we'll see the results.' In Szczecin the strike was over. Gierek promptly went to Gdańsk (23 January) and performed the same conjuring trick again. The Roman Catholic episcopate played its part too, appealing on 27 January for order and calm, as 'the best guarantees of independence'.

The women textile workers of Łódź were the only group to resist the regime's blandishments. On 12 February seven textile mills went on strike there, demanding a pay increase of 20–25 per cent and the abandonment of the December price increases. The Ursus tractor factory near Warsaw also came out. Jaroszewicz tried to emulate Gierek by visiting Łódź on 14 February and asking the women 'Are you going to help us?', to which they replied, 'No. You have to help us first.' The strike continued until the authorities capitulated, bringing prices back to the pre-December level and dismissing local party leaders for their incompetence on 15 February. With this the great social upheaval of 1970–1 finally came to an end and the communist party could return to the business of running the country.

The Gierek regime differed in several ways from that of Gomułka. Gierek's style was more populist, less austere, and initially he relied on personal meetings to put his policies across to ordinary people. He held no less than two hundred of these meetings during the year 1971. A joke current in Warsaw at the time was that the answer to the question 'Why during one week was there a shortage of milk?' was 'Because Gierek forgot to attend a meeting with the cows, so the cows did not produce any milk.'[16]

The essence of Gierek's policy was to substitute growth in production for economic reform, and wage increases for political change. The events of 1970–1 had shown that the workers could exercise a veto on the economic policy of their rulers. The Jaszczuk reforms were scrapped, and the Szydlak

Commission, set up to modernize the functioning of the economy and to 'overhaul the whole system of economic management', saw its recommendations ignored. Gierek had promised the internal democratisation of the trade unions, but he assigned the most reactionary member of the Politburo, Władysław Kruczek, to run them. In the short term, growth without reform was possible, and this was the policy adopted by the 6th Party Congress, in December 1971. The original version of the Five Year Plan for 1971–5 was drastically revised, and the previous economic priorities were now reversed. Individual and social consumption was to go up by 38%, real wages by 18%, housing construction targets were increased by 25%; and an extra one million eight hundred thousand jobs were to be created to ensure full employment. In fact real wages went up by 40% between 1970 and 1975.

For industry, the new stress on consumption meant a shift from Group A (producer goods) to Group B (consumer goods). Whereas between 1966 and 1970 Group A had grown by 9.4% and Group B by 6.6% per annum, in the period 1971–5 Group A grew 10.6% and Group B 10.4%. Moreover, within Group A energy production lagged behind engineering and chemicals.[17] On the face of it, Gierek's strategy, or, as Fallenbuchl has described it, his 'economic manoeuvre', was outstandingly successful. The share of accumulation in national income reached the uniquely high level of 38% in 1974. One million nine hundred thousand new jobs were provided; the productivity of labour rose at 7.6% per annum, and contributed 90% of the increase in production. But there were hidden difficulties. The productivity of capital continued to stagnate. The increase in production had only been secured by a tremendous input of capital. Hence the productivity of fixed assets, i.e. the ratio of national income to capital stock (Y/K) had only risen to 108.8% by 1975 in comparison with the baseline index of 100 in 1970.[18]

One reason for this was the inadequate performance of agriculture. The productivity of fixed assets in 1975 in agriculture was only 76.8% (1970 = 100). In part, this reflected bad weather. But, more importantly, the reversal of policy towards agriculture after 1970 was not consistently implemented. Gierek's initial policies towards agriculture were very promising. He abolished compulsory deliveries (1972); he raised the procurement prices of meat and milk; he extended health insurance to the countryside; he abandoned the policy of restricting the production of livestock; he allowed the State Land Fund (in which abandoned farms were vested) to sell more of its land to private individuals (the proportion went up from 24 per cent in 1970 to 39 per cent in 1973). The peasants reacted well: they invested in agricultural machinery (there was a 45 per cent increase in sales in 1971) rather than simply consuming their higher profits.

The party leaders, however, continued to hanker after their traditional aim of collectivisation. After 1973 there was another change in policy. Emphasis was again placed on socialised agriculture, via state farms, collectives, and Agricultural Circles; the result was a substantial increase in production in this sector of agriculture. Its share of gross agricultural output rose from 15 per cent in 1970 to 23 per cent in 1980. There were discriminatory measures against private farming, such as a reduction in sales from the State Land Fund from 39 per cent in 1973 to 5.5 per cent in 1975. But the socialised sector, despite its assumed superiority, performed far less efficiently than the private sector. The inferior capital/output ratio is one measure of this: it was five times as high as that of the private sector.[19]

The result of the post-1973 policy of discouraging private farmers was that Poland moved from being a net exporter of agricultural produce ($650m-worth in the 1960s) to an importer ($4.5bn-worth in the 1970s). By 1978 food constituted 23 per cent of Poland's imports. The very success of Gierek's policy in other spheres increased the food supply problem. As workers received more money, their consumption rose. Meat consumption was 118 pounds a head in 1970; by 1975 it was 156 pounds a head. Agriculture could not keep pace with this burgeoning demand.

Agricultural failure was compounded by, and in part caused by, Poland's rocketing foreign debt, which rose from $700m in 1971 to $6bn in 1975. Heavy foreign indebtedness was the natural consequence of Gierek's strategy of 'import-led growth'. Credit was cheap in the early 1970s, and it seemed to be the perfect way to achieve growth without lowering living standards. Poland imported not just Western machinery, but Western raw materials and components. Exports rose 153 per cent during the period 1971–5; but imports rose 196 per cent. A small balance of payments surplus in 1971 had turned into a deficit of $2bn by 1975; this continued to be the pattern for the rest of the decade. Gierek and his team had hoped that a massive injection of Western technology would lead to growth in the advanced sectors of the economy. The opposite happened. Not the 'advanced sectors' but the old-fashioned iron and steel industries benefited. The Katowice steel plant, in Gierek's own fiefdom of Silesia, was an example of inappropriate investment, producing lower quality steels, which were already in plentiful supply, instead of higher grades which still had to be imported. Five billion dollars' worth of investment was sunk in this project in the 1970s. Pressure from the CMEA and the Soviet Union played a part here, because the project went in tandem with the construction of a special broad-gauge railway line to link Katowice with the Soviet Union.

The failures of the Gierek regime were not just economic. It was unable to reach a modus vivendi either with the intelligentsia or the Roman Catholic Church. Gierek did make a number of concessions to the church in the earlier part of the decade. The clergy and their property were partially exempted from income tax; property titles to churches and other property in the former German territories were transferred to the church as an institution between 1971 and 1973. In return the Pope conceded a point in the long-running dispute over the Western Territories by appointing Polish resident bishops, thereby for the first time conferring full papal recognition of Polish sovereignty over those areas. But all this was very little compared with the failure to make progress either in education or church-building. The militia continued to intervene to tear down makeshift chapels and shrines; and the education bill of 1973 was denounced by the Episcopate as 'based purely on atheistic principles which completely excluded any influence by the Catholic Church.' Religious instruction continued to be excluded from the school curriculum.

The failure to achieve reconciliation with the Church was an important factor, both in strengthening the opposition of the intelligentsia (large sections of which were Catholic) and in influencing the workers to broaden the scope of their demands so that they covered human and civil rights. Already in 1970 the Episcopate had spoken of the 'righteous struggle of the Polish workers'. Church leaders advanced from their traditional stress on the rights of the clergy and church property to broader concerns. Successive attempts by communist governments to weaken the Church had resulted merely in 'bestowing a new virginity' (Singer) upon it, turning it into a symbol of resistance to oppression rather than an ally of reaction.[20]

The dissenting intelligentsia for their part were flexing their muscles again by 1975, after the period of quiescence initiated by the repressive measures of 1968. They began with protests against the new Polish Constitution, which formalised Poland's dependence on the Soviet Union and specifically referred to the 'leading role of the Party in the state'. Fifty-nine leading intellectuals submitted a petition to the *Sejm* calling for the inclusion of democratic rights in the new constitution. The party retreated under this attack, a sign of weakness that was to be repeated again and again in the future. The phrase about 'unshakeable fraternal bonds with the Soviet Union' disappeared; the leading role of the party was no longer stressed so emphatically. Hence the PZPR was now described as 'the leading political force of the society in the building of socialism'. These concessions did not still the voices of protest, however, and the atmosphere was thus prepared for the crisis of 1976.

In 1976 the government decided to grasp the economic nettle, and attack the growing overhang of purchasing power by raising prices; this would also make it possible to cut down on food subsidies and raise the prices charged to the peasants for industrial products. On 24 June 1976 the prime minister, Piotr Jaroszewicz, announced new, higher prices, which would come into operation on the 28th. The increase would have added 16 per cent to the cost of living overall, and 69 per cent to the price of meat. It is hard to say whether this was overconfidence or desperation on Gierek's part. He had by now abandoned his strategy of direct discussions with the workers, and the only people consulted in advance were party representatives in selected large factories. In any case, the reaction was immediate and devastating. The tractor workers at Ursus, near Warsaw, blocked the railway lines, including the main Paris-Moscow express route; at Radom the General Walter Armaments Works struck, brought out other factories, marched on the party headquarters and sacked it. The militia put down these revolts successfully, but the strike started to spread all over the country, and the next day the prime minister simply withdrew the price increases, explaining that 'many questions had been raised in the factories'.

The regime drew a political and an economic lesson from this crisis. Politically it decided to root out 'ringleaders' among the workers. Trials at Radom and Ursus were followed by a big purge. Thousands of workers were sacked and blacklisted. Hundreds were arrested and beaten. But this was not 1970. The dissident intelligentsia, already activated by the campaign of 1975 against the constitution, now took up the workers' cause, feeling a strength they had lacked five years before. An immediate declaration of 'solidarity with the workers of Poland' (June 1976) was followed up by the founding of KOR (Committee for the Defence of the Workers), which in September 1976 issued an Appeal, signed by twenty leading intellectuals, representing a kaleidoscope of different generations and tendencies. There were pre-war socialists like Edward Lipiński; ex-members of the Home Army; historians, economists, novelists, poets, literary critics; and the new generation of former students active in the 1960s such as Adam Michnik. A priest and an actress completed the list.[21]

KOR initially set itself the limited task of defending, materially supporting, and eventually gaining an amnesty for, the workers who had suffered as a result of their participation in the events of June 1976. Once again the regime retreated. First a partial amnesty was declared (February 1977); then, when KOR said this was unacceptable, all those in jail were released (July 1977). That was just the beginning. It soon became clear that Jaroszewicz's failed price increase had sparked off a political ferment which could not be dampened down. In September 1977 KOR expanded its concerns to broader human rights issues, becoming the Committee for Social Self-Defence – Committee for the Defence of the Workers (KSS-KOR). It also began to issue a periodical directed at workers, *Robotnik*.

Now the crisis started to spawn other organisations, smaller, with less working-class support, but significant in their more nationalist outlook. ROPCiO, or the Movement for the Defence of Human and Citizens' Rights, and KPN, or the Confederation for an Independent Poland, raised their sights to a higher target: Soviet control and the position of the party itself. KSS-KOR's point of view, which ultimately prevailed, was that the regime could be transformed from within through pressure on the party; the Soviet Union would not permit anything else.

A new development, even more threatening for the regime, emerged in 1978: embryonic trade unions founded by the workers themselves, bypassing both the official trade union movement (CRZZ) and the practically defunct Self-Management Conferences (KSR). A Committee for Free Trade Unions was formed at Katowice in February 1978, and a Committee of Free Trade Unions on the Coast followed in April. The latter was founded by a group which included the engineer Andrzej Gwiazda and the electrician Lech Wałęsa. It published its own newspaper, the 'Worker on the Coast' (*Robotnik Wybrzeża*), distributed at the factory gates and after Mass. The workers' movement was not entirely distinct from the activities of KOR, however. As Ash points out, 'It is difficult to separate the workers' own autonomous political learning process from the direct influence of KOR.'[22]

Thus the party's attempt to dampen the fires of political and trade-union activity after 1976 was a complete failure. Gierek did, however, make an attempt to rebuild an economic strategy, which we shall examine briefly. The final version of the Five Year Plan for 1976–80 took into account the workers' veto on the 1976 price-increases. It involved 'halting the investment drive in order to save a larger slice of the smaller cake for consumption.' Planned growth in gross investment for 1976–80 was set at the very low figure of 2.3 per cent per annum. Actual growth fell far behind this. It was 0.07 per cent per annum over the years 1976–79.[23]

Cuts were made in transport and electricity generation, areas the economy was least able to spare, as it turned out. The severe winter of 1978–9 practically brought the country to a standstill. This was reflected in the way actual production fell far short even of the modest targets set. The plan had provided for a 7.3% annual rise in the net domestic material product, or 'produced national income'. The annual figures actually achieved were: 1976, 6.8%; 1977, 5%; 1978, 3%; 1979, –2.3%; 1980, –6%. Agriculture continued to be a problem, because there was no serious revision in policy after 1976, despite minor concessions. The private farming sector declined from 75% of arable land in 1970 to 68.8% in 1977. The state farms continued to expand and to swallow up most of the input of fertilizer and animal fodder. They continued to be far less efficient than the private farms (1979 figures of net income per hectare: private farm land 13 600 złoty; state farms 1700 złoty.)[24] Agriculture performed badly in the second half of the 1970s. Output fell by 2.1% in 1975 and 1.1% in 1976, rose slightly in 1977 (1.4%) and 1978 (4.1%) possibly in response to the post-1976 reductions in the prices of consumer goods, but then declined slightly in 1979 (–1.5%) and catastrophically in 1980 (–10.7%).

Foreign trade displayed a similarly dismal picture. The planned growth in exports for 1976–80 was 11.8% per annum; the actual growth (in constant prices) was 6.2%. The only way to keep in balance was to cut imports savagely; this in turn reacted back adversely on domestic production. The burden of foreign debt continued to grow in the late 1970s, from $12 billion in 1977 to just under $18 billion in December 1979. By 1980 interest payments alone amounted to $2 billion.

By 1979 the feeling that something would have to change was well-nigh universal. It was not so much that a Polish cardinal was elected Pope in 1978 or that he visited Poland the following summer, to be greeted by very large crowds, which certainly made the relative popularity of Church and party very clear.[25] John Paul II discreetly avoided discussing Poland's problems on this trip. It was rather that these problems themselves continued to pile up. Not only were the oppositional intellectuals multiplying their activities, and there were few serious attempts at repression; within the party a group which wished to reform rather than undermine communist rule produced a devastating study of the situation, under the title 'Experience and the Future' (DiP). Although this had begun as a semi-official report, its conclusions were so unwelcome that it was refused official publication. The underground publishing group *Nowa* brought it out in October 1979. The DiP report pulled no punches. It spoke of popular resentment at a wage differential of 1:20; of mounting public frustration bordering on open conflict; of the gulf between the party and society; of flagrant violations of the standards of social justice; of a system of almost total secretiveness in the public domain; of a highly disturbing tendency to manipulate culture 'in recent years'; of privileged groups 'with access to a second economy'; and of the 'danger of an explosion'.[26]

There would indeed be an explosion very soon. The problems we have outlined provided the background; but what actually set off the explosion of discontent in 1980 was the decision of the party to implement only the part of the DiP report that suited it, and in the narrowest possible interpretation: an increase in economic efficiency, which, as far as the party leaders were concerned, meant simply price rises. We shall examine the premature Polish revolution of 1980–1 in the next chapter.

9 The Premature Revolution: Poland 1980–81

The DiP group had painted a devastating picture of Poland's problems and future; its concrete proposals for reform were however both moderate and vague. This was not unexpected, given the group's semi-official status. The 'three main lessons' drawn in the report were the need to 'preserve a national identity, so that the national culture can thrive unfettered', the need to 'develop the skills and talents of democratic co-operation, of self-government', and the need to 'develop the economic efficiency of society'.[1]

But there was no sign of any response from Gierek to the DiP proposals. At the Eighth Party Congress, held in February 1980, he jettisoned a few colleagues but made no changes in policy. Jaroszewicz was made a scape-goat for economic failure, and replaced as prime minister by Edward Babiuch; Kruczek ceased to be head of the official trade unions. His replacement was Jan Szydlak. Liberals and hard-liners were dropped in equal proportions from the Politburo, and replaced in similar proportions by hard-liners and liberals.

The regime's real answer, which turned out to be a serious mistake, was given in April by Babiuch. Poland's food supply problems, he said, neces-sitated a policy of austerity. Supplies to the domestic market would be cut by 15 per cent. Prices would accordingly have to rise. That the workers were not very likely to accept this had already been shown in December 1979, when workers at the Polkowice Copper Mine in Lublin had gone on 'the biggest strike in Poland since 1976' to secure pay parity with the coal miners. They succeeded. It was a sign of things to come.[2] In January 1980, the Lenin Shipyard at Gdańsk struck to enforce the return of the crane driver Anna Walentynowicz, transferred elsewhere as a troublemaker. The authorities were forced to bring her back. The government's room for manoeuvre was narrowing fast.

It had learned from the events of 1970 and 1976 that price rises could not be introduced directly. A more subtle approach was therefore chosen. On 1 July 1980 the amount of meat sold through the commercial shop network, at double the price charged by the state shops, was increased by 2.5 per cent. The better kinds of meat now disappeared from the latter and were trans-ferred to the former. This was a cleverly concealed price rise. No one was taken in, however. The giant Ursus Tractor Factory struck immediately.

Localised strikes followed in many other places. Again the party's response was apparently cleverer than on previous occasions: on 11 July the managers of major factories were told by the CC to buy 'social peace' by negotiating on a local basis, and conceding the demands if necessary. An element of farce now entered the situation: wherever a strike broke out refrigerated lorries full of meat and sausage were rushed to the spot.

But even this was no longer enough. Strikers at a lorry works in Lublin, which employed 10 000 people, now embarked on a new tactic: an occupation strike. They stayed in their factory and drew up a list of thirty-five demands which foreshadowed those made a month later at Gdańsk. The authorities managed to end this strike on 18 July by partial concessions, but the strike committee refused to dissolve itself afterwards; another harbinger of the future.

Finally the scene of the action shifted to Gdańsk. On 9 August Anna Walentynowicz was dismissed yet again by the management of the Lenin Shipyard. Five days later a strike broke out. Its main demands were her reinstatement, and a two thousand złoty pay rise. The leadership of the strike was quickly assumed by a man who had been sacked from the same shipyard in 1976: Lech Wałęsa. The new and safer tactic of an occupation strike rather than a march through the streets was soon in evidence. Other shipyards along the coast followed suit. So did factory workers in Gdańsk. On 16 August the Lenin Shipyard strike committee decided to settle for 1500 złoty. This was perhaps the turning-point in the growth of Solidarity. Strikers from other shipyards and factories rejected this purely monetary settlement. This, and the encouragement of the crowd outside the shipyard gates, led Wałęsa to change course, and go for a 'solidarity strike' with wider demands. The formation of the Inter-Factory Strike Committee (MKS), with a presidium headed by Wałęsa, and the emergence of the Twenty One Demands (17 August) marked a historic breakthrough.

A comparison between the Gdańsk demands of August 1980 and the Szczecin demands of January 1971 shows a number of significant changes. Instead of 'democratic elections to the trade unions' (1971) they called for 'free trade unions, independent of the party' (Demand no. 1 of 1980). Instead of calling for 'no reprisals against strikers' (1971) they wanted a guarantee of the right to strike (Demand no. 2). Instead of calling on the security services to 'stop harassing and arresting workers taking part in the strike' (1971) they asked for the release of all political prisoners (Demand no. 4). The demand for 'honest information on the political and economic situation' (1971) was taken up again in 1980 (Demand no. 6), but now 'freedom of speech, print and publication' and 'access to the mass media for representatives of all religions' was added (no. 3). Publication of the strikers' demands was a common feature. Wage rises were naturally asked for in both cases.

But the 1980 list then went on to cover practically the whole range of Polish discontents, from the exclusive job privileges of party members (the *nomenklatura* system) through inadequate maternity leave (no. 18) to Saturday working (no. 21). Four main areas were left out of these demands; agriculture, foreign policy, parliamentary elections, and the ending of censorship. The last three were thought to be dangerous, given Poland's 'geopolitical situation'. The first was later included by the MKS negotiators themselves when they added to point 6 a demand for 'lasting prospects for developing peasant family farms', 'equal access to all means of production, including land', and 'the rebirth of rural self-government'.

Both the immense scope and the essential realism of the twenty-one demands reflected the influence of the oppositional activists grouped in KOR and the Committee for Free Trade Unions. But would the rulers of Poland accept them? At first, Gierek tried to get away with a few cosmetic gestures. On 24 August the prime minister, Babiuch, was replaced by Józef Pinkowski, and six out of the eighteen members of the politburo were removed. On 26 August Jagielski admitted that the old trade unions had failed in their task, but did not offer any new ideas.

A week went by before the party leaders were forced to surrender. When they did so, it was for two reasons. First, the tremendous pressure exerted by workers all over the country. The three coastal cities did not remain alone. To the west of Gdańsk, Szczecin was on stride; to the south-west Wrocław set up an MKS on 26 August; on 27 August the same happened in Wałbrzych; on 29 August Jastrzębie and the steel mills of Katowice struck work. These events meant that the party would have to take 'strong measures' to stay in control. But a second factor entered here to rule out even this option: the Soviet Union wanted the Poles to reach a 'political solution'. Brezhnev did not want Poland to catch fire, given his deep involvement in the problem of Afghanistan.

The government's surrender came in the shape of three local agreements, signed with the Szczecin MKS on 30 August, the Gdańsk MKS on 31 August, and the Jastrzębie (Upper Silesia) MKS on 3 September. There were significant differences between the three protocols. The Szczecin Agreement did not mention the 'leading role of the party', although it did specify the 'socialist character' of the new self-governing trade unions. The Gdańsk Agreement was the longest and rather than being a simple acceptance of the twenty-one demands, it was a detailed description of the ways in which they could be implemented, including a number of time limits on the introduction by the government of the necessary measures.[3]

The Gdańsk Agreement made the recognition of independent and self-governing trade unions dependent on their recognising 'that the PZPR plays the leading role in the state' and their denial of any intention to 'play the role of a political party'. The demands were then examined one by one and met in each case with promises of action in the future. It remained to be seen how far the government genuinely intended to implement them. Most of the conflicts of the subsequent sixteen months revolved around the attempts of the workers to enforce both the spirit and the letter of the Gdańsk Agreements on an unwilling party and government.

The first step was to establish the 'independent, self-governing trade union' envisaged in the agreements. The spontaneous formations of August led naturally in the direction of a national umbrella body, via the intermediate stage of the Inter-Factory Founding Committees (MKZ). On 17 September, at Gdańsk, delegates from 38 MKZs, in an assembly in which intellectual oppositionists from the 1960s such as Modzelewski and Kuroń sat side by side with young working-class leaders thrown up by the movement, such as Marian Jurczyk of Szczecin and Zbigniew Bujak of Ursus Tractors, founded the Independent, Self-Governing Trade Union Solidarity. The union already had promises of membership from 3 000 000 people in 3500 factories.[4] By November Solidarity had 7 500 000 members, and by June 1981 the figure was 9 486 000, which constituted 70 per cent of all workers in the social (i.e. state) sector of the economy.[5] Unlike the old communist-run trade unions, Solidarity was highly decentralised. The National Coordinating Commission (KKP) was at the top of the structure, but it could do no more than coordinate the activities of the regional committees of Solidarity, the MKZs.

Although it had signed the agreements of August/September 1980, the government had no intention of honouring them if it could possibly avoid it. As early as 3 October Solidarity decided to call a one hour 'warning strike' in view of what it saw as the failure of the authorities to implement the agreements reached a month earlier. Wage rises had not been introduced; the union had not been given access to the mass media. The 3 October strike set a pattern; it was well observed all over Poland, and it was followed by apparent concessions. On 4 October the Sixth CC Plenum resumed its sessions, which had been interrupted in September. It removed seven leading members of Gierek's team (Gierek himself had already been replaced by Stanisław Kania on 6 September), proposed an emergency congress of the party to reform it, and reaffirmed the 'social accords' of August.

On no less than seven subsequent occasions in the next seven months the party first dug its heels in, and then retreated (at least in appearance) when challenged by the strike weapon. First there was the 'registration conflict'.

On 24 October the Warsaw Provincial Court registered Solidarity, but added phrases about the 'leading role of the party' and the 'socialist system and Poland's international alliances', which were not in the text of the statutes as submitted. The reaction was a threat to strike on 12 November if the offending phrases were not taken out. The crisis was settled, and a strike avoided, by a compromise according to which both sides would abide by the decisions of the Supreme Court. That court accordingly met on 10 November and removed the insertions, only to reinsert them as an appendix.

The next crisis was the Narożniak Affair. Jan Narożniak was a print worker arrested in effect for trying to secure freedom of information (20 November). He had photocopied a secret instruction, passed to him by a clerk in the public prosecutor's office, on the prosecution of anti-socialist activities. Again a strike was threatened, again it was averted at the last moment (27 November) by the release of Narożniak and his informant.

Then there came the dispute over free Saturdays, or the length of the working week. Poland had a 46-hour working week, but the Jastrzębie Agreement provided for a 40-hour week of 5 days. The government offered two Saturdays off per month (December 1980). Solidarity replied by simply proclaiming that all Saturdays were holidays. After two free Saturdays of this kind, on the 10th and the 24th of January, and the threat of a strike on 3 February, a compromise was reached (30 January) whereby there would be three free Saturdays a month during 1981 and the government stated its intention of introducing the 40-hour week when practicable. A fourth crisis was ended (after a strike) by the registration of the Independent Union of Students on 17 February. There were also two local crises at this time. A general strike took place in the province of Bielsko-Biała between 27 January and 6 February, to enforce the sacking of twenty top local officials for peculation; on 9 February a strike at Jelenia Góra compelled the authorities to hand over a special police sanatorium to the public health service.[6]

Finally, an extremely serious crisis blew up over the question of 'rural Solidarity'. Rural activists had been trying for months to get recognition for a rural counterpart to the urban Solidarity movement. As early as 29 October 1980 the Warsaw Provincial Court had refused registration; this ruling was defied on 14 December by those who set up Rural Solidarity, and they proceeded to put on the pressure by an occupation-strike at Rzeszów (2 January to 18 February 1981). Events came to a head on 19 March, with a police attack at Bydgoszcz on local Solidarity activists who had occupied the headquarters of the United Peasant Party (ZSL) to press for the recognition of Rural Solidarity.

The beatings administered by the police were severe enough to put Jan Rulewski in hospital with concussion. He was the regional Solidarity leader, and Solidarity nationally took the line that this was a provocation by hard-liners in the party and the security services. The furious reaction of the rank-and-file members of Solidarity was understandable, and Wałęsa's advisers Geremek and Mazowiecki had some difficulty in gaining a hearing for their more cautious approach.

The National Coordinating Commission narrowly avoided calling for an immediate general strike on the issue, which had now expanded to become two issues, i.e. both the registration of Rural Solidarity and the punishment of those responsible for ordering the beating of the Bydgoszcz activists. Wałęsa, who had continuously exerted a moderating influence on his colleagues throughout these months, was able to gain acceptance instead for a four-hour warning strike, to be followed by an indefinite strike on 31 March if no agreement could be reached.

The warning strike, held on 27 March, was absolutely solid. Many communists took part too, which was remarkable, considering that it had been called in defiance of the PZPR Politburo. But it did not shift the position of the party leaders. Three days later the decision was taken to call off the planned general strike, for Wałęsa had successfully negotiated a compromise with Mieczysław Rakowski, the government's representative, bypassing the National Coordinating Commission. Modzelewski accused Wałęsa of turning into a medieval monarch, and resigned as the Solidarity spokesman. It should however be added that on this issue Wałęsa was acting in concert with his closest advisers Geremek and Mazowiecki and with the Primate's representative Professor Kukułowicz. The substance of the compromise of March 1981 was that Rural Solidarity would be registered, and the Bydgoszcz incident would simply be 'investigated'.

The Bydoszcz incident was not in itself an important turning-point. There had been on–off strikes before; compromises between the union and the government had been arrived at before; there is no evidence of a change of heart on either side after March. But it did mark the beginning of a period of uncertainty, lasting until July, in which all sides were groping for a suitable position. As far as the party and the government were concerned, there were divided counsels. The Kania leadership came under fire from extreme hard-liners (the Katowice Forum declaration of May, attacking Kania for failing to combat the infection of 'Trotskyite-Zionist views, nationalism, clericalism' and so on); from the Soviet Union (the letter of 5 June, attacking Kania for surrendering 'one position after another', making 'no correction whatever to the policy of concession and compromise', and allowing 'forces hostile to socialism to set the tone of the election campaign' for the next party congress); and from Tadeusz Grabski, a member of the Politburo, who openly demanded the removal of Kania, at the Eleventh CC Plenum (9–10 June 1981).

These threats came from within the bureaucratic apparatus; but the party leaders also faced a threat from below, for the first time in many years. This was the movement of 'horizontal structures', which arose out of the Bydgoszcz crisis. It started with rank-and-file defiance of the Politburo on 27 March. At the Toruń Forum, on 15 April, 750 delegates from 13 provinces, representing a million party members, called for the election of party officials on a free, secret vote. This was already happening in some places. The party leaders wanted to defeat this movement; they were helped by the fact that workers who aimed at a democratic renewal of Polish society looked to Solidarity rather than the party: this was no longer 1956. The Tenth Plenum (29–30 April) saw a reaffirmation of the 'Leninist structure of the party', but at the same time an endorsement of the democratic election of delegates to the forthcoming Party Congress, with a choice of candidates and secrecy of the ballot. This combination did the trick. The 'horizontal activists' failed to surmount the hurdle of the May 1981 party elections. There were various reasons for this. One factor was the requirement that successful candidates gain more than 50 per cent of the vote: this worked in favour of faceless moderates who had not offended anyone. Another factor was the perceived irrelevance of the party: 1.5 million of its members had joined Solidarity and saw that union as their preferred field of action. Attempts to create links between the movement within the party and Solidarity were largely unsuccessful. Only in Łódź and Toruń was any contact achieved. Workers generally preferred to leave the party rather than stay and fight for the removal of the old apparatus. Finally, those who did participate in the elections saw their main purpose as to make a clean sweep of the team inherited from the Gierek era; their votes were negative rather than positive. By the end of May the leader of the 'horizontal structures' movement, Zbigniew Iwanów, had conceded defeat.

With the end of the movement for regenerating the party from below, the Ninth Party Congress (14–20 July 1981) was not likely to produce any radical initiatives. Appearances were deceptive, though. The Congress elected a Central Committee containing only 18 of the 142 members of the previous one; only four members of the old Politburo survived into the new one; and only nine out of a possible 49 district (*wojewódstwo*) secretaries were re-elected. But in terms of the factional line-up it was the mixture as before. The new leadership was a combination of conservatives (e.g. Olszowski and Siwak) and moderate centrists (e.g. Rakowski), and the party retained the traditional democratic centralist structure. The party's summit remained deeply divided, and the hard-liners who survived were able to ensure that radical political reform stayed off the agenda, although the economic reforms approved by the Congress were far-reaching at least in principle. This is what made Poland in 1981 different from Czechoslovakia in 1968, and it is the reason why direct Soviet intervention was unnecessary. The election to the Politburo of Zofia Grzyb, a member of Solidarity, was a purely token gesture. The only speaker at the Congress to hold out a prospect of 'the co-participation of trade unions in taking strategic decisions', which implied taking Solidarity into partnership, was Tadeusz Fiszbach, and he was kept out of the new Central Committee.

The Ninth Party Congress opened a new period in which the authorities overcame their paralysis, while Solidarity, having drawn back from the brink in March, gradually began to advance more radical demands, in response to the catastrophic economic situation and the pressure from below. These two developments made conflict inevitable. General Jaruzelski, prime minister since February, probably started his preparations for a military coup at this point. The civilian leaders of the party did their part by mounting a campaign of denunciation of the union, with the general theme that it was anti-Soviet and anti-Party, and was poisoning the atmosphere by its agitation over the food shortages. An attempt at negotiation between the two sides (3–6 August) collapsed in an atmosphere of mutual recrimination. The government made unacceptable conditions, in effect demanding that Solidarity cease all trade union activities and devote itself to acting 'for the social support of the price reform', i.e. selling the government's economic reform programme to its members. Since the economic reform involved doubling the price of some foodstuffs, rationing, greater intensity of labour, and a projected 1.2 million unemployed, this was rather a tall order. Solidarity too began to raise its demands, calling for control over the 'production and distribution of food'; the party's negotiator, Rakowski, inaccurately but significantly described this as 'a programme for the takeover of power'.

Solidarity's answer to the social and economic problems of 1981 was threefold. There should be 'a democratic reconstruction of local institutions', involving democratic elections to local councils and even the *Sejm*; workers' self-management should be introduced; and Solidarity members should work on their free Saturdays to produce goods which would be exchanged with the farmers for food by Solidarity Factory Commissions.[7]

This programme went substantially beyond the August 1980 agreements, and even the party's post-July leadership could not accept it. Only on the issue of workers' self-management was there any progress. Difficult negotiations between Solidarity and a parliamentary commission led eventually to a compromise, whereby the right to appoint the manager of an enterprise belonged either to the workers' council, or the administration, but in case of conflict between the two either side could appeal to a tribunal which would deliver a binding verdict. This compromise was passed by the *Sejm* on 25 September.[8]

But in general the government refused to accept Solidarity as a partner. This placed the union before the choice of either making a direct challenge for power, or scaling down its demands. It did neither. At its first National Congress, which was spread over two sessions, between 5 and 10 September and 27 September and 7 October, there was fierce conflict between the proponents of alternative strategies. Political divisions between 'radicals' and 'moderates', 'fundamentalists' and 'pragmatists', 'economic liberals' and 'socialist economists', 'True Poles' and the rest, gave the Solidarity Congress the aspect of a seventeenth century Polish parliament. It re-elected Wałęsa as its chairman, but he only received 55 per cent of the votes; the other votes were distributed among more radical candidates. It worked out an economic programme which essentially followed the Yugoslav model, involving 'social ownership of the means of production' combined with 'self-government and the market'. There would be free elections to parliament, equality before the law, freedom of information, no private hospital places, and an increase of incomes to the 'social minimum'. The 'only way to save Poland from ruin', the programme concluded, was by 'restructuring the state and the economy on the basis of democracy and all-round social initiative'. How would this programme be put into effect? That was left unclear, but clearly the authorities could not simply be ignored, and the Congress offered to hold 'honest and loyal talks' with them.

Jaruzelski, however, had his own plans for solving the crisis, into which Solidarity only entered as an obstacle to be destroyed. Further negotiations with the union in mid-October were carried on against a background of press attacks by the government, and Solidarity's proposal for a 'Social Council of the National Economy' consisting of persons of 'unquestioned moral authority', who would 'cooperate with the government in carrying out functions of economic policy and management' was not taken seriously. An offer of 17 November to endorse harsh economic measures in return for a share of power was admittedly followed by more desultory talks (17–26 November), but they collapsed when the government demanded that the proposed Social Council be 'a purely advisory body within the state structure'. Solidarity insisted on the Council's independence 'of all state institutions'.[9]

The replacement on 18 October of First Secretary Kania, the cautious embodiment of the party's paralysis, by General Jaruzelski, representative of the army's determination to surmount the crisis, marks the beginning of a period in which military preparations were quickly pressed forward, while a propaganda offensive was mounted against Solidarity, presenting the union as responsible for the wave of protests and strikes which swept over Poland in the autumn of 1981. This was true as a general statement: without the existence of Solidarity these activities would hardly have happened. In the particular situation of autumn 1981 it was false, however. Solidarity was trying to dampen down the fires of discontent, but the deterioration of the economy was such that 'the people standing in the queues began to lose their patience, and the workers their self-discipline'.[10]

The union's loss of control should not be exaggerated, however. There were a number of strikes at the end of October, involving 250 000 people, but the Solidarity leadership reduced the number to under a tenth of that by the end of November. By then only two significant workers' strikes were going on, by coal transporters and oil and gas workers – 20 000 people in all.[11] A survey completed in late October shows that ordinary workers were beginning to oppose strikes. Only 12 per cent 'thought the recent strikes had been necessary'; and if strikes were forbidden only 45 per cent would join a sit-in protest strike against this.[12]

The government, in contrast, claimed that the country was sliding into economic chaos, so as to provide a propagandistic justification for the forcible military solution which was now being planned in earnest. They were able to make this claim because certain groups which were not organised in Solidarity continued to press their own sectional interests by occupation strikes, despite the appeals of the union. This applies to the students (the occupation strike of 26 October by engineering students at Radom, lasting until 13 December; the strike of 20 November by the Independent Students' Union) the farmers (the occupation of the local administration in Siedlce to secure guarantees of inviolability of private property) and the apprentice firemen (the occupation of the Warsaw Fire Officers' Academy, brought to end on 2 December when the riot police stormed the building). It is in this sense only that Solidarity lost control of the situation.[13]

Jaruzelski's step-by-step progress towards his coup is easily outlined. On 25 October he sent army patrols into the countryside 'to help with food distribution', but really to collect information; on 22 November Jacek Kuroń's flat was raided to provide 'evidence' that Solidarity was aspiring to the role of a political party; on 23 November Jaruzelski ordered his army patrols to withdraw from the countryside and move into the cities; on 28 November the PZPR Central Committee demanded that he assume emergency powers; on 11 December Marshal Kulikov arrived from Moscow to discuss the final details of the coup; on 13 December Jaruzelski imposed martial law and interned leading members of Solidarity.

The reaction of the union's leaders to this challenge was rather hesitant. No one thought in terms of a seizure of power. The nearest they got was the Radom meeting on 3 December, tape-recorded secretly by government agents. At that meeting Wałęsa said 'confrontation is inevitable', but he added that a general strike would be stupid; Zbigniew Bujak suggested they set up the 'Social Council for the National Economy' unilaterally. It would be 'something like a provisional government,' he added. Grzegorz Palka called for the creation of a 'workers' militia, armed with helmets and batons'.[14] None of this was very terrifying. Moreover, it was unofficial. Only in Łódź was the decision taken (locally) to proceed on 21 December with an active strike, which would 'provide a solid foundation on which to demand free elections'.[15] When the Solidarity National Commission met on 11–12 December in Gdańsk it ignored these ideas, and adopted a resolution that the response to the government's use of its emergency powers, if it did use them, would be a general strike; for the rest it simply reaffirmed the old demands for democratic elections to local councils, free access to the media and union control of food distribution. A referendum would be held in February 1982 on the Jaruzelski government, it added. If the result was a vote of no confidence, the union would organise its own provisional government. This was certainly a threat, but much could happen during three months.

When the National Commission's delegates dispersed to their hotel rooms in Gdańsk, the plan for their internment was already in place. A few hours later (on 13 December) the majority of them were picked up by the police. Resistance to the coup was far weaker than expected, given Solidarity's ten million membership. It was also unorganised. The union had no plan of resistance, leading Norman Davies to comment: 'From this flowed Solidarity's lasting moral victory'.[16]

Wherever people felt strongly enough to do so, they resisted. There were strikes in 199 enterprises. There were some street battles on 16–17 December, notably in Gdańsk, Łódź, and Warsaw. The most dramatic events were at the Wujek mine, where nine people were killed in clashes with the mobile riot police. The most stubborn resistance came from the miners at the Piast mine in Silesia, who maintained an occupation strike underground until 27 December, unaware that the movement had collapsed elsewhere.

The Jaruzelski regime started out with relatively severe repressive measures. 1713 people went to prison, 34 000 were fined, strike organisers received three year sentences, and a total of 28 people were killed in the first year of martial law. But Jaruzelski cannot be compared either with Kádár in the decade after 1956 or Husák after 1969. Jaruzelski's was a regime of a 'non-ideological character', relying on economic pressures such as sackings and increases in work norms for troublemakers, on keeping good relations with the Roman Catholic Church, and on avoiding any alienation of the peasantry.[17] There were no systematic purges, there was no direct involvement of Soviet personnel, although General Viktor Dubynin, who commanded Soviet troops in Poland, later claimed that 'if General Jaruzelski had not acted we would have invaded'.[18] The immense powers possessed in theory by the Military Council of National Salvation (WRON) were not exercised to the full. Moreover, it proved impossible to arrest the decline of the party, which had already begun in 1980. The million people who left between 1980 and 1984 were largely young workers; between 1978 and 1986 the proportion of party members classified as 'workers' fell from 46 per cent to 30 per cent, and the proportion of members over 50 years old rose from 17 per cent in 1954 to 36.3 per cent in 1986. Only 2.2 per cent of the age-group 18–29 belonged to the party in 1986. At the same time professional people in non-managerial positions left in large numbers. All ruling communist parties were inevitably parties of management and *nomenklatura*; but the PZPR was now this and precious little else. 900 000 of the 1 200 000 managerial posts in Poland were held in 1987 by party members, at a time when total party membership was roughly 2 100 000.[19]

The Jaruzelski regime was good at solving problems of public order, and keeping the lid on political discontent. Attempts by Solidarity to organise disturbances on key anniversaries (1 May and 31 August 1982) were put down successfully by the riot police. By the end of 1982 Jaruzelski felt strong enough to 'abolish' Solidarity (October), release Wałęsa (November) and other internees (December), and finally end martial law (21 July 1983). Solidarity's Interim Coordinating Commission called a general strike on 10 November 1982 in protest against the union's abolition; it was a 'dramatic failure' (Smolar). After 13 December 1981 the majority of Poles returned to silence and withdrew from public life, and this is what Jaruzelski wanted to achieve. This is not to deny the importance of the heroic minority (larger than in other communist states) who continued to oppose.[20]

The economic problems, of course, remained, and it was eventually the conjunction of these problems with the continuing resentment of society which brought down the regime. Jaruzelski's answer in this area was the reform of January 1982, which attempted, on 'Hungarian' lines, to combine economic reform with continuing political tutelage, in the hope that economic success would make the political problems go away. Under the new system, enterprises were to be independent and self-financing (though not self-managing; workers' councils were not included): the choice of what to produce was no longer constrained by a central plan; central planning was to be implemented only indirectly through taxes and the allocation of credits. Most prices, however, remained fixed. 72 per cent of agricultural and 20 per cent of industrial prices were fixed by the government in 1983. Managerial independence was reduced by the obligation imposed on firms to meet government orders for goods of national importance.

The lack of consistency in Jaruzelski's reforms was certainly a weakness. But still worse than this was his unwillingness to confront the Polish workers directly. Managers, given the freedom to make wage bargains with the workers, did so, and the level of wages began to drift upwards again, thereby eroding the effect of the austerity measures of 1982. In politics, too, Jaruzelski sought to compromise. Solidarity's wings had been clipped. But that did not rule out negotiations between representatives of the regime and Polish society. We shall see later that this was the distinctive Polish route initiated by its temporary military ruler: the path of negotiation with the non-communist opposition. But for that to begin, two conditions needed to be fulfilled. First, the atmosphere in the Soviet Union would have to change, to deprive the old guard in the PZPR of backing in their resistance to such a course. Second, the opposition itself, which in the early 1980s was determined to call for all or nothing, would have to shift towards a less Manichaean view of the world. That most oppositionists made this transition in the late 1980s was largely the achievement of Adam Michnik.

The apparent defeat of the Solidarity movement in 1981 was highly discouraging to the rather weaker dissident movements elsewhere in Eastern Europe. It also gave fresh hope to the old guard of communist leaders. There followed a period of apparent deadlock, underwritten by the implicit Soviet guarantee of intervention if the 'achievements of socialism' were put in danger. Yet political, economic and cultural trends were ripening beneath the surface, ready to appear in the open when the heavy hand of the USSR was lifted, gradually and ambiguously, by the new Soviet leader, Mikhail Gorbachev.

10 Decline and Fall

The suppression of the Solidarity movement in Poland seemed to have returned Eastern Europe to uniformity. There were, however, two sets of differentiations, one a deep-going divergence in historical development, the other a result of short-term policy decisions. The deep division between 'East Central Europe' and the Balkan lands remained, with its contrast between still relatively undeveloped countries where communist-led modernisation had not collapsed into crisis (Romania, Bulgaria, Albania) and the more advanced north where the necessity of a radical transformation of the economic system was ever more apparent (the GDR, Poland, Czechoslovakia, Hungary).[1]

There was also a division specific to the eighties, between regimes which, owing to a feeling of insecurity rooted in memories of earlier social cataclysms, were prepared both to exercise a relative toleration of dissent and to attempt economic reforms (Poland, Hungary) and those which continued to be founded on pure repression (the GDR, Czechoslovakia, Romania, Bulgaria, Albania). Yugoslavia does not fit well into any category, but was clearly nearer Poland and Hungary in tolerance and readiness to reform.

These fundamental divisions had important consequences for the manner in which, and the degree to which, communist rule finally collapsed. Tolerant and reforming regimes were able to enter into a dialogue with their opponents, and assure a smooth transition to the post-communist era. We shall see this in both Poland and Hungary. Repressive regimes rejected dialogue and attempted to hold on to their power until the last moment. They were then faced with the choice between a Tienanmen Square style bloodbath and the ultimate abandonment of their position. Where they belonged to the first type (advanced economies) the decision went in favour of abandoning power (GDR, Czechoslovakia); countries of the second type (Bulgaria, Romania, Albania), where communist élites retained their morale, and dissident movements were weak, could postpone collapse for a little longer, though not for ever. The episode of Ceauşescu's overthrow in Romania, despite its highly dramatic features, does not invalidate this typology, since it was in essence a palace coup within the élite itself, backed up by popular protest.

The single unifying factor in the 1980s remained the looming presence of the Soviet Union, and of the common institutions underpinned by Soviet power, namely the CMEA and the Warsaw Pact. The death of Leonid

Brezhnev in 1982 and the periods in office of his short-lived successors Andropov and Chernenko seemed to make no difference to the Soviet policy of intervening where necessary to ensure that the countries of Eastern Europe pursued a common policy. In 1984 both Honecker and Zhivkov were forced by Soviet pressure to cancel state visits to West Germany. Even the election of Mikhail Gorbachev to the leadership of the Soviet communist party in March 1985 seemed to bring little change. It was of course of tremendous long-term significance. But Gorbachev's direct impact was far smaller than might be imagined. In the first two years (1985–7) the Kremlin remained silent about its relationship with Eastern Europe.[2] Hence V. V. Kusin could write in 1986 'Gorbachev has fine-tuned rather than bulldozed. No Eastern European leader has been toppled and no established government has been changed. The Hungarians continue their reforms, and the Czechoslovaks continue not to reform'; and as late as August 1987 a group of oppositionists from Poland and Czechoslovakia were sufficiently uncertain of Gorbachev's policies to issue a call that he undertake 'concrete actions' and show 'a deeper respect for the independent interests and traditions of other countries'.[3]

Gorbachev's attitude began to change in 1987 and by mid-1988 he had reached the view that the governments of Eastern Europe should be left to govern as they wished, without outside interference: in other words the Brezhnev Doctrine of limited sovereignty was finally thrown overboard. Straws in the wind at this time were the decision of May 1988 to start withdrawing Soviet troops from Afghanistan, and the statement in the Theses prepared for the Nineteenth Party Conference, also May 1988, that 'other countries are free to choose their own social systems'. Gorbachev himself may have wanted to renounce the Brezhnev Doctrine all along. As in domestic politics, his freedom of action was limited by conservative forces in the Politburo. The Nineteenth Party Conference (June–July 1988) marked the defeat of those forces. This was confirmed by the demotion of Gromyko and other leading members of the Brezhnevite old guard at the September CC Plenum. The Plenum also abolished the 'CC department for liaison with communist parties in the socialist countries', which had run Soviet policy towards Eastern Europe. From then on it was clear that perestroika would go ahead, in internal and external affairs. As Gorbachev said in February 1989: 'The new approach is based on unconditional independence, fully equal rights, strict non-interference in others' internal affairs, and the righting of earlier wrongs'. When the Hungarian Prime Minister Miklos Németh visited Moscow in March 1989 he was told 'every ruling communist party works out its policies in sovereign fashion.'

But this also meant that until late in 1989 the Soviet leader forswore any attempt to export his reforms abroad. To do this would merely have been to practise 'the Brezhnev Doctrine in reverse'. He visited Prague in April 1987 and allegedly had a 'frank' discussion with Husák. But it had no discernible consequences. Husák retired in December, only to be replaced by Miloš Jakeš, who was committed to maintaining the system he had inherited without major changes. Gorbachev consistently stayed silent on the subject of the Warsaw Pact intervention of 1968 against Czechoslovakia. To condemn it would have provoked a political crisis in Prague; it was argued, perhaps with excessive subtlety, that this would also constitute a kind of intervention.

Nevertheless, from 1988 onwards those in power in Eastern Europe felt themselves to be under threat. They had been restored by force in 1956, 1968 or 1981 or kept in power by the threat of force. Now they would have to rely on their own resources. We have already noted the divergent reaction of communist rulers to this situation. Some of them saw the writing on the wall and instituted strategies of defensive liberalisation (in Hungary and Poland). The rest rejected the idea of concessions altogether and held onto the system they were used to (Honecker in the GDR, Zhivkov in Bulgaria, Jakeš in Czechoslovakia, Ramiz Alia in Albania, Ceauşescu in Romania).

But the threat to the rulers of Eastern Europe did not come just from the changed attitude of the Soviet Union. There were also internal weaknesses, of increasing seriousness during the 1980s, cracks in the outwardly imposing edifice of 'really existing socialism', and I shall now turn to examine these. I shall ignore long-term structural weaknesses, such as the practical impossibility of planning an economy in detail, the unsatisfied hunger for freedom, democracy and consumer goods, and the lack of legitimacy of communist regimes, given their forcible imposition after 1945 and their failure to achieve popular consent after that. Such explanations, because of their general character, fail to explain why the communist system collapsed in Eastern Europe in 1989 and not at some other point. I shall look instead at the decade of the 1980s: a decade of decline.

First of all, there is the somewhat imponderable factor of morale. Revolutions have often been preceded by a collapse of morale among the former rulers, which renders them incapable of acting decisively. 1989 was no exception. The former East German dissident Jens Reich recalls the increasing tendency of members of the ruling party to avoid discussion: 'In the fifties,' he says, 'when a political discussion occurred at work, there was always a comrade who stepped in and defended the position of the party. In the seventies and eighties they avoided ideological work and preferred to walk out of the canteen or change the topic of conversation.'[4] This example is particularly telling because Erich Honecker's SED in general had things very firmly in hand until the late 1980s. There was also a creeping ideological collapse, i.e. a failure of even party ideologists to retain their faith in Marxism-Leninism. This was very pronounced in Poland, where a writer in the party periodical *Nowe Drogi* in 1987 openly admitted that 40 years of socialism had not 'abolished the exploitation of man by man or done away with social injustice' adding that 'those who oppose the changes equate socialism with the preservation of the current power structure.'[5] The very phrase 'really existing socialism', so popular as a self-description of the Eastern European systems in the 1980s, implies not only an admission that the ideal of socialism has not been achieved, but a readiness to settle for what exists simply because it is there – not a very exciting programme. Boris Kagarlitsky quotes the acute comments of the Hungarian dissidents Bence and Kis, writing in 1979: 'The requirements of ideology were now entirely negative: not to challenge the supremacy of the official ideology, or rather to celebrate ritually (on rare occasions only) a willingness to submit to that ideology.'[6] C. S. Maier's pithy summary is apposite here: 'The authoritarian rulers no longer believed in their own original political vision.'[7] The ruling ideology was losing its armour-plating.

Warning signs abounded in the economic sphere too. The growth of the 'second economy', a term which describes a multiplicity of private-enterprise activities, partly legal, and partly illegal, side by side with the official, state-controlled economy, was a feature of the late 1980s especially in Hungary and Poland. The Hungarian economist János Kornai, who described the second economy as 'a special kind of civil disobedience'[8] estimated that it accounted for one third of the total working time of Hungarians in the mid-1980s.[9] A considerable amount of resources and labour seeped away into this sphere, and *nomenklatura* bureaucrats were often heavily involved. This led Western writers like Winiecki to predict a gradual disintegration of the communist economic system from within. This was a piquant and rather Marxist idea: the revolution against communism would consist in the transformation of the relations of production, and political changes would then follow.[10]

But the expansion of the second economy should not be exaggerated. To the end it remained not just second but secondary. Even in Hungary, as R. István Gábor wrote, it was 'an important but not a dominant activity within the national economy'.[11] The performance of the official economy, the first economy, remained the decisive factor. The communist regimes of Eastern Europe had always sought justification and legitimation in the claim that their method of running the economy guaranteed rapid growth.

For many years the statistics seemed to bear them out. Broadly speaking the trend was as follows. The 1950s saw an average 6–7 per cent per annum growth in Net Material Product. After the general Soviet bloc economic crisis of the early 1960s, when growth fell to 2–3 per cent p.a., a recovery set in. This lasted until about 1975. But from then onwards it was downhill all the way. This downward trend in the rate of growth gave added urgency to calls for reform from within the ruling élite. Economic reforms were indeed introduced in the early 1980s in Poland and Hungary. They did not arrest the decline. The figures for 1985–9 are even worse than those for previous years. Brus, writing in 1985, identified a 'progressive tendency to stagnation' in communist countries.[12] It should be admitted, however, that the permanence of this trend is disputed. C. S. Maier, looking back in 1991, considered that 'the performance of Eastern Europe was creditable in terms of percentage growth'.[13]

This is partly, though not entirely, a matter of different ways of measuring growth in national income. Judged by Western standards, i.e. rate of growth of Gross National Product (GNP), including services, rather than Net Material Product (NMP), Eastern Europe's performance is less impressive. GNP growth per annum in constant prices, 1985–9 was 0.7% overall, and the figures range from Czechoslovakia 1.5% to Poland 0.2%.[14] NMP looks better than GDP, but it is still bad – Czechoslovakia 2%, Hungary 0.8%, Romania –1.3%. Poland, the GDR and Bulgaria roughly 3%.[15] Whichever measure one takes, there was a definite downturn in the late 1980s. The *Economic Survey of Europe* concluded, in its review for 1989: 'the output results are the worst since 1947'. Moreover, these measures of growth are purely quantitative. The quality and composition of output are taken for granted.

Why did the economies of Eastern Europe go into decline in the 1980s? The progressive integration of Eastern Europe into the system of world capitalism was a decisive factor. It took two forms: trade and debt. The direction of trade was increasingly towards the West. By 1989 over half the trade of Poland (56%), Hungary (53%) and the GDR (50%) was with the advanced capitalist countries. In Czechoslovakia it rose from 28% in 1980 to 34% in 1989. Only Bulgaria and Romania were moving in the other direction, with a fall in Bulgaria's Western trade to 18% by 1989, and Romania's to 14%. This meant that the big oil price rises of 1973 and 1979 were indirectly transmitted eastwards through their impact on the prices of other imported commodities. Oil itself could be had relatively cheaply from the Soviet Union until 1985, but then things changed. The Soviet authorities refused to reduce their prices to fall into line with the steep decline in the world price of oil, so that between 1986 and 1988 Eastern European oil importers were actually paying double the current world market price.

They were unable to pay for their imports by exporting more, because of ferocious competition from the low-wage and low-cost 'newly industrialising countries' of Asia and Latin America. But they had to have the products of Western technology because of their inability to copy the microelectronics-based 'third industrial revolution' of the 1970s and 1980s (Eastern backwardness in this respect resulted partly from the US embargo on the export of advanced technology imposed in 1951, maintained through a Coordinating Committee based in Paris and not relaxed until June 1990). Even securing the out-of-date technological products which could be imported involved a mounting burden of foreign debt, which went on increasing until 1987. By then it had reached $76 billion for the six Eastern European members of the CMEA. Almost half of this – $36 billion – was owed by Poland. For the next two years the burden of debt remained roughly constant, except in Romania, which wiped out its debt completely, and was $1.5bn in credit by 1989, at a cost of tremendous mass deprivation.

These debt figures certainly look spectacular, but a *caveat* should be entered. Lavigne has pointed out that the *debt service ratio*, i.e. the ratio between interest payments on debt plus annual amortisation and exports, was falling throughout the 1980s. It was 67 per cent in 1981 and 41 per cent in 1987. The other important ratio, the ratio of *net debt to exports*, was over the OECD's 200 per cent danger threshold in only two cases in 1987: Poland and Hungary.[16] Nevertheless, what the debt burden did mean was that Western creditors such as the IMF could demand austerity measures as conditions for rescheduling, and the communist rulers themselves were held responsible for such measures. Hence the strikes of 1988 in Poland, which were not unconnected with the 0.6 per cent per annum fall in the Polish standard of living between 1985 and 1989.

There were also a number of threatening social and political forces gaining strength in the 1980s. Some writers, e.g. Elemér Hankiss, have identified not just a 'second economy' but a 'second society' running parallel with the 'first' or official society, underpinned by a 'second culture', which was often a youth culture. The rock and jazz rebellion was very important in Czechoslovakia. It was lovingly chronicled by the novelist Josef Škvorecký in the book *Talking Moscow Blues*. Police actions by the authorities against rock concerts led to bloody battles with the fans. The pop group Plastic People of the Universe were jailed in 1976 for singing that a certain important citizen was 'not God but a piece of excrement', and the main dissident movement, Charter 77, emerged out of the protest against their imprisonment. In the early 1980s, when the punk phenomenon spread from the West, defiant bands like Lady Pank (Poland), Coitus Punk (Hungary), Patent (Czechoslovakia) and Pankow (the GDR) shouted out their often politically subversive songs, exploring the limits of the authorities' tolerance, narrow in Czechoslovakia and the GDR, broader in Hungary and Poland.[17]

There were also less spectacular but no less real changes in consciousness, involving the growth, or resuscitation, of religious, populist, nationalist, and liberal attitudes. As Hankiss reports, 'it was fascinating to see in 1987 and 1988 how fast the fortress of official ideology and world-view was crumbling to pieces.'[18] The strength of the second society in the 1980s led many people to refer to the growth of a 'civil society', or even to postulate an opposition between 'society' *tout court* and the communist state. The second society (a passive rejection of the system) shades into the dissident movement (an active rejection of it), but on this view the dissident movement was merely the tip of the iceberg, or at least the directly political articulation of initially non-political trends.

Despite the warning signs in all these spheres, the economic, the social, the ideological, the cultural, very few outside observers predicted the collapse of communist rule in the 1980s. It is easy to collect examples of the lack of foresight displayed by commentators on Eastern Europe right up to 1989. The historian Joseph Rothschild, writing as late as 1988, maintained that 'Soviet hegemony over East Central Europe cannot be relinquished without jeopardising Soviet legitimacy. These considerations will override Soviet awareness that the objects of that hegemony are sullen'.[19] The political scientists Lovenduski and Woodall wrote in 1987 that 'Eastern Europe remains firmly within the Soviet sphere. The prospects for it to break away are the same as for the Western countries to leave NATO, the EC, or the IMF'. Moreover, they added, 'the successful establishment of socialist ideals' provided a 'framework for the legitimation' of 'state socialist regimes' if they were able to deliver the 'promised social equality'.[20] Even Zbigniew Brzezinski, writing in 1988 from a much more hostile position than Lovenduski and Woodall, considered that the most probable outcome would be 'a protracted and inconclusive systemic crisis which might eventually subside into a renewed period of stagnation'.[21] Ronald Asmus, writing in August 1989, thought it 'premature to assume that the Brezhnev Doctrine is dead'.[22] The list could be continued.

As we have indicated, signs of decline were plentiful in Eastern Europe. But not of impending collapse. In 1989 the police and the army seemed reliable enough. Nowhere except in Romania (a special case) did the security forces mutiny or refuse to obey orders to break up demonstrations in the 1980s. This was true even in Poland. The Soviet bloc economies continued to function, to provide increases in real wages, and in exports, in most cases. When the end came, it came for the most part suddenly and unexpectedly.

Even the most astute observer would have been unable to predict the speed of the collapse of communism from the vantage-point of early 1989. When it happened it was a kind of chain-reaction. The weakest link in the chain broke first. That was Poland. The shift from defensive liberalisation to power-sharing, which was tantamount to abdication, can be dated precisely – the 10th Plenum of the CC of the PZPR in January 1989, at which it was agreed to hold talks with Solidarity. The rest of the Eastern European countries followed in rapid succession. Poland showed the way to Hungary. Talks with the non-communist opposition were opened there in June. Hungary then undermined the GDR by allowing freedom of movement across its borders: 10 September 1989, a decisive date in the fall of communism in Eastern Europe. The spectacle of the dismantling of the Berlin Wall set off the 'velvet revolution' in Czechoslovakia. There followed, though without any clear inner connection, the overthrow of Ceauşescu in Romania. The backwash of these events eventually destroyed communist regimes in Bulgaria and the northern part of Yugoslavia. Even Albania did not remain immune. This is of course a bald summary. Let us now look at the events in somewhat more detail, starting with Poland.

POLAND AND HUNGARY: A SMOOTH TRANSITION FROM COMMUNISM

In Poland the path of gradualism and compromise was taken. This required the kind of collaboration between government and opposition which was anathema to many who remembered the coup of 1981. Yet there were strong reasons for such a compromise. Despite the suppression of the Solidarity movement and the official announcement of its abolition (8 October 1982) Poland remained the country where communist rule was closest to collapse. The situation in Poland in the 1980s was characterised by three main elements: the continuing strength of the opposition, General Jaruzelski's own deep awareness of the weakness of his regime, and the problem of economic reform, which turned out to be insoluble without taking Solidarity into partnership.

The strength of the Polish opposition under Jaruzelski was somewhat obscured by the general's initial success in suppressing the various anniversary protests mounted in 1982. But underground Solidarity continued to be a force, and the range of dissident activities in the mid-1980s was truly unique for a communist country. Dissident publishing houses published 400 journals a year, reaching three million people; 500 books a year appeared via the 'second circuit' of independent publishing. These results were a testimony to the strength of the Polish dissident movement, and, paradoxically, to the tolerant character of the Jaruzelski regime. 'As for the so-called "second circuit",' admitted the Minister of Culture in 1987, 'we do not particularly support it, but we also do not go out of our way to persecute it.'[23]

The amnesty of Solidarity activists in September 1986 was a sign of the government's recognition that the opposition was a permanent feature of the Polish political landscape, not to be suppressed or ignored. It was also a sign that the regime was no longer totalitarian, and that it lacked the self-confidence to carry out an offensive of its own. In this context the murder of Father Popiełuszko in 1984 was of less significance than the government's readiness to punish members of its own security service for carrying out the crime (they were given jail sentences of between fourteen and twenty-five years in 1985). The foreign policy context should not be ignored, but it is still a matter for speculation how far the relative liberalisation of the years after 1985 in Poland was a response by party leaders to the change in atmosphere in the Soviet Union. There is no evidence of direct political pressure.

Finally, and most important of all, there was the worsening economic situation and the continuing problem of economic reform. Despite the imposition of martial law, and the ending of the strike movement, Poland's economy continued to deteriorate. It was suffering from 'the Polish disease', a complaint which, as Jan Drewnowski has pointed out, was not unique to Poland.[24] The symptoms were industrial overmanning, quiet sabotage by workers in reaction to the suppression of their trade unions, relative agricultural backwardness, and increasing national insolvency. The foreign debt was $39bn by 1988, real wages were 20 per cent lower in 1988 than 1980, national product per head was 13 per cent lower in 1988 than in 1978. The catastrophic decline of the period between 1978 and 1982 had it is true been followed by a partial recovery, but this was too slow to reach the former level by the end of the decade. After a period of recentralisation between 1982 and 1987, the government decided to confront the problem of economic reform, but to do it in collaboration with the Polish public. Professor Zbigniew Messner's market-oriented, austerity-based reform was put to the vote in November 1987. Its defeat (44 per cent of the eligible voters supported it) meant that the government's only plan for reform had been torpedoed. There followed a reversion to the hand-to-mouth policies of previous decades. The crisis of 1988 was set off by an attempt to stimulate agricultural production with incentives. In January 1988 farm procurement prices were raised by an average of 48 per cent. To pay for this, retail prices were raised by up to 40 per cent, and that is the economic background to the strikes of May and August 1988. The strikers wanted compensatory wage increases of 15 000 to 20 000 *złoty*, but they soon broadened their objectives in a way reminiscent of the strikes of 1970, 1976 and 1980 to the restoration of Solidarity, the release of political prisoners, and the reappointment of people sacked for political reasons. A wage-increase was conceded, but the political demands were ignored, as in 1970 and 1976.

This time, however, the story ended differently. There had since 1986 been fierce internal conflict between rival groupings within the opposing camps on the issue of compromise. Many Solidarity activists had an 'all or nothing' stance. There could be no compromise with evil, they said. But Adam Michnik, who started to advocate a compromise with the government in 1986, eventually brought the leading figures in Solidarity round to his point of view. It was a difficult choice, because compromise implied movement towards a free market which would damage the interests of workers in state industries. Radical veterans of Solidarity like Andrzej Gwiazda, Marian Jurczyk, Jan Rulewski, and Anna Walentynowicz rejected this, as did the PPS (Polish Socialist Party) founded by the KOR veteran Jan Józef Lipski. But the Church-influenced wing of the movement, including Bronisław Geremek and Lech Wałęsa himself, favoured what they called an 'anti-crisis pact' with the authorities. Similarly on the government side Jaruzelski and Mieczysław Rakowski were at first in a minority facing anti-reformers like Alfred Miodowicz, head of the official trade union movement. Hence the paradox of the strikes of 1988, which were opposed by Wałęsa and the government[25] and supported by the PPS, 'Fighting Solidarity', and the official trade unions. Jaruzelski offered 'round table discussions' with Wałęsa and other Solidarity leaders, and in January 1989, at the 10th CC Plenum, he forced his unwilling colleagues to agree to this by threatening his resignation. Later on, Adam Michnik publicly praised Jaruzelski for the 'political courage' he had shown in 'reversing seven years of anti-Solidarity policy' (April 1989). Jaruzelski's readiness to compromise was matched by Wałęsa's. The round table talks with Solidarity (February to April 1989) resulted in what was in effect a PZPR surrender, though it looked like a compromise. Free elections, it was agreed, would be held to a resurrected

Polish Senate, or upper house, and to 35 per cent of the seats in the *Sejm*. Thirty-eight per cent of the seats in the *Sejm* would be guaranteed to the PZPR, while the remaining 27 per cent would go to the hitherto obedient 'coalition parties' and 'Catholic organisations'. In return the opposition agreed to the creation of a new office of President, with power over the army and foreign policy. It was intended that Jaruzelski would be elected to this office.

The dimensions of the government's surrender were made apparent by the elections of June 1989. Predictably, Solidarity candidates swept the board, standing as representatives of 'Citizens' Committees', in both sets of elections. The whole of the open seats in the *Sejm* went to Solidarity, and 99 out of the 100 seats in the Senate went the same way. In strict numerical terms this was not sufficient to form a government, but the pull of the opposition was so strong that the former coalition partners of the PZPR, the United Peasant Party and the Democratic Party, kicked over the traces and formed a coalition with Solidarity. This opened the way to the formation of Tadeusz Mazowiecki's government in August. Twelve of the cabinet seats were given to Solidarity, making a majority. The PZPR was given four seats, but these included the Ministries of the Interior and Defence. It was assumed incorrectly that the Soviet Union would not tolerate anything less, such was the uncertainty about Gorbachev's position. Yet the PZPR's apparently key role was in reality window-dressing. The real force in the government was Solidarity; the programme was Solidarity's; and the policy was the progressive dismantling of the communist system of control over the state and the economy.

A similar path of compromise and conciliation was taken in Hungary, but whereas in Poland the process started rather suddenly and unexpectedly in Hungary it had long been ripening, starting perhaps as far back as 1956. János Kádár's decision to consolidate his regime by a partial compromise on the basis 'who is not against us is with us' set a policy framework which lasted until the late 1980s. There were it is true some ups and downs. The short-lived movement of 1966–73 towards greater ideological permissiveness and economic reform was followed by a tighter regime, involving a witch-hunt against the Budapest School of Marxist humanists (1973), the dismissal of Rezső Nyers (1974) and some economic recentralisation.

The harder line taken by the HSWP in the early 1970s must be seen as an attempt to ward off the continuous 'erosion of power' (Hankiss)[26] that inevitably accompanied moves towards liberalisation. When in 1977 the HSWP felt able to move forward again, primarily in the direction of economic reform, the erosion of its power was considerably accelerated. This was certainly not what the party leaders intended in making the reforms. In the political sphere, multiple candidatures were introduced for the Hungarian elections of June 1985, but Kádár stressed that a one-party system would still prevail in Hungary. The rival candidates in the elections were obliged to adhere to the Patriotic People's Front (PPF) programme (which did not differ materially from the HSWP party programme). Nonetheless, it was significant that 43 seats (11 per cent) were won by independents.

In the economic sphere, certain restrictions on private agriculture had already been removed in 1980 (private farmers were allowed to buy tractors), and this resulted in an increase in the contribution of the private sector to agricultural production (from 31 per cent in 1980 to 34 per cent in 1985), even though it constituted a mere 13 per cent of the arable land. In industry change was harder to achieve. There were a number of relatively minor liberalising moves in the early 1980s, such as the breaking up of some large enterprises into smaller units, and increased freedom of entry for small private firms, but the well-nigh insoluble problem the government faced was the contradiction between its links with monopolistic producers and its economic aim of retrenchment and stabilisation. The 'stabilisation programme' of 1979 started off with ruthless austerity measures and price reforms to bring domestic prices closer to those on the world market. In 1982 Hungary was admitted to the IMF and the World Bank. But by 1985 the industrial managers' lobby, supported by Kádár himself, had defeated the economic experts within the party. The latter responded to their disappointment at the 1985 Party Congress by defecting to the dissident opposition. The loss of these economic advisers was a key element in the decline of the party's confidence.[27]

Meanwhile, stirrings were felt within the PPF, so obedient hitherto. Its chairman, Imre Pozsgay, was himself a leading party reformer. His appointment in 1982 to head this organisation, which was then still a typical 'transmission belt', was clearly a demotion. But he was able in the changed conditions of the late 1980s to convert it into an independent power base. In 1986 the PPF commissioned a study by thirty-five leading Hungarian economists, entitled 'Turning Point and Reform' (*Fordulat és Reform*), which pulled no punches in its analysis of the situation. The report called for 'political, organisational, institutional and social reform'. An 'open society' should be established, it said, with 'a government responsible to parliament', and 'a plurality of interest representation'. It just stopped short of demanding a multi-party system, but avoided mentioning the leading role of the party. On the economy itself the recommendations could hardly have been more radical: 'the government's task is the constant and conscious elimination of the constraints on the market'.[28]

It is a measure of the curious form of partial liberalisation that prevailed in Hungary in the late 1980s that the party allowed this reform programme to be published in the official periodical of the Hungarian Academy of Sciences, but denounced it for ignoring the 'leading role'. This confused response reflected 'leadership drift', a phenomenon observable in other communist states as well,[29] caused by factional conflict at the top of the party. After his many years in power, Kádár's position was now in decline, and he was being challenged by the faction around Pozsgay. In the centre, between Pozsgay and Kádár, there was Károly Grósz, who took over as Prime Minister in July 1987, then as First Secretary of the party in May 1988. The 'palace revolution' of 22 May 1988, when Kádár and many of his Politburo colleagues were removed from their positions, seemed like a decisive step in the direction of a multi-party system, but Grósz rapidly disappointed the hopes that had been placed in him; he tried to block the debate on reform within the party. This brought further disillusionment.[30]

Nevertheless, compromise continued to be the name of the game in Hungary. The moderate opposition and the party's reformers joined forces in September 1987, with the establishment of the Hungarian Democratic Forum (HDF). Imre Pozsgay himself spoke at the founding conference of the HDF. His words carried weight, as he was included in the HSWP Politburo in the May 1988 reshuffle. There followed a period of cautious advance, in which Grósz tried to hold the opposition at arm's length, while nevertheless allowing the reforming wing of the party to get on with the implementation of the economic parts of the reform programme (Mihály Bihari's 'Programme Basket for Democracy', presented to parliament in June 1988, and enacted point by point in 1988–9). In the meantime, there was a certain amount of pressure by more radical elements. Their programme was the 'New Social Contract', a set of proposals published in the *samizdat* periodical *Beszélő* in June 1987 by a group led by the philosopher János Kis.[31] It called for surrender by the party rather than compromise: free elections, the restoration of local self-government, and a government responsible to parliament.[32] Having formed the Alliance of Free Democrats early in 1988, the radicals occasionally took to the streets. There was a demonstration against the Romanian leader Ceauşescu's 'systematisation policy' (April 1988), which was having a bad effect on the Hungarian minority in Transylvania. This was a fairly harmless subject. But there was also a demonstration on 16 June 1988 commemorating Imre Nagy and the Hungarian Revolution of 1956. This was to attack the legitimacy of HSWP rule at its roots, and the demonstration was suppressed.

The pressure from below, and the dawning realization that under

Gorbachev the Soviet Union would not intervene whatever happened, enabled the reformers to overcome the opposition of the conservative wing of the party at the decisive CC meeting of 10 February 1989. The defeat of Grósz was followed by a series of measures during 1989 which in effect dismantled party rule, and, by their impact externally set off the chain-reaction which destroyed communist rule elsewhere. First the HSWP committed itself to a multi-party system (February 1989); then it renounced democratic centralism (April); then it abandoned the *nomenklatura* system (May); then it rehabilitated the 1956 revolution, and allowed a funeral to be held for Imre Nagy (June); then it signed an agreement with the opposition for free parliamentary elections (13 September). In October the old parliament showed its independence by banning party cells in the workplaces, abolishing the 60 000 strong Workers' Militia, and converting Hungary from a People's Republic into a Republic. Finally, on 7 October, the party dissolved itself. Two rivals for the communist succession emerged: the Hungarian Socialist Party, set up by the reformers, and the Hungarian Socialist Workers' Party, representing the more conservative faction.

It was an unusual situation. The party élite had destroyed its own position. Why? Szelényi explains this 'astonishing readiness of the élite to dissolve itself and its organisations' by referring to the 'changing pattern of recruitment into the party and state bureaucracy after 1970'. The loyalties of the 'able young professionals' brought into the *nomenklatura* in the 1970s and 1980s 'did not lie with communism'. They naturally wanted to look after their own interests, so the phenomenon of what Hankiss calls 'the conversion of power' arose: 'The ruling élite in Hungary gave up its power ... because it realized that it had a good chance of *converting* the power it had possessed in the old system into a new kind of power.' Hence public firms could be transformed into the private property of their former managers. The point is of general application in Eastern Europe, in economic and social, though less in political, terms.[33]

But it was the change in Hungarian foreign policy that had the greatest external impact. In May 1989 the barbed-wire fence on the Austrian border was taken down. It was the end of the 'iron curtain'. East German holiday-makers flooded into Hungary to take advantage of this. In August the West German embassy in Budapest had to close because its grounds were over-crowded with East German refugees. Finally on 10 September the Hungarian government threw open the border with Austria, allowing 12 000 East Germans to leave within 72 hours. This was a breach of a longstanding agreement with the GDR, and led inexorably to the collapse of that country.

THE GDR, CZECHOSLOVAKIA AND THE REST: A CHAIN-REACTION OF COLLAPSE

Until the intervention of external forces, the ruling party had the situation well under control in East Germany. The 1970s and 1980s had seen increasing international recognition. the German Democratic Republic began to be described as the state that had 'come in from the cold'. West Germany's strategy ever since 1973 had been to 'make reunification superfluous' by a 'policy of reassociation'. Successive credits of 2 billion marks were granted to the GDR in 1983 and 1984. The Soviet Union at first attempted to oppose the gradual improvement in relations between the two countries. Honecker was prevented by Chernenko from visiting Bonn in 1984. The change in Soviet attitudes brought about by Gorbachev opened the way to a *rapprochement* between East and West Germany. In September 1987, when Honecker visited Bonn, he was treated with the full ceremonial honours due to the head of a foreign country.[34]

Many people interpreted the Honecker visit as meaning that the Federal Republic had accepted the division of Germany into two states. This was in a sense true but Bonn's policy was double-edged. The GDR became increasingly dependent on West Germany as a trading partner (18 per cent of imports in 1988, 20 per cent in 1989). For Honecker, the opening to the West was a huge gamble. But internally the all-pervasive state security force (the *Stasi*) was able to suppress and nip in the bud any movements of dissent. Really obstinate opponents were expelled to the West. The GDR economy appeared to be performing well in the early 1980s. A successful export drive in the period 1981 to 1985 allowed the burden of debt to be reduced from $10.1bn to $7.1bn.[35] Honecker's gamble, wrote one prominent Western analyst in 1988, 'has generally paid off'.[36]

But the GDR was not immune from the underlying weaknesses outlined earlier in this chapter. Foreign trade stagnated in the late 1980s, owing to competition from South-East Asia. The country's reliance on oil from the Soviet Union meant that it could not benefit from the fall in the price of oil in the mid-1980s. By 1986 it was buying oil from the Russians at three times the world market price. The burden of debt increased progressively from 1985 onwards. It was back to $10.1bn by 1987, $11bn in 1989. There was a distinct decline in the rate of growth of national income in the late 1980s (from 4.5 per cent per annum in 1981–5 to 3.1 per cent per annum in 1986–9).[37] These problems were certainly serious, but the real weaknesses lay in the psychological sphere. The population could not remain unaware of the level of pollution, in particular sulphur dioxide emissions, which resulted from the one-sided stress on production for production's sake; they could not be insulated from West German television, with its constant demonstration that however much the GDR had progressed it was still far behind the Federal Republic in material terms. What Glaessner calls 'the emancipation of society from the SED's claim to direct and rule everything'[38] proceeded apace in the 1980s.

The reforms of Gorbachev in the Soviet Union also had a considerable indirect effect. There was increasing alienation from the Honecker regime from 1985 onwards because of the comparison between liberalisation in the Soviet Union and continuing resistance to this by the SED. Censorship of news from the Soviet Union, even the banning of Soviet publications and films, was not effective because West German radio and television stations reported Gorbachev's activities in full.

Yet there was very little open dissidence in the GDR. As late as 1989, the Minister for State Security estimated the total number of 'hostile forces' in the GDR at about 2 500. One reason for this was repression: the ever-present and massive (100 000 strong) network of the *Stasi* intelligence service. Another was the existence of the safety-valve of emigration. Although the Wall was impenetrable for ordinary citizens, troublesome people were either permitted to leave or forced out. In 1984 32 000 people were deprived of GDR citizenship and allowed to leave the country. A total of 382 481 people left the GDR legally between 1961 and 1988.

Where dissidence did exist it was so moderate in its aims that it could be tolerated by the regime. This toleration was itself perhaps a sign of weakness. 1987 saw the emergence of two major unofficial journals, 'Ecology News' and 'Borderline Case', the former concentrating on issues of environmental protection, the latter on developing a programme of peace and human rights. From 1987 onwards 'peace discussions' took place at the *Nikolaikirche* in Leipzig, under the aegis of the Evangelical Church. The subject of many of these discussions, namely the reduction of armaments in both East and West, was not necessarily unwelcome to the GDR authorities. But in the spring of 1989 the church and peace groups raised their sights to the more political arena of the local elections. In April 48 prominent clergy called on people to boycott them; in May a number of people were arrested in Leipzig for attempting to monitor the extent of electoral fraud.

It was this movement, harmless at first, that gave birth in the tense and emotional circumstances of September 1989 to the New Forum, a body initially intended to promote a dialogue on change between the dissidents and the authorities, but quickly swept by a swelling tide of discontent into confrontation. From the middle of September the masses started to intervene. Hundreds of thousands of ordinary East Germans attempted to get away to the West; others took part in the marches and demonstrations mounted under the auspices of New Forum in Leipzig. The authorities were thus faced with two problems. The first was the more serious. Until the beginning of October there was drift and uncertainty in governmental circles. Published records of ministerial discussions show that the security chiefs in the Interior Ministry did not know how to react to the 'GDR tourist problem'. Erich Mielke was told by his advisers 'That is naturally a complicated question at the moment, Comrade Minister'. General Major Hähnel pointed out that 'the people are discontented with the level of services, with housing and with the interruptions in production'.[39] The migrants could simply have been allowed to leave quietly from the West German embassy in Prague where they had taken refuge. Instead the Politburo insisted that they pass through the GDR on their way west so that they could be formally 'expelled' rather than just melt away: a face-saving gesture. This decision meant that 'freedom trains' passed through the GDR itself, quite unnecessarily, and it resulted in a three-hour riot in Dresden, where 15 000 people attempting to board were driven away by the police.

The key question then became: was the ruling group in the country prepared to go as far as a 'Chinese solution', on the lines of the Tienanmen Square massacre five months before? A demonstration on 7 October was suppressed by force; much more force would be needed two days later (to deal with 70 000 people). Honecker was in favour of using live ammunition; he was overruled 'by one vote'[40] in circumstances as yet unclarified. The local party leaders in Leipzig advised against the use of force. Egon Krenz claimed that his opposition was decisive. Gorbachev may well have intervened in the course of his visit to East Germany. He allegedly spoke sharply to the SED Politburo behind closed doors on the need for concessions. His public comment that 'dangers only exist for those who don't grasp the situation, who don't react to life' could be construed as encouraging those who favoured a softer line. The 9 October demonstration, and all subsequent ones, went ahead peacefully. It was the first of a series of surrenders, each of which was intended to take the sting out of the movement, and none of which succeeded. Honecker was replaced by Krenz as First Secretary on 18 October; the whole of the government and the party Politburo resigned on 8 November. The opening of the border with West Germany on 9 November was the really crucial surrender, and not just for the GDR. It was evident that Czechoslovakia was next on the list.

Or rather, it was time for the dissidents around Charter 77, who had been trying for years to bring some movement into a stagnant situation, mainly by demonstrating on important anniversaries, official and unofficial, to show that changes could be brought about in Czechoslovakia as well. Gorbachev publicly guaranteed for the first time on 25 October that the

Soviet Union would not interfere in the affairs of its neighbours. There was an interval of two weeks, and then the forces that had quietly been gathering strength went into action. On 17 November there took place in Prague a march in commemoration of the funeral of Jan Opletal, a student killed by the Nazis in 1939. It was permitted because of its apparently 'harmless' theme. The opposition, however, used the opportunity to call for 'freedom', 'justice', the release of political prisoners, the dismissal of Jakeš, and even the ending of communist rule. A hard core of students headed for Wenceslas Square after the demonstration had officially ended, and sat down there. The riot police intervened brutally. There was blood on the streets, and it was even suggested that one student had been killed. This turned out to be untrue, but it was a useful myth at the time, with tremendous mobilising power.

The Prague students were now joined by the actors (18 November) and the veteran dissidents from Charter 77, led by the playwright Václav Havel. On 19 November they set up Civic Forum to give direction to the protest movement. In Bratislava a group of Slovak intellectuals set up a similar movement, Public Against Violence. The decision by the authorities not to intervene against a demonstration by 100 000 people the next day against police brutality was the first in a series of surrenders to street pressure. There followed a succession of militantly non-violent demonstrations, each bigger than the previous one. A two-hour general strike on 27 November was observed almost unanimously throughout the country. In retrospect (though there was naturally uncertainty at the time) the process of unravelling communist rule unfolded with classic inevitability. It concluded provisionally with the formation on 10 December of a new government in which the communist party held only 8 out of 21 ministries, and the resignation of President Husák. The new president, elected unanimously on 29 December by the Federal Assembly, was Václav Havel. The rest of the story belongs to post-communist history.

That left the Balkans: Bulgaria, Romania, Albania, and one could well add Yugoslavia, still a communist state despite its forty years outside the Soviet bloc. The processes that took place in South East Europe were similar to those in East Central Europe, but they developed painfully, slowly and incompletely at first, owing to the weakness of the non-communist opposition and the superior staying-power of communist élites. Clever Hungarian-style footwork by Petŭr Mladenov in 1989 almost took the sting out of the crisis in Bulgaria. A number of warning signs had appeared there in the late 1980s. Agricultural output, still a very important component of the Bulgarian economy, fell by 5.1 per cent in 1987, and by 0.1 per cent in 1988. National income fell in 1989 by 0.4 per cent, the volume of exports to the West by 3.4 per cent. The net debt to the West rose from 5.9 billion dollars in 1988 to 9.3 billion dollars in 1989. A kaleidoscopic spectrum of dissidence and opposition emerged in 1989: from hunger strikes by the Turkish minority to demonstrations by the ecological pressure group Ecoglasnost. There was also an independent trade union, *Podkrepa* (Support), a Club for the Support of Perestroika and Glasnost, and a Committee for the Defence of Religious Rights.

Mladenov and his faction in the BCP decided to forestall what was coming by measures of defensive liberalisation. Zhivkov was overthrown by a palace coup on 10 November. A rapid series of concessions followed, including the promise of free elections. In January 1990, at its Fourteenth Congress, the BCP adopted the name 'Bulgarian Socialist Party' and committed itself to multi-party democracy and a 'socially oriented market economy'. This promising strategy ultimately failed because, firstly, the party was suspected of being incapable of renouncing violent methods (the relative fairness of the June 1990 elections which the BSP won was cancelled out in many people's minds by the discovery of a video recording showing President Mladenov calling for the use of tanks against demonstrators); and, secondly, the transition to a market economy destroyed any support the party retained among the industrial workers. In November 1990 the BSP government of Andrei Lukanov was forced to resign by a general strike jointly conducted by *Podkrepa* and the former official communist trade union. The opposition United Democratic Front was brought into a coalition government; the leader of the opposition, Zhelyu Zhelev, had already been made President in August. The new government then proceeded with the usual package of price increases, removal of subsidies, privatisation and decollectivisation. Further elections, in October 1991, resulted in a defeat for the BSP and its complete removal from office. Thus the transition to post-communism was made relatively smoothly and peacefully in Bulgaria.

Romania, in contrast, suffered from a series of special factors which made a violent dénouement inevitable. The regime of Nicolae Ceauşescu was both incurably Stalinist and fiercely repressive. In this respect Romania did not differ from Albania. Ceauşescu's own personal rule heightened the tensions, however. Alone among Eastern European rulers, he took pride in paying off his country's debts. This could only be done with the most extreme austerity measures. Moreover, the earthquake of 1977, centred on the country's oilfields, caused a drop in oil production from 14.7m. tonnes in 1979 to 11.5m. in 1980 and 10.7m. in 1985. As a result, Romania became a net importer of oil from the West. It was therefore severely affected by the 1979 increase in world prices. The attempt to replace oil with coal was a failure (coal production in 1985 was 46m. tonnes instead of a planned 86m.). The stagnant condition of electrical power generation (68 bn kilowatt hours in 1980; 71.8 bn in 1985) meant that the luckless Romanian consumer was harassed by constant power cuts.[41] Moreover, the range of Romanian exports was severely reduced in the 1980s by Asian competition. Food alone could be exported, and this meant less food for a population which was expanding rapidly, thanks to Ceauşescu's strongly pro-natalist policies. Nationalist demagogy against the Hungarian minority was not an adequate solution. As Jonathan Eyal commented, 'Ceauşescu could offer an endless supply of tricolour flags, but he could not make these flags edible.'[42]

It was the attack on the Hungarian minority which in fact sparked off the crisis in Romania. Ceauşescu's policy of 'systematisation' involved the destruction of half the country's villages and the relocation of the inhabitants in towns where they could be controlled more easily. The process was actually started in purely Romanian areas close to Bucharest. But it was in the Hungarian villages of Transylvania that it met with resistance, led by the pastor of Timişoara, László Tőkés. The authorities attempted to remove him from his parish. This sparked off the demonstrations of 15–17 December by Tőkés's parishioners, joined by many other inhabitants of the city, Hungarian and non-Hungarian. Ceauşescu ordered his state security force, the Securitate, to restore order by force. A massacre ensued in which, officially, seventy one people died. There may have been more. The news spread across the country. A feeling of revulsion for the regime grew among the people, including the army, which became increasingly unreliable. Finally, on 21 December, for the first time ever, a stage-managed rally in Bucharest failed to follow the script. Ceauşescu was interrupted by demonstrators. Subsequently large sections of the Romanian army changed sides. In pitched battles over the next four days the army and the people together defeated the Securitate. Power was taken over on 22 December by a National Salvation Front led by Ion Iliescu, not by any means a dissident but a communist who had remained in the Politburo until his removal in 1984. Ceauşescu and his wife were put on trial and quickly shot. The NSF was run by an inner circle of reform-minded communists, and it was concerned above all to stabilise the situation, and to preserve party rule under another name. By the judicious use of nationalist and class demagogy (the killing of Hungarian demonstrators in March 1990, the brutal beating and murder of protest demonstrators by miners brought in for the purpose in June 1990) and elections of a semi-fraudulent character (May 1990) the NSF remained in power. But it did not escape the logic of the process of communist collapse. It was compelled, willy-nilly, to preside over the process of transition. In its programme of March 1991 the NSF described itself as a 'social democratic party committed to the market economy'.

In Albania the same process as elsewhere in the Balkans took place, but with a delay of two years. As in Romania, the regime in place was determined to resist the wind of change. President Ramez Alia reacted to the news of the defection of the writer Ismail Kadare in October 1990 by asserting that 'we have no intention of emulating the rest of Eastern Europe'. Unlike Ceauşescu, however, Alia was prepared to give way to pressure from below. In December 1990 protests by students and workers in all Albanian cities were defused by concessions. The government allowed the formation of independent political parties, and announced that they would be allowed to take part in elections, to be held in March and April 1991. The ruling party, the Albanian Party of Labour, actually won these elections thanks to its support in the countryside, just as the former communists had won the elections of June 1990 in Bulgaria under the name of the Bulgarian Socialist Party. In Albania, as in Bulgaria, a second set of elections (March 1992) 'corrected' the previous year's verdict. Alia resigned as President a few days later (3 April 1992).

The country which remains to be considered, Yugoslavia, remained an exception, just as it had been throughout the epoch of communist rule. Though it shared in many of the other problems of economic stagnation, foreign debt, decline of morale and crumbling of ideological certainties which plagued the communist régimes of Eastern Europe during the 1980s, it was ethnic conflict which actually caused the disintegration of the state. The ethnic problems which affected several other Eastern European states paled into insignificance beside Yugoslavia's. To explain this we must take a short historical detour.

With a population composed in 1948 of Serbs (41.5%), Montenegrins (2.7%), Croats (24.0%), Slovenes (9.0%), Macedonians (5.1%), Muslims of Bosnia-Hercegovina and the Sandjak (5.1%), Albanians (4.8%), Hungarians (3.1%) and other assorted nationalities (4.7%) it displayed greater ethnic diversity than any other European state. The ideological basis of Yugoslavia had been the Yugoslav national idea, but very little progress was made towards creating a sense of 'Yugoslav' nationality in the interwar years. Moreover, the Serbs, who constituted the leading nation in terms of numbers and strength, were never in a position to enforce their will completely on the Croats. The Cvetković-Maček Agreement of 1939 marked Belgrade's recognition that a separate Croat nation existed and had to be given autonomy. Despite this, interethnic hatred subsequently reached depths unequalled elsewhere in Eastern Europe. As we saw earlier, the Communist Party of Yugoslavia drew much of its strength from its multinational, supra-ethnic character, and over much of the subsequent period a genuine attempt was made to resolve ethnic problems in a spirit of concord and unity, except in Kosovo where the claim of the local Albanians for national self-determination was rejected and an armed rebellion suppressed in 1945–6.[43]

Some time in the 1970s this sense of unity collapsed, and the old problems began to rear their heads again, alongside some new ones. The moves of the late 1960s towards decentralisation marked the abandonment of the attempt to create a unified and integrated 'Yugoslav' nation. The 1963 Constitution transferred sovereignty to the nations of the Yugoslav republics, despite the fact that only two of the republics were ethnically homogeneous (Slovenia, which was 96% Slovene, and Montenegro, which was 87% Montenegrin). From now on, Yugoslavia would consist of at least five separate nations. At the Ninth Congress of the LCY in 1969, it was confirmed that the League consisted of eight sections, one for each republic (Serbia, Croatia, Slovenia, Macedonia, Montenegro, Bosnia-Hercegovina) and one for each autonomous province (Vojvodina and Kosovo-Metohija); these sections increasingly represented the particular interests of the local nationality, whether Serb, Croat, Slovene, Macedonian or Montenegrin.[44] The situation was further complicated by the recognition in 1968 of two further nationalities. The Bosnian CC accepted the Muslims as a nationality in their own right (previously they had been forced to define themselves as Serbs or Croats),[45] and the Serbian Central Committee allowed the Albanians of Kosovo-Metohija to take charge of their own province, renamed Kosovo (in Albanian: Kosova), thereby beginning a process of political and cultural emancipation which continued until 1981.

Centralist elements in the party leadership, led by Tito himself, found these moves towards the creation of a genuine, rather than a sham, federation disquieting. In addition, the emancipation of Kosovo was perceived by nationalistically-inclined Serbs as an attack on them. The crisis of 1971, when Tito intervened against Croat national communists, was one warning sign. The second one was the conflict over Kosovo, which blew up in 1981, shortly after death removed Tito's restraining hand (May 1980). With every decade that passed, the proportion of ethnic Albanians in this province of Serbia increased. But at the same time it was falling behind the rest of the country economically. In 1991 the ratio between Gross Domestic Product per capita in Kosovo and in Slovenia was 1:7·5. Kosovo's severe and increasing economic backwardness, combined with a degree of harassment of the Serbian minority, led Serbians to leave the province in droves. Those who stayed behind had a lower birth rate than the majority community. In 1953 Kosovo was 65% Albanian. By 1990 the proportion was 90%. In 1981 the Kosovan Albanians demanded that their province be upgraded to the status of a Yugoslav republic, worthy of standing beside Slovenia or Croatia or Serbia itself. The reply of the Serbian police to the Kosovo demonstrations of 1981 and later was brutal; over 3 000 Albanians were arrested and 100 killed between 1981 and 1985 in the province.

The Kosovo issue was the nodal point around which the forces making for the disintegration of Yugoslavia on ethnic lines crystallized. The man who can be regarded as the embodiment of Serbian nationalism, Slobodan Milošević, came to power in and through the Kosovo question. The year 1986 saw two major developments: the election of Milošević as head of the Serbian section of the LCY (in May) and the publication, unauthorised by its authors, of the Memorandum of the Serbian Academy of Arts and Sciences on the Condition of Yugoslovia (September).[46] This document, 'the blueprint for . . . the 1991–92 war',[47] was an appropriate accompaniment to the ascent of Milošević to supreme power, for it condemned the whole of the previous nationality policy of the Yugoslav communist movement as fundamentally anti-Serb, and singled out in particular the failure of the LCY to oppose the 'neo-fascist aggression coming from across the border', which was the authors' way of describing the Albanian demonstrations in Kosovo. 'Genocide' was being practised against Serbs in Kosovo and the Belgrade leadership was doing nothing to oppose this. While the liberal party boss of Belgrade, Pavlović, immediately condemned the Memorandum, Milošević took up its main themes as the slogans of a demagogic campaign among the Kosovo Serbs. His speech of 27 April 1987 at Kosovo Polje was a fateful moment. He made himself the spokesman not just of the Kosovo Serbs but of ethnic Serbs everywhere in Yugoslavia. The combination of an appeal to nationalism and to a return to traditional communist values was irresistible within the Serbian part of the LCY, and in September 1987 at the 8th. Central Committee Plenum the conservative-nationalist wing completely routed the liberals. Pavlović and the former party leader Stambolić were both removed from the party presidency and the Central Committee and subsequently expelled from the party altogether.

There followed a period of orchestrated mass rallies all over Serbia, of purges of unreliable liberals, and of furious press campaigns against 'Albanian irredentism'. The final stage was reached in March 1989 when the Serbian Assembly approved a new constitution abrogating the autonomy of both Kosovo and Vojvodina, thereby 'returning sovereignty to Serbia' as the Belgrade newspaper *Politika* put it.[48] This change in the Yugoslav constitution, carried out unilaterally by Serbia, in its turn gave a strong impulse to tendencies towards separatism in Slovenia and Croatia. In September 1989 the Slovene Assembly, although it was still dominated by the League of Communists, declared Slovenia to be a 'sovereign and independent state' deleted the 'leading role of the league' from the constitution, and insisted on Slovenia's right to veto the use of armed force on its territory. It went on to set a date of April 1990 for multi-party elections. Yugoslavia could now disintegrate in two ways: by the ending of communist rule, and by the fragmentation of the League of Communists itself into its different national components. The LCY was the first to go, at a special party congress held on 20 January 1990. The Slovene delegates walked out in protest against the failure of the majority to accept their proposals for a multi-party system, the complete confederalisation of Yugoslavia, the abolition of democratic centralism and the introduction of democracy in Kosovo. All other delegates except the Serbs and the Montenegrins refused to continue the congress. With this the LCY in effect ceased to be a single entity. In the course of 1990 a series of free elections underlined the division of the country into separate national units. These elections made the unelected federal presidency of the old Yugoslavia an irrelevance. Non-communists (or at least ex-communists) came to power everywhere except in Serbia and Montenegro. In Serbia Milošević and his renamed Serbian Socialist Party were returned in December 1990 with a large majority (77% of the vote). Milošević was prepared ultimately to let Slovenia get out of Yugoslavia, but not Croatia. If Croatia tried to leave, he said, Serbia's borders would be 'an open political question'.[49]

With the declaration of independence by Slovenia and Croatia (June 1991) the future of Yugoslavia left the arena of political discussion and entered that of military force. The Serbian point of view was that if Yugoslavia was to be divided up, it would be on ethnic lines. Hence the Serb minorities in non-Serbian republics would have the right either to separate status or unity with Serbia. In many areas ethnic mixture made unfairness inevitable; the Serbs made sure that no-one was unfair to them, thanks to their control of the Yugoslav army, which had in fact increased during the 1980s.[50] Where geographically viable Serb areas did not exist they were created through the process of 'ethnic cleansing'. There was no effective opposition to this policy at home, since Milošević's main opponent, Drašković, was as strongly in favour of it as he was. Nor was there effective opposition abroad, since the international community was unprepared to go further than exerting moral pressure. The decision to recognise Bosnia-Hercegovina as an independent state and admit it to the United Nations (April 1992) simply hastened the coming of a three-cornered civil war there, between the Bosnian Muslim majority and the Serb and Croat minorities.[51]

What, then, has emerged from this account of the collapse of communism in Eastern Europe? The following points may be made by way of a conclusion:

(1)   Certain weaknesses in the structure of the Eastern European communist states were accentuated in the course of the 1980s. This applies especially in the economic and cultural spheres.

(2)   The dissident opposition movements were not strong enough to overcome the regimes by themselves, but they were growing in strength everywhere in the late 1980s.

(3)   External forces were of great importance in pushing the ruling élites of Eastern Europe towards a surrender of their position. Gorbachev's personal role was significant, but also the growing disintegration of the Soviet Union played a part. Direct pressure from the West was of little importance. In contrast, the indirect impact of growing economic and cultural interdependence was vital.

(4)   The precise mode of the abandonment of power varied from country to country – it was voluntary in some cases, done under tremendous pressure in others. Where it was voluntary, communist élites were able to retain some power in the new post-communist era. Tremendous changes in the political scene and the organisation of the economy masked a fundamental continuity in social structure.

(5)   The transformation was accomplished largely without violence except in Romania – and there the extent of the transformation itself remains in doubt.

(6)   The so-called revolutions of 1989–90 resemble a chain reaction rather than a simultaneous cataclysm. The 'demonstration effect', and the availability of full information on events in neighbouring countries, often in the form of television images, helped to spark off each of the movements.

One final comment needs making. The dissident movements which pressed for change throughout the 1980s on a broad range of issues, including alongside political freedom the reduction of armaments, the protection of the environment and an improvement in the condition of life for the mass of the people, were to find that their broader aims were often slow to be realised in the new post-communist environment. Problems the communists had sometimes wrestled with, sometimes themselves created, continued to exist. With the collapse of their old opponent, the dissident coalitions either split into their component parts or disappeared from the scene completely. Elections everywhere produced new governments, which were faced with some surprises and some disappointments in their attempts to combine a functioning democratic political system with a privatised and marketised economy, while moving towards economic recovery and the thorough integration of their countries into the global world system. History, far from coming to an end, continued to unfold in Eastern Europe, in ways I have tried to summarise above in the Introduction to the Second Edition.

ACHIEVEMENTS AND FAILURES OF EASTERN EUROPEAN COMMUNISM

It is no doubt too early to draw a balance of this sad epoch in the history of the region; still, the attempt must be made. This book has stressed the difficulties and problems of communist rule, and the towering events of 1989 have thrown a large shadow backwards, just as books written about Tsarist Russia have tended until recently to see its history as a prelude to the Bolshevik Revolution. Yet the communist regimes of the period between 1948 and 1989 were able to point to a number of achievements, on which their successors might well have built, although they are far more likely to destroy them. Here I shall comment very briefly on the progress made in national income, standard of living, social equality, and education during the four decades of communist rule; an adequate study of these matters would naturally require a separate book.

National income grew very satisfactorily all over Eastern Europe until the very end of the communist period, as Tables 3 and 4 indicate. Quantitative growth of this kind was of course part of the *raison d'être* of the communist system. It mattered very much to the rulers of Eastern Europe that successive economic plans were 'fulfilled' and 'overfulfilled'. But once the decision had been made, after 1953, to abandon overt Stalinist terror the consent of the ruled became an important objective as well. Columns of production figures in the newspapers would not be effective. In fact visible progress was achieved, even for the ordinary citizen. The standard of living, after declining in the years of high Stalinism up to 1953, underwent a well-nigh continuous improvement after that.[52] This was partly a result of the process of economic development and modernisation itself, which inevitably involved a population shift from country to town (only in the already highly urbanised GDR did the proportion of town-dwellers remain static throughout the period, at roughly three quarters) and from agricultural to industrial employment. Here was a vital social change which transformed the face of the region.[53]

The rising standard of living allowed improvements in diet, with a progressive move away from cereals and potatoes to meat, milk and sugar.

On the other hand, the failure of the system to provide adequate supplies of consumer goods meant that much of the improved personal income was simply salted away in savings accounts.

Moreover, improvements in the overall standard of living were accompanied by the rise of a new inequality between the classes, after the rigid egalitarian measures of the Stalin era had lost their strength. Differentiation took place among the former peasants and workers who had 'risen to the foreground' and, Matejko claims, 'ousted the higher levels of society' under Stalin.[54] Having reached the top, these members of the formerly oppressed classes made sure they stopped there, and passed on their privileges to their descendants. 'Economic reform', writes J. F. Brown, 'has been the motor of the new inequality in Eastern Europe'. The more radical the economic reform, the greater the inequality. According to Ivan Völgyes over a quarter of Hungarians were below the poverty level in 1983.[55]

The idea of equality between women and men was deeply embedded in Marxist-Leninist theory. Measures to secure this were enshrined in the constitutions of the Eastern European states. There were considerable, but incomplete, achievements in this sphere.[56] Let us take some examples from Czechoslovakia. Far more women went out to work than before (the female participation rate in labour rose from 54 per cent in 1950 to 85 per cent in 1970); women broke into previously all-male occupations (by 1970 46 per cent of specialists with higher education were women); more women were educated (between 1954 and 1965 the number of girls in secondary schools rose 114 per cent, while that of boys only rose by 16 per cent). The increase in female employment was somewhat facilitated by improved childcare arrangements. The number of crèches increased from 268 in 1948 to 1526 in 1964, the number of kindergartens from 4664 in 1948 to 7569 in 1965. The picture for relative income (which remained roughly static from 1946 to 1970) and for chances of promotion (again static throughout the period) was not so bright.

One way of improving the quality of life especially for women is to reduce family size. The communist regimes did not impose restrictions on birth control, but it always had a low priority. Hence by 1970 only six per cent of women in Czechoslovakia used modern methods of contraception, and the proportion would be lower for most other Eastern European countries. The main methods of birth control remained *coitus interruptus* and abstinence, and where these failed, abortion. In the Stalin era this was illegal, since a highly pro-natalist outlook prevailed. Changes came as part of de-Stalinisation. Abortion was legalised everywhere in the late 1950s (Bulgaria, Hungary, Poland, Romania in 1956, Czechoslovakia in 1957, the GDR in 1972, Yugoslavia in 1960). Later on, worries about the falling birth-rate led to a reversion to 'pro-natalist programmes' in many cases, which were sometimes negative in approach (making abortion harder to obtain) sometimes positive (increases in maternity leave and in family allowances).[57]

Education was another communist priority, though in many cases expansion had already been put in hand by the coalitions of 1945–8. The distinctive communist contribution was to use education as an engine of social change. Since there were no fees, and maintenance grants were paid, the sons and daughters of workers and peasants had a greater chance of progressing to higher levels. In the early years there was also positive educational discrimination in favour of working-class children. In Poland, for instance, as a result of these factors, the proportion of students of working-class and peasant origin rose from 11 per cent in 1946 to 63 per cent in 1950. Conversely, the proportion of children from professional families who graduated fell from 35.5 per cent in 1935–6 to 1.2 per cent in 1960–1. All over Eastern Europe there was a tremendous growth in the number and proportion of children undergoing education. Illiteracy was practically wiped out everywhere.[58]

Yet all these improvements in the situation of the mass of the people of Eastern Europe had the opposite effect from the one anticipated. The success achieved in increasing industrial production at any cost eventually fuelled ecological protest movements because of the resultant adverse impact on the environment. The continuous increase in the standard of living and the level of real wages created bitterness instead of gratitude, because there was nothing to spend the money on. Inability to supply appropriate consumer goods remained the Achilles' heel of the communist regimes. Cheap food was taken for granted. The structure of the welfare state was taken for granted. Security of employment was taken for granted. Educational opportunities were taken for granted. The growth of education widened people's horizons and raised expectations which could not be satisfied under the existing system, and seemed to be satisfied in the West.

Finally, the apparent permanence of a large and parasitic bureaucracy, enjoying privileges which increased in proportion as liberalising reforms were made in the economic system, deprived the communist regimes of any vestigial legitimacy they had possessed under the pseudo-egalitarian reign of terror which prevailed in the early 1950s. The revolutions of 1989 overthrew a structure which had long been hollowed out from within.

Appendix:
Statistical Tables

Table 1: Areas, population and agricultural employment

Country	Area (1000 sq. km.)	Population, millions			Agricultural Employment, per cent		
		1948	1968	1988	1939	1967	1989
Albania	28.8	1.2	2.0	3.1	80		49
Bulgaria	110.9	7.1	8.4	9.0	80	42	13
CSSR	127.9	12.3	14.4	15.6	26	19	10
GDR	108.3	19.1	17.1	16.7	23	16	8
Hungary	93.0	9.2	10.3	10.6	51	30	12
Poland	312.7	24.0	32.3	37.9	65	40	22
Romania	237.5	15.9	19.7	23.0	80	54	21
Yugoslavia	255.8	15.9	20.0	23.6	76	57	23

SOURCES: Spulber, *Economics*, p. 5; D. H. Aldcroft, *The European Economy*, (London, 1987), p. 213; *FAO Production Yearbook*, vol. 44, 1990, pp. 30–3; *Economic History of Eastern Europe*, vol. 1, p. 206.

Table 2: The movement of real wages (percentage growth per annum, five-year averages)

Country	1951–5	1956–60	1961–5	1966–70	1971–5	1976–80	1981–5	1986–9
Bulgaria	10.3[1]	6.1	1.9	5.4	3.0	0.5	2.2	2.1
CSSR	1.7	4.6	1.2	3.5	3.4	0.7	1.0	1.5
GDR	11.2	7.4	2.5	3.7	3.8	4.4	2.0	2.4
Hungary	0.8	8.0	1.7	3.5	3.4	0.7	1.0	2.3
Poland	1.7	5.1	1.5	1.9	7.3	2.0	–3.4	5.7
Romania	4.0	8.2	4.1	3.5	3.7	6.1	1.5	1.2
Yugoslavia	1.0	8.0	5.4	7.4	1.0	3.1	–4.7[2]	4.5

1 Average of 1953–5.
2 1979–85, from Lydall, *Yugoslavia in Crisis*, p. 41
SOURCES: Brus, *Economic History*, III, pp. 64, 95, 150 and 152; *Economic Survey of Europe*, 1981, p. 263.

Appendix

Table 3: The growth of the gross national product (GNP)

(Average annual growth rate of the gross national product at constant prices)

	Bulgaria	CSSR	GDR	Hungary	Poland	Romania	Yugoslavia	E. Europe
1950–65	7.1	4.8	5.6	4.7	6.2	7.7	9.2	5.8
1965–70	4.7	3.5	3.2	3.1	3.8	4.0	6.3	3.8
1970–75	4.5	3.4	3.5	3.4	6.6	6.2	4.6	4.8
1975–80	1.2	2.2	2.4	2.3	0.9	1.4	5.8	2.3
1980–85	0.9	1.4	1.8	0.9	1.2	1.2	1.3	1.3
1985–89	0.7	1.5	1.4	0.9	0.2	0.3	0.4	0.7

SOURCES: UN Economic Commission for Europe, *Economic Survey of Europe,* 1969, pt. 1, p. 42; T. P. Alton, *Research Project on National Income in East Central Europe. Occasional Paper No. 110,* (New York, 1990), table 18, p. 28.

Table 4: The growth of the net material product (NMP)

(Average annual growth rate of the net material product at constant prices)

	Albania	Bulgaria	CSSR	GDR	Hungary	Poland	Romania	Yugoslavia
1951–55		8.1	6.9	13.0	4.6	6.6	12.6	4.2
1956–60	7.0	9.6	7.0	7.1	6.0	6.5	6.6	8.0
1961–65	5.8	6.6	1.9	3.4	4.1	6.2	9.1	6.9
1966–70	9.2	8.8	7.0	5.2	6.8	6.0	11.2	
1971–75	6.6	7.8	5.5	5.4	6.2	9.8	11.3	5.7
1976–80	2.7	6.1	3.6	4.1	2.8	1.2	8.5	5.6
1981–85	2.0	3.7	1.8	4.5	1.3	–.8	–.2	0.6
1986–89	1.7	3.1	2.0	3.1	0.8	3.0	–1.3	1.4

SOURCES: for 1951–75, Brus, *Eastern Europe*, vol. 3, pp. 19, 95, 150, 152; for 1976–85, *Comecon Data 1989*, London, 1990, p. 56; for 1986–9, *Statisticheskiy Ezhegodnik Stran-Chlenov S.E.V.*, (Moscow, 1990), pp. 6–15.

Table 5: The socialisation of agriculture

Percentage of arable land in collective farms (1) and state and collective farms together (2)

Country	1950 (1)	1950 (2)	1953 (1)	1953 (2)	1956 (1)	1956 (2)	1960 (1)	1960 (2)	1975 (1)	1975 (2)	1985 (1)	1985 (2)
Albania	3	8	8	13	28	37	69	82	78	100	70	100
Bulgaria	11	13	53	56	65	72	80	91		90		90
Czechoslovakia	14	23	40	54	37	48	84	87	61	91	63	94
GDR	–	5	–	5	22	29	84	90	82	90	83	91
Hungary	3	7	26	39	22	39	60	77	70	85	72	87
Poland	2	13	7	19	10	23	1	13	2	19	4	22
Romania	3	12	8	21	18	31	61	84	54	84	55	85
Yugoslavia	18	24	21[1]	24[1]	4	10[2]	1	10		17		20

Percentage of agricultural land: (1) 1952; (2) 1955.

SOURCES: Brus, *Economic History*, III, pp. 52, 80 (tables 24.5 and 25.1); *Statisticheskiy Ezhegodnik Stran-Chlenov S.E.V.*, 1976, p. 186, and 1986, p. 168; N. Spulber, *The Economics of Communist Eastern Europe*, (Cambridge, Massachusetts, 1957), pp. 254–61.

Notes

1 INTRODUCTION

1. O. Halecki, *The Limits and Divisions of European History*, (London, 1950), p. 135.
2. François Fejtö excluded East Germany (the 'German Democratic Republic') from the first volume of his history of Eastern Europe (*Histoire des démocraties populaires*, Paris, 1952) but was forced to include it in the second (*A History of the People's Democracies*, London, 1971).
3. Manuscript, 'Political Change in Post-War Poland', as quoted by W. Brus, 'Stalinism and the "People's Democracies"', R. C. Tucker, (ed.), *Stalinism – Essays in Historical Interpretation*, (New York, 1977), p. 248.
4. As Dimitrov put it in a telegram of 1941 to the Yugoslav communist partisans, quoted by J. Marjanović in *Komunist* (Belgrade), January 1951, p. 116.
5. Ernst Fischer, writing in the official journal of the Communist International in October 1942, quoted in J. B. Urban, *Moscow and the Italian Communist Party*, (London, 1986), p. 158.
6. Quoted by N. Davies, 'Poland', in M. McCauley, (ed.), *Communist Power in Europe 1944–49*, (Macmillan, 1977), p. 47.
7. M. Djilas, *Conversations with Stalin*, (London, 1962), p. 90.
8. *Documents on Polish–Soviet Relations*, vol. 2, (London, 1969), p. 432, conversation of 18 October 1944. This is the official record of the conversation. Regrettably, I have found no trace either there or in Mikołajczyk's memoirs of Stalin's alleged remark that 'Communism fits Poland like a saddle fits a cow'.
9. J. K. Hoensch, *Sowjetische Osteuropa-Politik 1945–1975*, (Düsseldorf, 1977), p. 14.
10. According to Révai's own account, given later on, at the founding conference of the Cominform (*Informatsionnoye Soveshchaniye Predstaviteley Nekotorykh Kompartiy v Pol'she v Kontse Sentyabrya 1947 Goda*, (Moscow, 1948), p. 273).

2 THE SEIZURE OF POWER: THE NORTHERN TIER

1. The whole period of the communist seizure of power in Poland is the subject of Krystyna Kersten's massive study *The Establishment of Communist Rule in Poland 1943–1948* (Oxford, 1991), first published in Polish in 1984.
2. Quoted in M. K. Dziewanowski, *The Communist Party of Poland*, (Cambridge, Massachusetts, 1977), p. 385.
3. W. Gomułka, in *Nowe Drogi*, Sept.–Oct. 1948, p. 45.
4. A. Polonsky and B. Drukier, *The Beginnings of Communist Rule in Poland*, (London, 1980), p. 14.
5. Polonsky and Drukier, op. cit., pp. 203–7; J. Coutividis and J. Reynolds, *Poland 1939–1947*, (Leicester, 1986), p. 131.

204   *Notes to Chapter 2, pp. 8–17*

6. J. Pawłowicz, *Strategia frontu narodowego PPR*, (Warsaw, 1965), p. 170.
7. *Polska Partia Robotnicza. Dokumenty Programowe 1942–1948*, (Warsaw, 1984), pp. 554–61.
8. Coutividis and Reynolds, op. cit., p. 148.
9. W. Gomułka, *Artykuły i przemówienia*, (Warsaw, 1962), I, p. 281.
10. Coutividis and Reynolds, op. cit., pp. 167–8.
11. J. Gołębiowski, *Nacjonalizacja przemysłu w Polsce*, (Warsaw, 1965), p. 112; see also J. Reynolds, 'Communists, Socialists and Workers', *Soviet Studies*, 30, 4, Oct. 1978, 519–20; and Polonsky and Drukier, op. cit., pp. 39, 393.
12. W. Gomułka, a speech of 27 May 1945, in *Artykuły*, I, pp. 265–7; Reynolds, art. cit., p. 522.
13. Coutividis and Reynolds, op. cit., pp. 179–80.
14. Reynolds, art. cit., p. 522.
15. Gomułka, *Artykuły*, I, pp. 215–16.
16. Coutividis and Reynolds, op. cit., p. 240.
17. Coutividis and Reynolds, op. cit., p. 280.
18. Hoensch, op. cit., p. 28.
19. A. Korbonski, *Politics of Socialist Agriculture in Poland: 1945–1960*, (New York, 1965), p. 131.
20. C. Klessmann, 'Betriebsräte, Gewerkschaften und Arbeiterselbstverwaltung in Polen', *Jahrbücher für die Geschichte Osteuropas*, NF, vol. 29, 2, 1981, pp. 197–203.
21. Reynolds, art. cit., pp. 530–6; J. Malara and L. Rey, *La Pologne d'une Occupation à l'autre (1944–52)*, (Paris, 1952), pp. 134–5.
22. J. Bloomfield, *Passive Revolution: Politics and the Czechoslovak Working Class*, (London, 1979), p. 96.
23. K. Kaplan, *The Short March: the Communist Takeover in Czechoslovakia*, (London, 1987), p. 53, n. 17.
24. Bloomfield, op. cit., p. 101.
25. Kaplan, *Short March*, p. 53, n. 17.
26. Bloomfield, op. cit., p. 171.
27. P. E. Zinner, *Communist Strategy and Tactics in Czechoslovakia, 1918–48*, (New York, 1963), p. 162.
28. Z. Hejzlar, *Reformkommunismus. Zur Geschichte der Kommunistischen Partei der Tschechoslowakei*, (Cologne 1976), p. 37.
29. Bloomfield, op. cit., p. 202.
30. Kaplan, *Short March*, p. 15.
31. Hejzlar, op. cit., p. 31.
32. Text of the Košice Programme, in S. Schröder-Laskowski, *Der Kampf um die Macht in der Tschechoslowakei*, (Berlin, 1978), pp. 189–205.
33. K. Kaplan, *Znárodnění a socialismus*, (Prague, 1968), p. 110.
34. Speaking in December 1944, as quoted in M. Bouček, M. Klimeš, and M. Vartiková, *Program Revoluce*, (Prague, 1975), p. 235. The Slovaks also wanted to loosen their connection with Czechoslovakia, it should be added.
35. K. Gottwald, *Spisy*, vol. 12, (Prague, 1955), pp. 253–4.
36. Kaplan, *Short March*, p. 59.
37. Bloomfield, op. cit., p. 154.
38. Speaking to the September 1946 Plenum of the CC (Gottwald, *Spisy*, vol. 13, pp. 230–31).

39. Gottwald, *Spisy*, vol. 12, p. 83.
40. Kaplan, *Short March*, pp. 52, 62; P. Tigrid, 'The Prague Coup of 1948: the Elegant Takeover', in T. T. Hammond (ed.), *The Anatomy of Communist Takeovers*, (London, 1975), p. 420.
41. L. Kalinová, 'K poúnorovým změnám ve složení řídícího aparátu', *Revue Dějin Socialismu*, 4, 1969, p. 488.
42. Kaplan, *Short March*, p. 15.
43. *Foreign Relations of the US*, [FRUS], 1947, vol. 4, dispatch, 18 June 1947.
44. P. Tigrid, 'Prague Coup', p. 405; K. Kaplan, 'Úvahy o nevyhnutelností února', in *Svědectví*, 55, 1978, pp. 346–7.
45. Kaplan, *Short March*, p. 73.
46. F. Fejtö, *Le Coup de Prague 1948*, (Paris, 1976), quoting J. Švec, unpublished MS, pp. 206–7; extracts in Kaplan, *Short March*, p. 75.
47. See below, p. 33, for the criticisms made of the Hungarian communists at Szklarska Poręba.
48. M. Bouček, *Praha v únoru 1948*, (Prague, 1963), p. 16.
49. Fejtö, *Le Coup de Prague*, p. 96.
50. Kaplan, *Short March*, pp. 76–7.
51. J. Belda et al., *Na Rozhraní Dvou Epoch*, (Prague, 1968), pp. 196–7.
52. K. Gottwald, *Spisy*, vol. 14, (Prague, 1958), p. 192 (speaking at the November Plenum of the CC).
53. V. Pavlíček, 'Únor 1948', *Právník*, 3, 1968, p. 187.
54. Kaplan, *Short March*, p. 179.
55. Tigrid, art. cit., p. 423.
56. Kaplan, *Short March*, p. 175.
57. V. Kopecký, *ČSR a KSČ*, (Prague, 1980), p. 412; J. Veselý, 'K historii vzniku LM', in J. Sýkora (ed.), *Pražské milice v Únoru*, (Prague, 1964), pp. 33–9.
58. Fejtö, *Le Coup de Prague*, p. 154 (quoting Švec).
59. Tigrid, art. cit., p. 426.
60. Extracts from the resolution are printed in Bloomfield, op. cit., pp. 224–5.
61. J. Mlýnský, 'Úloha akčních výborů NF při zajišt'ování únorového vitězství', in *Sborník historický*, December 1964, p. 134.
62. J. Korbel, *The Communist Subversion of Czechoslovakia*, (Princeton 1959), p. 227, quoting J. Veselý, *Kronika únorových dnů 1948*, (Prague, 1958), pp. 122–3.
63. A directive of 26 February from the CC of the CPCz giving instructions to the Action Committees on purging all 'rightist elements' is printed in V. Král, *Cestou k únoru*, (Prague, 1963), pp. 411–12.
64. K. Kaplan, *Die politischen Prozesse in der Tschechoslowakei 1948–54*, (Munich, 1986), pp. 60–2.
65. J. Neumannová, 'K poúnorovým proměnám kulturní politiky', *Revue dějin socialismu*, 6, 1968, p. 821. On the degree of state control of the economy, see J. Krejči, 'The Czechoslovak Economy during the Years of Systemic Transformation 1945–49', *Jahrbuch der Wirtschaft Osteuropas*, Bd. 7, 1977, pp. 314–71.
66. H. Krisch, *German Politics under Soviet Occupation*, (New York, 1974), pp. 101–73.
67. R. Steininger, *Deutsche Geschichte 1945–1961*, vol. 1, (Frankfurt, 1983), p. 155.

68. D. Staritz, *Die Gründung der DDR*, (Munich, 1974), p. 6.
69. *Protokoll der I.Parteikonferenz der SED, 25. bis 28.Januar in Berlin*, (Berlin 1949), p. 333. The date of this speech should be noted. Grotewohl was rejecting 'people's democracy' in its new, post-1948 version, which encompassed a transition to full socialism and the dictatorship of the proletariat.
70. D. Staritz, *Geschichte der DDR 1949–1985*, (Frankfurt, 1985), p. 77.

3 THE SEIZURE OF POWER: HUNGARY AND THE AGRARIAN SOUTH

1. The events of the war altered this situation in Yugoslavia, but one should note Djilas's comment: 'When we got into Belgrade we encountered not one – literally not one – member of the party.' (M. Djilas, *Wartime*, London, 1977, p. 419).
2. A. Fontaine, *History of the Cold War*, vol. 1, (London, 1968), p. 212.
3. B. Kovrig, *Communism in Hungary: from Kun to Kádár*, (Stanford, California, 1979), p. 180.
4. Kovrig, op. cit., p. 159.
5. Kovrig, op. cit., p. 157.
6. I. Lahav, *Der Weg der KPU*, vol. 1, (Munich, 1985), p. 104.
7. Lahav, op. cit., vol. 1, p. 112.
8. Kovrig, op. cit., pp. 172–4.
9. F. Nagy, *The Struggle Behind the Iron Curtain*, (New York, 1948), p. 154.
10. Kovrig, op. cit., p. 193; H. Seton-Watson, *Nationalism and Communism*, (London, 1964), p. 107.
11. Kovrig, op. cit., p. 189.
12. Polonsky and Drukier, op. cit., p. 424.
13. E. Reale, 'The Founding of the Cominform', in M. Drachkovitch, and B. Lazitch (eds), *The Comintern – Historical Highlights*, (New York, 1966), p. 255.
14. G. Schöpflin, 'Hungary', in M. McCauley (ed.), *Communist Power in Europe 1944–1949*, (London, 1977), p. 105.
15. In a speech in 1952, quoted in W. Juhász, (ed.), *Hungarian Social Science Reader*, Munich, 1965, p. 150. It should be added that Zoltán Pfeiffer, of the Smallholders' Party, claimed that he invented the term himself in 1946, illustrating it to the President with a salami brought for the purpose. (C. Gati, *Hungary and the Soviet Bloc*, Durham, North Carolina, 1986, p. 22).
16. A. Bán, 'Hungary', in D. Healey (ed.), *The Curtain Falls: the Story of the Socialists in Eastern Europe*, (London, 1951), p. 73.
17. Lahav, op. cit., vol. 2, p. 268.
18. Kovrig, op. cit., p. 223.
19. Berry to US Secretary of State, 12 December 1944, FRUS, 1944, 4, pp. 280–1.
20. It also misled some later historians: 'The Russians held down radical local communists and supported King Michael.' (G. Kolko, *The Politics of War*, New York, 1968, p. 404).
21. Berry to Secretary of State, 19 Feb. 1945; and telegram of 23 Jan. 1945, FRUS, 1945, 5, pp. 469–71. General Rădescu himself contributed to the crisis of February 1945 by dismissing his communist under-secretary at the Minis-

ter of the Interior, Teohari Georgescu. (V. Georgescu, *The Romanians, A History*, London, 1991, p. 228).
22. FRUS, 1945, 5, pp. 488–502.
23. FRUS, 1945, 5, p. 489.
24. FRUS, 1945, 2, p. 510. Another motive for King Michael's surrender to Soviet pressure was his wish to recover Northern Transylvania, disputed between Romania and Hungary, which had been placed under Soviet administration in November 1944. (V. Georgescu, *The Romanians*, pp. 228–9).
25. Seton-Watson, *Nationalism and Communism*, p. 103.
26. FRUS, 1945, *Potsdam Papers*, I, p. 373.
27. F. Fejtö, *Histoire des démocraties populaires*, (Paris, 1952), pp. 435–6; J. M. Montias, *Economic Development in Communist Rumania*, (Cambridge, Massachusetts, 1967), p. 19.
28. FRUS, 1945, 2, Schuyler to Truman, 3 May 1945, pp. 541–2.
29. Given Tătărescu's political past this word can only be placed in quotation marks.
30. N. Oren, *Revolution Administered: Agrarianism and Communism in Bulgaria*, (Baltimore, 1973), p. 20.
31. N. Oren, *Bulgarian Communism: The Road to Power 1934–44*, (New York, 1971), pp. 167–8.
32. Oren, *Bulgarian Communism*, pp. 216–19.
33. *Pladne* ('Noon') was the name of their newspaper.
34. M. L. Miller, *Bulgaria during the Second World War*, (Stanford, 1975), p. 216; M. M. Boll, *Cold War in the Balkans. American Foreign Policy and the Emergence of Communist Bulgaria 1943–1947*, (Lexington, 1984), p. 60.
35. Oren, *Bulgarian Communism*, pp. 254–6.
36. R. L. Wolff, *The Balkans in our Time*, (Cambridge, Massachusetts, 1956), p. 293. Phyllis Auty gives a higher estimate of 20 000–100 000 in 'Bulgaria', p. 30, R. R. Betts, (ed.), *Central and South-East Europe*, (London, 1950).
37. According to exiled Bulgarian Anarchists writing in *La Bulgarie. Nouvelle Espagne*, (Paris, 1948), p. 21.
38. FRUS, 1944, III, p. 496 (Report by Maynard B. Barnes).
39. Boll, op. cit., p. 68 (letter of 29 November 1944 to Georgiev).
40. S. S. Biryuzov, *Surovye Gody*, (Moscow, 1966), p. 486.
41. Boll, op. cit., p. 89.
42. Byrnes to Barnes, 16 August 1945, FRUS, 1945, 4, p. 283.
43. Barnes to Byrnes, 29 March 1946, FRUS, 1946, 6, pp. 92–4.
44. FRUS, 1946, 6, p. 119, report of 16 July.
45. Fejtö, *Histoire*, p. 109.
46. Boll, op. cit., p. 187.
47. J. F. Brown, *Bulgaria under Communist Rule*, (London, 1970), p. 198.
48. D. Wilson, *Tito's Yugoslavia*, (Cambridge, 1979), p. 28 (quoting Milovan Djilas).
49. F. Singleton, *Twentieth Century Yugoslavia*, (London, 1976), p. 96.
50. P. Shoup, 'The Yugoslav Revolution', in T. T. Hammond, *Anatomy*, p. 255.
51. AVNOJ manifesto of 8 February 1943, printed in *Prvo i Drugo Zasjedenje AVNOJa*, (Belgrade, 1963), pp. 109–10.
52. J. Marjanović, 'Forme borbe i rada KPJ u narodnoj revoluciji', *Komunist* (Belgrade), Jan. 1951, p. 140.

53. P. Auty, *Tito, A Biography*, (London, 1970), p. 231.
54. FRUS, 1945, Potsdam Papers, II, p. 208.
55. V. Koštunica and K. Čavoški, *Party Pluralism and Monism. Social Movements and the Political System in Yugoslavia 1944–49*, (New York, 1985), p. 60. This is a translation of a work published legally in Belgrade.
56. Kostunica and Čavoski, op. cit., p. 63.
57. The official historian Branko Petranović was still in 1979 justifying the suppression of opposition newspapers on the basis that 'the country was in a revolutionary process of change'.
58. M. Djilas, *Rise and Fall*, (London, 1985), p. 45.
59. Kostunica and Čavoski, op. cit., p. 97.
60. Kostunica and Čavoski, op. cit., p. 177.
61. Fejtö, *Histoire*, p. 168; Wilson, *Tito's Yugoslavia*, p. 52.
62. J. Tomasevich, 'Collectivisation in Yugoslavia', ch. 7 of I. T. Sanders, (ed.), *Collectivisation of Agriculture in Eastern Europe*, (Lexington, 1958).
63. *FRUS*, 1947, IV, p. 842.
64. See the detailed studies by P. R. Prifti, *Socialist Albania since 1944*, (Cambridge, Massachusetts, 1978); N. C. Pano, *The People's Republic of Albania*, (Baltimore, 1968); and B. Tönnes, *Sonderfall Albanien*, (Munich, 1980).

4   HIGH STALINISM

1. D. J. K. Peukert, *The Weimar Republic*, (London, 1991), p. 82.
2. It was published on 1 July 1948 in the Cominform's journal, *For a Lasting Peace, for a People's Democracy*.
3. L. Marcou, *Le Cominform*, (Paris, 1977), p. 221.
4. See K. Kaplan, 'Třídní boje po únoru 1948', *Příspěvky k dějinám KSČ*, 1963, 3, p. 330.
5. Fejtö, *Le Coup de Prague*, p. 216.
6. *For a Lasting Peace, For a People's Democracy*, No. 13, 1 July 1948.
7. *Nowe drogi*, Sept.–Oct. 1948, p. 144.
8. A. Korbonski, *The Politics of Socialist Agriculture in Poland 1945–1960*, (New York, 1965), p. 152.
9. As quoted in Kaplan, 'Třídní boje', p. 328.
10. M. K. Dziewanowski, *The Communist Party of Poland*, 2nd edn, (Cambridge, Massachusetts, 1976), p. 219; R. Hiscocks, *Poland: Bridge for the Abyss?*, (London, 1963), p. 143.
11. Speaking on 15 December 1948 at the Fifth Congress of the Bulgarian Communist Party. See J. K. Hoensch, *Sowjetische Osteuropapolitik 1945–1975*, (Düsseldorf 1977), pp. 28–9.
12. J. F. Brown, *Bulgaria under Communist Rule*, (London, 1970), p. 20.
13. Kovrig, op. cit., p. 257.
14. Hejzlar, op. cit., p. 51.
15. K. Kaplan, 'Zamyšlení nad politickými procesy', *Nová mysl*, 6, 1968, p. 772.
16. K. Kaplan, *Utváření generální linie výstavby socialismu v Československu*, (Prague, 1966), p. 131.
17. J. Kosta, *Abriss der sozialökonomischen Entwicklung der Tschechoslowakei 1945–1977*, (Frankfurt-am-Main, 1978), p. 65; see also S. J. Kirschbaum,

'The Cooperative Movements in Socialist Slovakia', in A. Balawyder (ed.), *Cooperative Movements in Eastern Europe*, (London, 1980).

18. See K.-F. Wädekin, *Sozialistische Agrarpolitik in Osteuropa*, vol. 1, (Berlin, 1974), p. 103.
19. Brus, *Economic History*, vol. 2, p. 593.
20. Kovrig, op. cit., p. 257.
21. Korbonski, op. cit., pp. 153, 157; Hiscocks, *Poland*, p. 154.
22. See Table 5, p. 202; W. Brus, in M. Kaser (ed.), *The Economic History of Eastern Europe 1919–1975*, vol. 3, (Oxford, 1986), p. 9; V. R. Berghahn, *Modern Germany*, (Cambridge, 1987), p. 294.
23. V. Brabec, 'Vztah KSČ a veřejnosti k politickým procesům na počátku padesátých letech', *Revue dějin socialismu*, 1969, 3, p. 374.
24. Korbonski, op. cit., p. 163; Kovrig, op. cit., p. 259; J. R. Lampe, *The Bulgarian Economy in the Twentieth Century*, (London, 1986), p. 148; J. F. Brown, *Bulgaria*, p. 29; V. Georgescu, *The Romanians*, p. 235; Brus, *Economic History*, III, p. 52. Discrepancies in figures for collectivisation arise from differing definitions of cultivable land and cooperative holdings.
25. Kosta, op. cit., p. 70.
26. Korbonski, op. cit., p. 182.
27. J. Rothschild, *Return to Diversity. A Political History of East Central Europe since World War II*, (Oxford, 1989), p. 20.
28. See the discussion on pp. 610–17 of W. Brus, 'Postwar Reconstruction and Socio-Economic Transformation', in chapter 22 of *Economic History*, vol. 2, (Oxford, 1986). See also, on the defeat of the social democratic planners in Poland, J. Drewnowski, 'The Central Planning Office on Trial. The Beginnings of Stalinism in Poland', *Soviet Studies*, 31, 1, 1979, pp. 23–42.
29. K. Kaplan, *The Council for Mutual Economic Aid 1949–1951*, (London, 1979).
30. Kaplan, ibid, pp. 15–16.
31. V. Prucha et. al., *Hospodářske dějiny Československa v 19. a 20. storoči*, (Bratislava, 1974), p. 344.
32. W. Brus, *Economic History*, vol. 3, pp. 19–20.
33. *Economic Survey of Europe since the War*, (Geneva, 1953), table 11, p. 30.
34. Kosta, op. cit., p. 75; V. Brabec, in *Revue dějin socialismu*, 1968, special issue, p. 1066.
35. *Economic History*, vol. 3, p. 19, table 23.3 (official estimates).
36. *Economic History*, vol. 3, pp. 29–34. It should be added that real wages rose in Romania (110 in 1953) and the German Democratic Republic (177 in 1953). 1950 had been a bad year in both countries, so the starting base was low. See E. Hankiss, *East European Alternatives*, (Oxford, 1990), pp. 16–17 for further examples of what he calls 'the appalling and grotesque proliferation of socialist emulation movements' propagated in Hungarian factories in 1952.
37. L. Labedz, 'Sociology and Social Change', in *Survey*, July 1967, p. 34.
38. A. Matejko, *Social Change and Stratification in Eastern Europe*, (New York, 1974), pp. 11–12.
39. K. Kaplan, *Die politischen Prozesse in der Tschechoslowakei 1948–54*, (Munich, 1986), p. 82.
40. Hankiss, op. cit., p. 22. Hankiss, pp. 11–49, is a valuable summary of Hungarian Stalinism in all its aspects.

41. K. Bartošek, 'Les procès politiques 1948–54', *Communisme*, 4, 1983.
42. Kaplan, *Die politischen Prozesse*, p. 70.
43. Hankiss, op. cit., pp. 40–1.
44. Fejtö, *Histoire*, p. 241.
45. In Romania Pătrăşcanu was purged in February 1948 for 'nationalist deviation'. This was connected not with Titoism but with Pătrăşcanu's opposition to the policy of conciliating the Hungarian minority in Transylvania.
46. Kovrig, op. cit., p. 244; G. Litván, 'Nouvelles enquêtes sur le procès Rajk', *Communisme*, 26–7, 1990, pp. 45–52. The ÁVO was renamed ÁVH (State Defence Authority) in December 1949.
47. J. Pelikan, (ed.), *The Czechoslovak Political Trials 1950–54*, (London, 1971), p. 78.
48. M. McCauley, *The German Democratic Republic*, (London, 1983), p. 52.
49. Pelikan, op. cit., p. 106.
50. J. Krulic, 'Affirmation nationale et discours révolutionnaire dans la diplomatie Yougoslave 1945–49', *Revue d'Histoire Moderne et Contemporaine*, t. 38, Jan.–Mar. 1991, pp. 154–67.
51. M. Djilas, *Rise and Fall*, (London, 1985), p. 174.
52. D. Wilson, op. cit., pp. 58–9. M. Djilas, *Tito: the Story from Inside* (New York, 1980), pp. 86–7.
53. D. Rusinow, *The Yugoslav Experiment 1948–74*, (London, 1977).
54. See H. Lydall, *Yugoslavia in Crisis*, (Oxford, 1989), for a discussion of the reasons for Yugoslavia's decline in the 1980s.

5 EASTERN EUROPE AFTER STALIN

1. T. Aczél and T. Méray, *The Revolt of the Mind*, (New York, 1959), p. 159.
2. Published in Hungarian in *Irodalmi Újság* (Paris), 36, 3, pp. 11–14; a French translation appeared in *Communisme*, no. 9, Dec. 1986. The report in which Imre Nagy presented and justified this resolution to the CC on 27 June 1953 was published in English in 1985 in a translation by Bill Lomax, in *Labour Focus on Eastern Europe*, vol. 8, no. 1, pp. 5–14.
3. I. Nagy, *On Communism: In Defence of the New Course*, (London, 1957), p. 275.
4. T. Méray, *Thirteen Days that Shook the Kremlin*, (London, 1959), pp. 25–8.
5. B. Lomax, *Hungary 1956*, (London, 1976), p. 25; Kovrig, op. cit., p. 283.
6. Lomax, op. cit., p. 35.
7. Nagy, op. cit., pp. 57, 15.
8. E. Murphy, 'Higher Education in Communist Hungary 1948–56', *American Slavic and East European Review*, 19, 1960, pp. 395–413.
9. Lomax, op. cit., p. 39.
10. F. Toke, in J.-J. Marie and B. Nagy, (eds) *Pologne–Hongrie 1956*, (Paris, 1966), p. 242.
11. Kovrig, op. cit., p. 296.
12. Kovrig, op. cit., pp. 297–8.
13. The Sixteen Demands, drawn up on the night of 22 October, publicised on the 23rd, are printed in Méray, *Thirteen Days*, pp. 67–8.
14. Lomax, op. cit., pp. 109–10.

15. F. Fehér, and A. Heller, *Hungary 1956 Revisited*, (London, 1983), p. 168.
16. Lomax, op. cit., pp. 140–1.
17. Lomax, op. cit., p. 116.
18. M. Molnár, *Budapest, 1956*, (London, 1971), p. 134.
19. Interview with the Polish journalist Wiktor Woroszylski, quoted by Lomax, op. cit., p. 132.
20. Fehér and Heller, op. cit., p. 146.
21. P. Zinner (ed.), *National Communism and Popular Revolt*, (New York, 1956) pp. 419–20.
22. Nagy, op. cit., pp. 49–50.
23. Molnár, op. cit., p. 98.
24. Zinner, *National Communism*, pp. 428–32.
25. N. S. Khrushchev, *Khrushchev Remembers*, (Boston, 1970), p. 418.
26. C. Gati, *Hungary and the Soviet Bloc*, (Durham, North Carolina, 1986) pp. 147–8.
27. V. Mićunović, *Moscow Diary*, (New York, 1980), pp. 130–42.
28. Lomax, op. cit., p. 144.
29. S. Kopácsi, *In the Name of the Working Class*, (London, 1989), pp. 200–04.
30. Fehér and Heller, op. cit., p. xvii.
31. I. Deutscher, *Russia, China and the West*, (London, 1970), p. 88.
32. J. Mindszenty, *Memoirs of Jozsef Cardinal Mindszenty*, (London, 1975), pp. 331–3.
33. This is F. A. Váli's estimate, in *Rift and Revolt in Hungary*, (Cambridge, Massachusetts, 1961), pp. 439–40. See Kovrig, op. cit., pp. 326–8, for details of repressive measures.
34. F. Fejtö, 'Hungarian Communism', in W. E. Griffith (ed.), *Communism in Europe*, vol. 1, (Oxford, 1969), pp. 230–1.
35. G. Mond, 'Les échos et les conséquences du XXième Congres du PC de l'URSS en Pologne', in *Le Vingtième Congrès*, published as vol. 24 of *Collection historique de l'Institut d'études Slaves*, (Paris, 1977), p. 80.
36. *Economic History*, III, p. 42.
37. Khrushchev allegedly opposed the appointment of Roman Zambrowski on this occasion, arguing that there were already too many Jews in the leadership, and unsuccessfully upheld the candidacy of the ultra-conservative Zenon Nowak. (Z. A. Pelczynski, in R. F. Leslie (ed.), *The History of Poland since 1963*, (Cambridge, 1983), p. 345).
38. T. Torańska, *Oni*, (London, 1987), p. 69.
39. *Economic History*, III, pp. 64, 66.
40. Mond, 'Les échos', p. 81.
41. C. R. Hiscocks, *Poland: Bridge for the Abyss?*, (London, 1963), p. 190; M. J. Kryński, 'Poland's Literary Thaw', *Polish Review*, 1, 4, 1956, p. 16.
42. A. Brzeski, 'Poland as Catalyst', *Polish Review*, 16, 2, 1971, p. 3.
43. K. Pomian, *Pologne: Défi a l'impossible*, (Paris, 1982), p. 198.
44. G. Sakwa, 'The Polish October: A Re-appraisal through Historiography', *The Polish Review*, 23, 3, 1978, p. 75.
45. Zinner, *National Communism*, pp. 239–40; K. Syrop, *Spring in October*, (London, 1957), p. 64.
46. Z. Brzezinski, *The Soviet Bloc*, 2nd edn, (Cambridge, Massachusetts, 1967), p. 250.

47. Marie and Nagy, op. cit., pp. 18–19.
48. Mond, 'Les échos', p. 115.
49. Jan Kott, quoted in Hiscocks, op. cit., p. 212.
50. In an interview with Teresa Torańska. (Torańska, op. cit., p. 78).
51. Syrop, op. cit., p. 163.
52. M. K. Dziewanowski, *The Communist Party of Poland*, 2nd edn, (Harvard, 1976), p. 284.
53. See Korbonski, op. cit., p. 262.
54. Syrop, op. cit., p. 157.
55. W. Gomułka, *Przemówienia*, (Warsaw, 1957), p. 112.
56. O. Anweiler, 'Die Arbeiterselbstverwaltung in Polen', *Osteuropa*, 8, 4, April 1958, pp. 230–1.
57. *Economic History*, III, p. 101.
58. Gomułka, op. cit., p. 213.
59. Richard Hiscocks, writing in 1963, before the disillusionment of the late 1960s, considered that 'since October *Po Prostu* had sometimes gone to extremes, and Gomułka was to some extent justified in saying that it did not fairly present the Polish situation.' (Hiscocks, op. cit., p. 264).
60. M. L. Danilewicz, 'The Polish Literary Scene', *Soviet Survey*, July–September 1958.
61. Pelczynski, in Leslie, (ed.), op. cit., p. 378.
62. P. Raina, *Political Opposition in Poland 1954–1977*, (London, 1978), p. 73.
63. Raina, op. cit., pp. 86–9.
64. *Eastern Europe*, III, p. 95.

6 THE QUIET YEARS, 1957–68

1. A. H. Smith, *The Planned Economies of Eastern Europe*, (London, 1983), p. 43.
2. Figures from *Economic History*, III, p. 150.
3. J. Kosta, *Abriss der sozialökonomischen Entwicklung der Tschechoslowakei 1945–77*, (Frankfurt, 1978), p. 124.
4. Cf. W. Brus, 'The East European economic reforms: What happened to them?', *Soviet Studies*, 21, 2, 1979, pp. 257–67; G. Grossman, 'Economic reforms, a balance sheet', in *Problems of Communism*, Nov.–Dec. 1966, pp. 43–55.
5. A. Matejko, *Social Change and Stratification in Eastern Europe*, (New York, 1974), p. xix.
6. Figures from D. Staritz, *Geschichte der DDR 1949–1985*, (Frankfurt, 1985), p. 166; standard of living figures from T. P. Alton, *Research Project on National Income in East Central Europe*, Occasional Paper no. 113, (New York, 1990), table 5, p. 14.
7. M. McCauley, *The German Democratic Republic since 1945*, (London, 1983), p. 123.
8. Staritz, op. cit., p. 200. It has now been revealed that Ulbricht was removed from office largely because of his resistance to negotiating a treaty with West Germany. The appointment of Honecker was followed rapidly by the signing of a full treaty between the two Germanies, in December 1972 (T. G. Ash, *In Europe's Name*, London, 1993, p. 78).

9. M. Melzer, 'The GDR', ch. 3 of A. Nove, H.-H. Höhmann and G. Seidenstecher, (eds). *The East European Economies in the 1970s*, (London, 1982), pp. 50–1.
10. Kovrig, op. cit., p. 353.
11. E. Hankiss, *East European Alternatives*, (Oxford, 1990), p. 56.
12. A. Zwass, *The Economies of Eastern Europe in a Time of Change*, (London, 1984), p. 7.
13. IMF, *Direction of Trade Statistics*, Yearbook for 1989.
14. G. Gross, 'Rumania: the Fruits of Autonomy', *Problems of Communism*, 15, 1, Jan.-Feb. 1966, p. 23.
15. Zwass, op. cit., p. 87.
16. Zwass, loc. cit. On the cultural concomitants of this policy, see Katherine Verdery, *National Ideology under Socialism*, (Berkeley, 1991).
17. M. Kaser, 'Romania', in H.-H. Höhmann, M. Kaser and K. Thalheim (eds), *The New Economic Systems of Eastern Europe*, (Los Angeles, 1975), p. 172–4.
18. M. Kaser and I. Spigler, 'Economic reforms in Romania', in Nove, Höhmann and Seidenstecher, op. cit., p. 274.
19. Zwass, op. cit., pp. 97–8.
20. R. Daviddi, 'Bulgaria', in P. Joseph, *The Economies of Eastern Europe*, (Brussels, 1987), pp. 81–2; G. Feiwel, 'Economic development in Bulgaria', in Nove, Höhmann and Seidenstecher, op. cit., p. 246.

7 CZECHOSLOVAKIA IN 1968: CLIMAX AND DEFEAT OF REFORM COMMUNISM

1. Petr Pithart quotes with approval a statement by the philosopher Karel Kosík, who was prominent in the intellectual movement of the 1960s: 'the Slovak question forms the essence of the Czech question.' (P. Pithart, *Osmašedesatý*, (London, 1987), p. 83).
2. V. Mencl, and F. Ouředník, 'Jak to bylo v lednu', *Život strany* (Prague), 1968, no. 16, p. 20; Zdeněk Hejzlar (*Reformkommunismus*, (Frankfurt, 1976), p. 108) and Eugen Steiner (*The Slovak Dilemna*, (Cambridge, 1973), p. 110) on the contrary see the 12th Congress as the beginning of the period of liberalisation.
3. Quoted in J. Batt, *Economic Reform and Political Change in Europe*, (London, 1988), p. 187.
4. Hejzlar, op. cit., p. 121; Brus, *Eastern Europe*, III, pp. 95, 150; Kosta, *Abriss*, p. 75.
5. P. Tigrid, *La chute irrésistible d'Alexander Dubček*, (Paris, 1969), p. 42; P. Tigrid, *Kapesní průvodce inteligentní ženy po vlastním osudu*, (Toronto, 1988), p. 26.
6. See an interview given by Smrkovský shortly before his death, quoted in H. G. Skilling, *Czechoslovakia's Interrupted Revolution*, (Princeton, 1976), p. 879.
7. Z. Mlynář, *Night Frost in Prague*, (London, 1980), p. 97.
8. Špaček, writing in *Život strany*, (Prague), 1968, no. 5, pp. 1–4.
9. In *Student* (Prague), 3 April 1968.
10. An English translation (without the section on science) is printed in R. A.

Remington, ed., *Winter in Prague*, (Cambridge, Massachusetts, 1969), pp. 88–137.

11. In *Práce*, (Prague) 11 April 1968, printed in translation in P. Tigrid, *Le Printemps de Prague*, (Paris, 1968), pp. 217–20.

12. Šik, speaking in May 1968, quoted in Batt, op. cit., p. 218.

13. A. Pravda, 'Some aspects of the Czechoslovak economic reform and the working class in 1968', *Soviet Studies*, vol. 25, no. 1, July 1973, p. 112.

14. Brus, in *Economic History*, III, p. 213.

15. A. Oxley, A. Pravda and A. Ritchie (eds), *Czechoslovakia, The Party and the People*, (London, 1973), p. 170; Batt, op. cit., p. 197.

16. Batt, op. cit., p. 218; Brus, op. cit., p. 215.

17. *Rudé právo*, (Prague) 11 April 1968.

18. *Život strany*, (Prague) 1968, no. 10, p. 18.

19. A translated text is printed in Remington, ed., *Winter in Prague*, pp. 196–202.

20. Skilling, op. cit., p. 278.

21. I. Aleksandrov, in the issue for 11 July. See Pithart, op. cit., p. 72; Skilling, op. cit., p. 285.

22. Remington, op. cit., p. 240.

23. Hejzlar, op. cit., p. 174.

24. Remington, op. cit., pp. 257–8.

25. Skilling, op. cit., p. 316.

26. Mlynář, op. cit., p. 170; Remington, *Winter in Prague*, p. 268.

27. G. Golan, *Reform Rule in Czechoslovakia*, (Cambridge, 1973), p. 142.

28. Hejzlar, op. cit., p. 181.

29. Golan, op. cit., p. 238.

30. P. Tigrid, *La chute irrésistible d'Alexandre Dubček*, (Paris, 1970), p. 88.

31. Hejzlar, op. cit., p. 267.

32. The full details of the resistance are presented in the 'Black Book' (Seven Prague Days) compiled by Czechoslovak historians at the time and later published in English under the title *The Czech Black Book* (ed. R. Littell), (New York, 1969).

33. The text of the secret Moscow Protocol, which was leaked to the Paris Czech-language journal *Svědectví*, is printed in English in Remington, *Winter in Prague*, pp. 379–82.

34. Hejzlar, op. cit., pp. 292–3.

35. Forms of working-class action at this time are outlined in Golan, op. cit., pp. 283–94.

36. Hejzlar, op. cit., p. 312.

37. As quoted in J. Skála, *Vom Prager Frühling zur Charta 77*, (Berlin, 1978), p. 61.

38. J. Kavan, 'From the Prague Spring to a Long Winter', in J. Pehe (ed.), *The Prague Spring*, (London, 1988), p. 109.

39. It consisted of Dubček, Husák, Černík, Svoboda, Erban, Sádovský, Štrougal, Bil´ak, Piller, Colotka, Poláček. Both Černík and Svoboda had by now changed sides.

40. Tigrid, op. cit., p. 210.

41. Hejzlar, op. cit., p. 354.

42. V. V. Kusin, *From Dubček to Charter 77*, (Edinburgh, 1978), p. 85.

43. M. Šimečka, *The Restoration of Order*, (London, 1984), chs 3 and 4.

44. Skilling, op. cit., p. 852.
45. Pithart, op. cit., p. 66.
46. Quoted in B. Kagarlitsky, *The Thinking Reed*, (London, 1988), p. 201.

8 THE BREZHNEV YEARS: DITHERING AT THE TOP AND REVOLT FROM BELOW

1. Quoted in Hoensch, op. cit., p. 329.
2. Hoensch, op. cit., p. 384, n. 3.
3. W. Brus, 'The East European reforms: what happened to them', *Soviet Studies*, 31, 2, 1979, pp. 257–67.
4. M. Myant, *The Czechoslovak Economy 1948–88*, (Cambridge, 1989), p. 183.
5. Speaking at the Tenth Congress of the HSWP. (Hoensch, op. cit., p. 367).
6. There are sharply divergent views in the literature on this point. Compare Höhmann: 'Hungary's New Economic Mechanism stood the test of time and was maintained despite some restriction' (in Nove, Höhmann and Seidenstecher, op. cit., p. 5) and Brus: 'The Hungarian reform was far from being a failure: its crucial features remained' (p. 185 of *Economic History*, III) with Zwass: 'The reform simply ceased functioning after 1973' (A. Zwass, *The Economies of Eastern Europe*, (London, 1984), p. 8) and Hankiss: 'The counter-attack of the bureaucracy . . . halted this process (of reform) already in 1972–3, and strengthened bureaucratic state control over the economy.' (Hankiss, op. cit., p. 64).
7. Kovrig, op. cit., p. 393.
8. Quoted in Z. A. Pełczyński, 'The Downfall of Gomułka', in A. Bromke and J. W. Strong, (eds), *Gierek's Poland*, (New York, 1973), p. 8.
9. M. Rakowski, 'December 1970: the Turning Point', in Bromke and Strong, op. cit., p. 30.
10. See W. Rozenbaum, 'The Anti-Zionist Campaign in Poland, June–December 1967', *Canadian Slavonic Papers*, 20, 1978, pp. 218–36; and Z. Bauman, 'The End of Polish Jewry', *Bulletin on Soviet and East European Jewish Affairs*, Jan. 1969.
11. H. Laeuen, 'V. Kongress der Polnischen Kommunisten', *Osteuropa*, May–June 1967, p. 370.
12. Pełczyński, art. cit., pp. 19–21; P. Unger, *Die Ursachen der politischen Unruhen in Polen im Winter 1970–71*, (Bern, 1975), p. 136.
13. Unger, op. cit., p. 128.
14. Speaking at the February 1971 CC Plenum, quoted in Unger, op. cit., pp. 118 and 124.
15. The demands are given in full in 'Polish Workers Speak', *New Left Review*, 72, March–April 1972, pp. 36–7.
16. Quoted in G. Blazynski, *Flashpoint Poland*, (New York, 1979), p. 96.
17. W. Brus, in Nove, Höhmann and Seidenstecher, *The East European Economies in the 1970s*, (London, 1982), p. 94.
18. Brus, in op. cit., p. 99.
19. W. Brus, 'Economics and Politics – the Fatal Link', in A. Brumberg, (ed.), *Poland, Genesis of a Revolution*, (New York, 1983), p. 36.
20. D. Singer, *The Road to Gdańsk*, (New York, 1981), p. 190.

21.   J. J. Lipski, himself a participant, tells the story in *KOR. A History of the Workers' Defense Committee in Poland 1976–1981*, (Berkeley, 1985); see also P. Raina, *Political Opposition in Poland 1954–77*, (London, 1978), and *Independent Social Movements in Poland*, (London, 1981).

22.   T. G. Ash, *The Polish Revolution*, (London, 1983), p. 24.

23.   W. Brus, in Nove, Höhmann and Seidenstecher, op. cit., pp. 127, 132.

24.   S. Gomułka, 'Macroeconomic Reserves, Constraints and Systemic Factors in the Dynamics of the Polish Crisis 1980–82', *Jahrbuch der Wirtschaft Osteuropas*, vol. 10, 1, 1987, p. 218.

25.   T. G. Ash suggests that 'it is hard to conceive of Solidarity without the Polish Pope.' (op. cit., p. 30).

26.   M. Vale, (ed.), *Poland, the State of the Republic*, report by the DiP group, (London, 1981), part 1. These are simply some of the more startling comments in this long and complex report.

9   THE PREMATURE REVOLUTION: POLAND 1980–81

1.   Vale, (ed.), *Poland, the State of the Republic*, pp. 218–19.

2.   Lipski, op. cit. p. 344.

3.   The text of the Szczecin and Gdańsk Agreements is given in Appendix 2 of N. Ascherson, *The Polish August*, (London, 1981), pp. 280–295.

4.   Ash, *Polish Revolution*, p. 75.

5.   K. Pomian, *Pologne: Défi a l'impossible*, (Paris, 1982), p. 201.

6.   T. G. Ash gives several other examples of local conflicts between Solidarity and the authorities at this time (op. cit., ch. 4).

7.   Appeal of 12 August 1981, summarised in Ash, op. cit., pp. 202–3.

8.   Laws of 25 September 1981 on Workers' Self-Management, and on State Enterprises, printed in P. Raina, *Poland 1981*, (London, 1985), pp. 396–419.

9.   Raina, op. cit., p. 443.

10.   Ash, op. cit., p. 295.

11.   C. Barker, *Festival of the Oppressed*, (London, 1986), p. 134; and Raina, op. cit., p. 431, quoting a Solidarity statement of 7 December 1981.

12.   J. Staniszkis, *Poland's Self-Limiting Revolution*, (Princeton, 1984), p. 327.

13.   J. Holzer, *Solidarität*, (Munich, 1985), pp. 375, 381.

14.   Barker, op. cit., p. 138.

15.   Z. Kowalewski, in *Labour Focus on Eastern Europe*, 5, 1–2, spring 1982, p. 28.

16.   N. Davies, *Heart of Europe. A Short History of Poland*, (Oxford, 1984), p. 19.

17.   Staniszkis, op. cit., p. 334.

18.   Quoted in *The Guardian*, 14 March 1992, p. 16. It has since been claimed by Ryszard Kukliński, who defected from Poland to the USA in 1981, that there was a real possibility of a Soviet invasion, rather than an internal coup, in December 1980, and that Brezhnev was restrained by Western warnings that severe financial penalties would be imposed (R. Kuklinski, 'The Suppression of Solidarity', *Orbis*, 32, 1988, pp. 7–31).

19.   A. Sułek, 'The PUWP: from mobilisation to non-representation', *Soviet Studies*, 42, 3, 1990, pp. 499–511.

20.   See A. Smolar, 'The Polish Opposition', in F. Fehér and A. Arato, (eds), *Crisis and Reform in Eastern Europe*, (London, 1991), p. 185, and *passim*.

10   DECLINE AND FALL

1.   The Royal Institute of International Affairs recognised this contrast when it commissioned two separate studies on the collapse of communism in Eastern Europe, namely Judy Batt's *East Central Europe from Reform to Transformation* and Christopher Cviic's *Remaking the Balkans* (London, 1991, in both cases).

2.   It should be added that this view has been contested by Eduard Shevardnadze himself, who writes: 'starting in April 1985 we abandoned interference in their internal affairs and stopped imposing solutions' and by Giulietto Chiesa, who writes, 'the doctrine of limited sovereignty had been disavowed ever since the 27th Congress (held in 1986)' (R. Medvedev and G. Chiesa, *Time of Change*, (London, 1991), p. 264–5).

3.   J. Bugajski and M. Pollack, 'East European Dissent', in *Problems of Communism*, 37, 2, March–April 1988, p. 67.

4.   J. Reich, 'Reflections on becoming an East German dissident', in G. Prins, (ed.), *Spring in Winter*, (Manchester, 1990), p. 83.

5.   *Nowe Drogi*, 6, 1987, quoted by Z. Brzezinski, *The Grand Failure*, (New York, 1989), p. 124.

6.   B. Kagarlitsky, *The Thinking Reed*, (London, 1988), p. 211.

7.   C. S. Maier, 'The Collapse of Communism', *History Workshop Journal*, 31, Spring 1991, p. 54.

8.   J. Kornai, *The Road to a Free Economy. The Example of Hungary*, (London, 1990), p. 40.

9.   Kornai, op. cit., p. 37.

10.   J. Winiecki, 'Are Soviet-type economies entering an era of long-term decline?', *Soviet Studies*, 38, 3, 1986, pp. 325–48.

11.   Quoted in Hankiss, op. cit., p. 85.

12.   W. Brus, writing in *New Left Review*, No. 153, Sept.–Oct. 1985, p. 52.

13.   Maier, art. cit., p. 56.

14.   See Table 3, p. 200.

15.   See Table 4, p. 201.

16.   M. Lavigne, *International Political Economy and Socialism*, (Cambridge, 1991), pp. 327–8.

17.   On the musical rebellion see also T. Ryback, *Rock Around the Bloc*, (New York, 1990).

18.   Hankiss, op. cit., pp. 97–8.

19.   Rothschild, op. cit., p. 75.

20.   J. Lovenduski, and J. Woodall, *Politics and Society in Eastern Europe*, (London, 1987), p. 430.

21.   Brzezinski, *The Grand Failure*, p. 245.

22.   Quoted in Batt, *East Central Europe*, p. 27.

23.   A. Smolar, 'Polish opposition', in F. Feher and A. Arato (eds), *Crisis and Reform in Eastern Europe*, (New Brunswick, 1991).

24.   J. Drewnowski (ed.), *Crisis in the East European Economy: the Spread of the Polish Disease*, (London, 1982).

25.   T. G. Ash, *The Uses of Adversity*, (Cambridge, 1989), p. 199.

26.   Hankiss analyses this process in detail in op. cit., pp. 113–19.

27.   Batt, *East Central Europe*, p. 11.

28.   'Turning Point and Reform', summarised by László Antal and others, in *Acta Oeconomica* (Budapest), vol. 38, nos 3–4, 1987, pp. 187–213.
29.   See *Studies in Comparative Communism*, vol. 22, no. 1, spring 1989, for a discussion of this concept.
30.   F. Tökes, 'Hungary's new political élites', *Problems of Communism*, vol. 39, 6, Nov.–Dec. 1990.
31.   Translated in *East European Reporter*, vol. 3, no. 1, 1987, pp. 54–8.
32.   Ash, *The Uses of Adversity*, p. 135.
33.   Hankiss, op. cit., pp. 253–4.
34.   K. W. Fricke, 'Der Besuch Erich Honeckers in der BRD', *Europa Archiv*, 42, 23, 10 Dec. 1987, p. 687.
35.   *Economic Bulletin For Europe*, vol. 41 (New York, 1989), table 2.16. The much lower figure of $5.5bn is given by M. Haendcke-Hoppe, 'The German Democratic Republic: Foreign Economic Relations', p. 75, in P. Joseph (ed.), *The Economies of Eastern Europe and their Foreign Economic Relations*, (Brussels, 1987).
36.   J. F. Brown, *Eastern Europe and Communist Rule*, (Durham, North Carolina, 1988), p. 261.
37.   This is the rate of growth of Net Material Product at constant prices, from Lavigne, *International Political Economy*, p. 386. The rate is lower but the trend is the same if we use Western measures of GNP growth (1.8 per cent p.a., 1980–85; 1.4 per cent p.a. 1985–9, figures from T. P. Alton, (ed.), *Research Project on National Income in East Central Europe*, Occasional Paper no. 110, New York, 1990, p. 28). See Tables 3 and 4.
38.   G.-I. Glaessner, 'RDA: Premières réflexions sur l'effondrement d'un régime', *Communisme*, nos 24–5, p. 158.
39.   A. Mitter and S. Wolle, *Ich liebe euch doch alle*, (Berlin, 1990), p. 117.
40.   Prins, op. cit., p. 81, Markus Wolf, the retired head of State Security, testified to this.
41.   See A. H. Smith, 'Romania: Internal Economic Development and Foreign Economic Relations', in P. Joseph (ed.), *The Economies of Eastern Europe and their Foreign Economic Relations*, (Brussels, 1987), pp. 255–74.
42.   J. Eyal, 'Why Romania could not avoid bloodshed', in Prins, op. cit., p. 155.
43.   P. Shoup, *Communism and the Yugoslav National Question*, (New York, 1968), pp. 266, 103.
44.   S. L. Burg, *Conflict and Cohesion in Socialist Yugoslavia* (Princeton, 1983), p. 81.
45.   W. Höpken, 'Die Jugoslawischen Kommunisten und die bosnischen Muslime', in A. Kappeler, ed., *Die Muslime in der Sowjetunion* (1989), p. 198.
46.   The text is printed in M. Grmek, *Le Nettoyage Ethnique* (Paris, 1993), pp. 231ff.
47.   B. Magaš, *The Destruction of Yugoslavia*, (London, 1993), p. 4.
48.   G. Stokes, *The Walls Came Tumbling Down. The Collapse of Communism in Eastern Europe* (Oxford, 1993), p. 235.
49.   Speech of 26 June 1990, quoted in G. Stokes, *The Walls Came Tumbling Down*, p. 247.
50.   J. F. Brown, *Hopes and Shadows. Eastern Europe after Communism* (London, 1994), p. 283.
51.   It would clearly be out of the question to attempt a detailed account of the

post-1989 Yugoslav crisis. There are already several excellent books: L. J. Cohen, *Broken Bonds. The Disintegration of Yugoslavia* (Boulder, 1993); M. Glenny, *The Fall of Yugoslavia: The Third Balkan War* (London, 1992); M. Thompson, *A Paper House. The Ending of Yugoslavia* (London, 1992); B. Magaš, *The Destruction of Yugoslavia. Tracking the Break-Up 1980–92* (London, 1993).

52. See the tables in Brus, *Economic History*, III, pp. 46, 64. Real wage statistics give the same picture (e.g. Brus, III, pp. 95, 150, 152). The years after 1970 are covered in T. P. Alton, op. cit., O. P. no. 113, p. 14. Alton's tables make it clear that the rise in the standard of living continued to the end except in Poland, Romania and Yugoslavia.

53. See Tables 25.4 and 25.5 on p. 84 and 86 of *Economic History*, III.

54. A. Matejko, *Social Change and Stratification in Eastern Europe*, (New York, 1974), p. 63. The specific reference here is to Poland. G. Gömöri, in contrast, writing in D. Lane and G. Kolankiewicz, (eds), *Social Groups in Polish Society*, (New York, 1973), p. 160, considers that the workers and peasants 'gained access' to the ruling class rather than actually 'pushing out' the old classes.

55. Quoted by J. F. Brown, in *Eastern Europe and Communist Rule*, p. 409.

56. See A. Heitlinger, *Women and State Socialism*, (London, 1979), pp. 135–90 for a study of the position in Czechoslovakia.

57. See R. J. McIntyre, 'Pronatalist Programmes in Eastern Europe', *Soviet Studies*, 27, 3, July 1975, pp. 366–80.

58. See Matejko, op. cit., Tables 2.6 and 2.8, and the *Economic History of Eastern Europe*, vol. I, ch. 2 (by M. Hauner) for changes in educational levels in Eastern Europe between 1950 and 1972.

Index